SOFTWARE TESTING

Software Testing

Techniques, Principles, and Practices

JJ Shen

SOFTWARE TESTING

TECHNIQUES, PRINCIPLES, AND PRACTICES

Copyright © 2019 by Jianjun Shen
All rights reserved

No part of the book may be reproduced or transmitted in any form, by any means, including but not limited to electronic, mechanical, or photocopying without prior written approval from the author, except for the inclusion of brief quotations in critical articles and reviews. The author may be contacted by email at jjshen99@gmail.com.

FIRST EDITION

ISBN: 9781693054907

DAHUO BOOKS

Contents

Preface

Part 1: Software Test Cases

1. Introduction
   1.1 Software Quality 3
   1.2 Software Testing 4
   1.3 Traditional Classifications of Software Testing 5
      1.3.1 Knowledge of Software Internal Structure 6
      1.3.2 Development Stage Level 6
      1.3.3 Test Coverage 7
      1.3.4 Software Architectural Layers 8
      1.3.5 Non-Functional Real-World Situations. 9

2. Software Test Cases
   2.1 Test Case Definitions 10
   2.2 Characteristics of Test Cases 14
      2.2.1 A Test Case Is Deterministic 14
      2.2.2 A Test Case Is Reproducible 16
      2.2.3 A Test Case Is Atomic 17
      2.2.4 A Test Case Is Independent 17
      2.2.5 Other Properties of Test Cases 18
   2.3 Test Vectors 19
   2.4 Classification of Test Cases 21
   Exercise Problems 26

Part 2: Test Case Generation Techniques

3. Equivalence Partition Testing
   3.1 Equivalence Partitioning 31
   3.2 Limitations of Base Case Equivalence Partitioning 36
   3.3 Boundary Value Partitioning 38
   3.4 Equivalence Partitioning with Multiple Dimensions 42
   3.5 Category Partitioning 53
   3.6 Equivalence Partitioning with Dependent Variables 65
   3.7 Summary of Equivalence Partitioning 70
   Exercise Problems 71

4. Combinatorial Testing
- 4.1 Pairwise Testing 74
- 4.2 Limitations of Pairwise Testing 81
- 4.3 T-wise Testing 83
- 4.4 Orthogonal Arrays 84
- Exercise Problems 90

5. Decision Table Testing
- 5.1 Decision Table 92
- 5.2 Decision Table Construction and Rule Count 93
- 5.3 Cause-effect Graphing 104
- Exercise Problems 109

6. Structural Testing
- 6.1 Control Flow Graph 110
- 6.2 Node and Edge Coverages 116
- 6.3 Prime Path Coverages 119
  - 6.3.1 Prime Path Coverages 119
  - 6.3.2 Infeasible Requirements and Best Effort Touring 124
  - 6.3.3 Cyclomatic Complexity 128
- 6.4 Condition Coverages 128
  - 6.4.1 Basic Condition Coverage 128
  - 6.4.2 Condition and Edge Coverage 129
  - 6.4.3 Compound Condition Coverage 130
  - 6.4.4 Modified Condition/Decision Coverage 132
- 6.5 Call Graph 136
- 6.6 Application to Use Case Testing 138
- 6.7 Finite State Machine Model 141
- Exercise Problems 149

Part 3: Principles & Practices of Software Testing

7. General Principles of Test Case Design
- 7.1 Atomic Principle 155
- 7.2 Independency Principle 156
  - 7.2.1 Order Independency 157
  - 7.2.2 Path Independency 158
  - 7.2.3 State Independency 158
  - 7.2.4 Environment Independency 159
  - 7.2.5 Time Independency 159
- 7.3 Modularization Principle 160
  - 7.3.1 Modularization Principle 160
  - 7.3.2 Hierarchical Finite State Machine 162
- 7.4 Coverage Principle 165

CONTENTS

8. Regression Testing
- 8.1 Regression Testing 168
- 8.2 Regression Test Selection 170
  - 8.2.1 Predefined Test Sets 170
  - 8.2.2 Strategic Test Sets 171
  - 8.2.3 Prioritized Test Sets 171
  - 8.2.4 Random Test Sets 172
  - 8.2.5 Test Sets Annotation 172
- 8.3 Weighted Prioritization 173
- 8.4 Regression Testing with Continuous Integration 176

9. Unit Testing (Type 0 Tests)
- 9.1 Characteristics and Benefits of Unit Tests 179
- 9.2 Writing Unit Tests 182
- 9.3 Dependencies and Coding Practices 191
- 9.4 Stubbing 193
- 9.5 Mocking 196
- Exercise Problems 199

10. Integration Testing (Type 1 Tests)
- 10.1 Integration Testing and Functional Testing 201
- 10.2 Integration Testing Approaches 203
- 10.3 Test Case Generation Strategies 205
- 10.4 Test Data Design 210

11. Performance Testing
- 11.1 Mathematical Basics for Performance Testing 216
  - 11.1.1 Statistical Terms 216
  - 11.1.2 Normal Distribution 217
- 11.2 Performance Requirements and Indicators 219
- 11.3 Performance Testing Types 221
- 11.4 Performance Testing Processes 224
  - 11.4.1 Performance Testing Processes 224
  - 11.4.2 Metrics to Collect 226
  - 11.4.3 Performance Monitoring 226
- 11.5 Performance Testing Principles and Practices 227
  - 11.5.1 Test Case Design 227
  - 11.5.2 Valid Performance Testing Simulation 228
- 11.6 Case Study: Performance of Database Operations ... 230
  - 11.6.1 The Application Under Test & Test Design 230
  - 11.6.2 Testing Environment & Testing Approach 230
  - 11.6.3 Performance Benchmarks & Analysis 231
  - 11.6.4 Performance Comparison of Four Versions of the Application 238
  - 11.6.5 Sever Processing Time Analysis 240

CONTENTS

12. Case Study One: Web Service API Testing
    12.1 The API Requirements 244
    12.2 Test Case Generation 246
        12.2.1 Equivalence Partitions 246
        12.2.2 Different Parameter Orders 252
        12.2.3 Smaller Number of Parameters 254
        12.2.4 Multiple Entries for the Parameters 256
    12.3 Test Data Generation, Verification Strategies, & Test Automation 258

13. Case Study Two: Record Filtering Testing
    13.1 The Application Under Test 262
    13.2 Test Case Generation 265
        13.2.1 Filtering Operations 266
        13.2.2 Conditions with AND and OR Operators 268
        13.2.3 Sorting 271
    13.3 Test Data Generation & Test Automation 271

About the Author 277

Index 279

FIGURES:

Figure 2.1: Black box representation of a test case 11
Figure 2.2: A XOR gate 12
Figure 2.3: First XOR gate implementation 13
Figure 2.4: Second XOR gate implementation 13
Figure 2.5: A test case is reproducible: it holds at any time 16
Figure 2.6: Illustration of testing types 23

Figure 3.1: Illustration of boundary value selections 40
Figure 3.2: Input space for example 3.5 44
Figure 3.3: Input space for example 3.5 with more specific invalid zones 46
Figure 3.4: Input space for example 3.6 48
Figure 3.5: Input space with variables *l* and *t* for example 3.8 60
Figure 3.6: Input space for example 3.10 67

Figure 5.1: Decision tree for example 5.2 95
Figure 5.2: Cause-effect graph for example 5.4: Loan rate under different conditions 105

Figure 6.1: Graph for example 6.1 112
Figure 6.2: A 'for' loop and it's control flow graph 113
Figure 6.3: A 'while' loop and it's control flow graph 114
Figure 6.4: A 'if else' loop and its control flow graph 114
Figure 6.5: A 'switch' loop and its control flow graph 114
Figure 6.6: Graph for example 6.2 116
Figure 6.7: Graph for example 6.3 118
Figure 6.8: Graph for example 6.1 119
Figure 6.9: Graph for example 6.4 121
Figure 6.10: Tour, tour with sidetrip, and tour with detour examples 125
Figure 6.11: Graph for example 6.5 127
Figure 6.12: Call graph for example 6.10 137
Figure 6.13: Activity graph for example 6.11 139
Figure 6.14: Illustration for example 6.12: Cat in a black box 142
Figure 6.15: State transition diagram for example 6.12 144
Figure 6.16: State transition diagram for example 6.13: A simplified alarm system 147

Figure 7.1: Graph for test modularization HFSM model 163
Figure 7.2: Graph for test modularization HFSM model: test clusters 163
Figure 7.3: Graph for test modularization HFSM model: test classes 164

Figure 10.1: Illustration of integration testing and functional testing 202
Figure 10.2: Illustration of top-down and bottom-up integration testing approach 203
Figure 10.3: Application architecture illustration 208

Figure 10.4: User connectivity graph for Example 10.2 213
Figure 11.1: Normal distribution density 218
Figure 11.2: Response time distribution for table creation 232
Figure 11.3: Response time over time and latency over time for table creation 233
Figure 11.4: Response time and latency over time for column insertion and deletion 235
Figure 11.5: Transaction throughput and response time vs number of threads 237
Figure 11.6: Latency over time when number of concurrent users increases 238
Figure 11.7: Response time comparison for four versions of the application 239
Figure 11.8: Server processing time 242
Figure 12.1: Vector space for start_time & end_time 247

TABLES:

Table 2.1: Truth table for XOR gate 12
Table 2.2: Summary of test case definitions 18
Table 2.3: Summary of test case characteristics 19
Table 2.4: Fundamental classification of test cases 23
Table 2.5: Fundamental type classification of certain common testing types 23

Table 3.1: Test cases for example 3.1 35
Table 3.2: Test cases for example 3.7 51
Table 3.3: Reduced test cases for example 3.7 52
Table 3.4: Test cases for example 3.8 58
Table 3.5: Test cases for example 3.10 69
Table 3.6: Number of test cases for different levels of equivalence partitioning 70

Table 4.1: All permutations of three parameters 75
Table 4.2: Pairwise test cases for example 4.1 76
Table 4.3: Requirements for example 4.2 77
Table 4.4: Pairwise test cases for example 4.2 78
Table 4.5: Configuration requirements for example 4.3 79
Table 4.6: Pairwise test cases for example 4.3 80
Table 4.7: Pairwise test cases when constraints are considered for example 4.3 80
Table 4.8: Pairwise test cases with extra requirements for example 4.3 81
Table 4.9: Requirement definition for example 4.4 82
Table 4.10: Pairwise test cases for example 4.4 82
Table 4.11: OA (1,2,3,3) array 85
Table 4.12: 1st and 3rd columns in OA (1,2,3,3) 85
Table 4.13: OA (1, 3, 4, 2) 87
Table 4.14: 3-wise test cases for example 4.4 88
Table 4.15: Pairwise test cases for OA (1,2,4,2) 88

Table 5.1: Decision table for example 5.1 92
Table 5.2: Decision table for example 5.2 93
Table 5.3: Decision table for example 5.2 with rule counts 94
Table 5.4: Decision table for example 5.2 with all combination of conditions 95
Table 5.5: Test cases for example 5.2 95
Table 5.6: Truth table for three Boolean conditions 97
Table 5.7: Condition part of the decision table for example 5.3 97
Table 5.8: Decision table for example 5.3 98
Table 5.9: Test cases for example 5.3 98
Table 5.10: Extended entry decision table for example 5.3 100

Table 5.11: Test cases based on extended entry decision table for example 5.3 101
Table 5.12: Intermediate steps collapsing the extended decision table for example 5.3 101
Table 5.13: Collapsed decision table for example 6.3 with rule counts 102
Table 5.14: Final extended decision table for example 5.3 102
Table 5.15: Test cases based on extended decision table 5.14 for example 5.3 102
Table 5.16: Causes for example 5.4 105
Table 5.17: Effects for example 5.4 105
Table 5.18: Individual cause-effect graphs for example 5.4 106
Table 5.19: Decision table based on cause-effect graphs for example 5.4 107
Table 5.20: Test cases for example 5.4 107

Table 6.1: basic blocks for example 6.2 115
Table 6.2: Simple paths for example 6.4 121
Table 6.3: Calculate test paths from prime paths 122
Table 6.4: Test cases for example 6.4 123
Table 6.5: basic blocks for example 6.5 123
Table 6.6: Simple paths for example 6.5 127
Table 6.7: Prime paths for example 6.5 127
Table 6.8: Compound coverage for example 6.6 131
Table 6.9: Compound coverage for example 6.7 131
Table 6.10: Compound coverage for example 6.8 131
Table 6.11: Compound coverage for example 6.9 132
Table 6.12: MCDC construction for example 6.6 133
Table 6.13: MCDC test cases for example 6.6 134
Table 6.14: MCDC construction for example 6.9 135
Table 6.15: MCDC test cases for example 6.9 136
Table 6.16: Edge coverage test cases for example 6.10 138
Table 6.17: Transition function for example 6.12 143
Table 6.18: Test cases generated from finite state machine for example 6.12 144
Table 6.19: Test cases generated from FSM for example 6.13 147

Table 7.1: Atomic test case definition from common test case generation technique 156
Table 7.2: An example of organizing test cases 165
Table 7.3: Recommended test coverages for common test case generation techniques 166

Table 8.1: 3-wise test cases for example 4.5 168
Table 8.2: A sample test case priority assignment 172
Table 8.3: Weights of factors in determining test case priority 174
Table 8.4: A sample test case priority assignment based on weighted sum 175

Table 9.1: Commonly used assertion statements in Junit 184

Table 10.1: Module pairs to be included in integration testing for Example 10.1 206
Table 10.2: Module triples to be included in integration testing for Example 10.1 206
Table 10.3: Integration points with database & external services for Example 10.1 209

Table 11.1: Classification of performance testing 224
Table 11.2: Response time for testing transactions 231
Table 11.3: Average response time for testing transactions 239

Table 11.4: Server processing time for testing transactions 242
Table 12.1: Parameters for the order API 244
Table 12.2: Test cases for start_time and end_time partitions 248
Table 12.3: Test cases for parameters order_type, user_id, and order_state 251
Table 12.4: Test cases for parameters order_id, and product_names 251
Table 12.5: Test cases for parameter limit 252
Table 12.6: Test cases for partitions from 29) to 32) 252
Table 12.7: Test cases for different parameter orders 254
Table 12.8: Test cases for different orders with reduced number of parameters 254
Table 12.9: Test cases for different parameter orders 254
Table 12.10: Number of permutations vs number of parameters 255
Table 12.11: Number of permutations to test 256
Table 12.12: Test cases for one parameter only 256
Table 12.13: Test cases for multiple parameter entries 257
Table 12.14: Test cases for multiple parameter entries 257
Table 12.15: Testing strategies for the api_user API 258
Table 13.1: Filter operations and possible values for Boolean column type 263
Table 13.2: Filter operations and possible values for Date and Time column type 263
Table 13.3: Filter operations and possible values for Integer column type 264
Table 13.4: Filter operations and possible values for Enum column type 264
Table 13.5: Filter operations and possible values for String column type 264
Table 13.6: Columns of the database table under test 265
Table 13.7: Selected table columns to use in testing 266
Table 13.8: Test cases for the five types of columns 268
Table 13.9: Boolean logic to cover 271
Table 13.10: Sorting test cases 271
Table 13.11: Test cases for an Enum column 272

CODE SEGMENTS:

Code Segment 2.1: Two threads in parallel computing 15
Code Segment 3.1: Java MonthNumber method for example 3.1 33
Code Segment 3.2: Java code segment for example 3.2 36
Code Segment 3.3: Initial Java implementation for example 3.3 37
Code Segment 3.4: Second Java implementation for example 3.3 38
Code Segment 3.5: Java implementation for example 3.5 42
Code Segment 3.6: Java implementation for example 3.7 triangle areas 49
Code Segment 4.1: Java Implementation with defect for example 4.4 83
Code Segment 5.1: Java implementation for example 5.3: 98
Code Segment 6.1: Example to illustrate syntactic and semantic reaches 112
Code Segment 6.2: Occurrence count of a character in a string 115
Code Segment 6.3: Java method to calculate the average of an integer array 126
Code Segment 6.4: Java methods for example 6.10 137
Code Segment 8.1: Tagging of test cases 173
Code Segment 9.1: A Java implementation of a test for example 9.1: prime number 182
Code Segment 9.2: A Java implementation of the test with try catch blocks 183
Code Segment 9.3: A sample test written in Junit for example 9.1: prime number 183
Code Segment 9.4: A alternative implementation for the test in example 9.1 184
Code Segment 9.5: Java implementation for example 9.2: average of two numbers 185
Code Segment 9.6: Java implementation of unit tests for example 9.2 valid zone 187
Code Segment 9.7: Implementation of unit tests for example 9.2 invalid zones (1) 188
Code Segment 9.8: Implementation of unit tests for example 9.2 invalid zones (2) 189
Code Segment 9.9: Implementation for example 9.3: a set address method 190
Code Segment 9.10: Implementation of unit tests for example 9.3 190
Code Segment 9.11: Java method `customerCanWriteReview()` 191
Code Segment 9.12: Refactoring Java method `customerCanWriteReview()` 192
Code Segment 9.13: Java implementation of class `UserNameService` 194
Code Segment 9.14: Stub class for example 9.5 194
Code Segment 9.15: A type 0 test with a stub for example 9.5 195
Code Segment 9.16: Java code for `DatabaseInterface` for example 9.6 196
Code Segment 9.17: Java class `UserAddressUpdateService` for example 9.6 197
Code Segment 9.18: Database interface mocking for example 9.6 197
Code Segment 9.19: A type 0 test using a mock for example 9.6 198
Code Segment 12.1: Testing method for a test case in the valid user partition 260
Code Segment 13.1: Implementation of test cases 5 and 14 for operator 'on' 275

EXAMPLES:

Example 2.1: A Length Converter 11
Example 2.2: A Simple Web Page 11
Example 2.3: Logical XOR Gate 12

Example 3.1: An Input Box for Integers 1 to 12 (Month numbers) 32
Example 3.2: An Application to Print Out the Season 36
Example 3.3: A Program to Return Factorial of a Number 37
Example 3.4: English Letter to Binary Code Conversion 41
Example 3.5: Average of Two Integers 42
Example 3.6: A Program Takes Two Integer Variables 47
Example 3.7: Area of a Triangle 48
Example 3.8: Password Creation Field on a Web Page 53
Example 3.9: An Order API 61
Example 3.10: Loan Rate under Different Conditions 65

Example 4.1: A Panel with Three on/off Switches 75
Example 4.2: A Custom Car Building Application 76
Example 4.3: A Web Application 79
Example 4.4: A Weather Condition Coding 82
Example 4.5: Visibility of Applications on a Web Page 87

Example 5.1: Gym Fee Structure 92
Example 5.2: Chicken Feeding at a Farm 93
Example 5.3: College Admission Initial Categorizing 96
Example 5.4: Loan Rate under Different Conditions 104

Example 6.1: Test Graph One 111
Example 6.2: A Function to Check Occurrence Count of a Character in a String 115
Example 6.3: Another Test Graph 117
Example 6.4: A Function to Check Occurrence Count of a Character in a String 120
Example 6.5: Average of Integers in an Array 126
Example 6.6: A Compound Boolean Expression 129, 133
Example 6.7: Compound Boolean Expression: (*a* OR *b* OR *c* OR *d*) 131
Example 6.8: Compound Boolean Expression: (*a* AND *b* AND *c* AND *d*) 131
Example 6.9: Compound Boolean Expression: ((((*a* AND *b*) OR *c*) AND *d*) OR *e*) 132, 134
Example 6.10: A Program to Calculate Unit Pay for a Specific Situation 136
Example 6.11: Online Ordering Process 139
Example 6.12: Cat in a Black Box 142
Example 6.13: A Simplified Alarm System 145

Example 7.1: Function Calls 160
Example 7.2: A Web Site with Common Breadcrumbs 161
Example 7.3: Shopping Site Workflow 161

Example 9.1: Prime Numbers 182
Example 9.2: Average of Two Numbers 185
Example 9.3: A Set Address Method 190
Example 9.4: A Customer Can Review Method 191
Example 9.5: User's Name from a Web Service 193
Example 9.6: User's Address Updates 196

Example 10.1: A Online Shopping Site 205
Example 10.2: Content Visibility on A Networking Web Site 212

PREFACE

Software testing has become a critical element in software development cycles, partly because software applications are becoming more and more complex (e.g.: real-time, high performance, machine learning capability), interactive, distributed (e.g.: cloud services, high availability), and are expected to perform well. Most importantly, software applications are playing a larger and larger role in our daily life, and are critical to the industries and the economy, and are an essential part of our human endeavors.

The trend of software development had already shifted to agile and a lot of time to test-driven, and the success of software development requires the early intervention of quality assurance and collaboration of software developers and quality engineers. As a result, quality engineers and software developers are required to have a better understanding of common testing techniques and principles.

In this book, basic software testing techniques are presented with abundant examples, and certain crucial strategies, principles, and best practices one can follow in real-world scenarios are discussed.

In the first part of the book software test cases are formally and concisely defined, and basic characteristics of test cases are discussed, and testing types are classified from a fundamental standpoint that was not covered anywhere else.

The second part of the book is the most important one in which major software testing techniques are covered. Equivalence partitioning techniques are discussed in detail with an abundance of practical examples, and some of the materials are handled differently from what you can find in other references or books. Other techniques covered include combinatorial testing, decision table testing, and structural testing.

General principles in test case design and regression testing are covered in part three of the book. Unit testing and integration testing are then introduced, followed by performance testing. Two case studies are presented in the last two chapters to demonstrate how to use some of the techniques discussed in the book.

For most of the testing techniques, complex mathematics is skipped. The main goal is to introduce the basic techniques with the help of relevant examples. In some chapters, certain advanced mathematics are presented to illustrate the theories for mathematically inclined people, aiming to provide a systematic view of the techniques. In most cases, the mathematics can be skipped, and the text can be followed without losing the content. Also, notice that majority of the code segments presented in the book are in Java.

Aside from the common techniques, a lot of the materials, especially those in chapter 2 (test case definition and classification), majority of chapter 3 (equivalence partitioning), are original works of the author and have never been published elsewhere. The author takes full responsibility for the context, in the meantime, and reproduction or quotation of the materials should include references to the book and the author.

In the chapters that common techniques are presented, the author developed the book materials independently, so no references have been listed at this point since the focus of this book is not on the full theories of any topic and is not research oriented. Any further interests in those theories/techniques can be found elsewhere in research journals, other books, or on the internet.

This book is targeted mainly to software quality engineers, software developers, and other IT professionals. The book is written in a textbook style, and there are also numerous exercise problems at the end of most chapters, especially the ones on testing techniques. Therefore, the book is suitable as a reference book for undergraduate or graduate students taking classes in software testing related subjects.

PART ONE

Software Test Cases

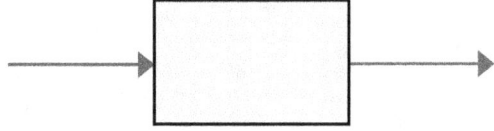

1 INTRODUCTION

1.1 SOFTWARE QUALITY

A piece of software serves its purposes, the quality of the software is how well it serves its purposes.

There are two main perspectives to view software quality. One is the functional view, it states that software quality is the degree to which a system, component, or process meets specified requirements; the other is beyond functional, often referred to as structural view, in which software quality means how well the software delivers its functionalities, such as performance, reliability, and maintainability.

From the perspective of software testing, different views translate to different types of testing and are all essential parts of the testing process. We will talk about various types of testing in the last section of this chapter and will introduce a new way to classify software testing into fundamental types in the next chapter.

Certain quality models seek to represent the requirements from shareholders of a software system. From a quality model's perspective, the quality of a system is how the system satisfies the stated and implied needs of its various stakeholders. Those stakeholders' needs (functionality, performance, security, maintainability, etc.) are represented in the quality model, which categorizes the product quality into characteristics and sub-characteristics. The quality model determines which quality characteristics will be taken into account when evaluating the properties of a software product.

There are many software quality models, one of them is ISO/IEC 25010. According to ISO/IEC 25010, there are eight product quality characteristics with a total of 31 subcategories. The eight product quality characteristics are functional suitability, performance efficiency, compatibility, usability, reliability, security, maintainability, and portability. Quality models are not covered in this book, the focus of the book are software testing techniques and principles.

From a software developer's point of view, the quality criteria can be achieved by proper architectural design, by a good selection of software design frameworks, by following software development standards and by exercising good coding practices in implementation, by providing proper documentation, and by following proper development and release procedures, etc.

A software quality engineer's tasks are to design and execute proper tests to verify that the software application meets the quality specification. We will discuss extensively how tests are defined and designed.

1.2 SOFTWARE TESTING

Engineering, in general, is to apply scientific and mathematical knowledge to the design, development, and operation of structures, machines, and processes, etc. Computer software quality engineering is to design and implement test cases for quality assurance, set up infrastructure and config relevant environments for test case execution, and to follow the development and testing processes that fit in the software development and product release cycles. Both computer science knowledge and mathematical knowledge are applied to a certain extent in quality engineering.

Software testing is the main component of quality engineering. The ultimate goal of software testing is to ensure that the software application under test meets both the specified functional requirements and the specified operational requirements such as those with performance, capacity, security, and usability.

The way software testing is done is to find *deviations* from the requirements, referred to as **defects**, and to verify that the software performs as expected in various real-world environments.

There are many reasons why defects exist in a software application. Here is a list of some of the common ones:

(1) Misinterpretation of requirements, miscommunications of requirements, or incomplete requirements.

(2) Constant requirement changes.
(3) Software architectural design issues.
(4) Poor coding practices.
(5) Development process issues, involving code review, source control, branch merging, and testing.
(6) Unrealistic development and release schedule.

While generally speaking, software testing is independent of how defects were introduced, there are indeed factors related to development processes that are worth considering in the testing process. Here are a few important ones:

(1) The stage of the software development cycle and release cycle: what kind of tests need to be performed in each development stage and each release stage.
(2) Cost of testing effort: time needed to test and how the testing fits in the development and release schedule.
(3) Test coverage: what's the testing scope in each stage.

The stage determines the kinds of tests to execute, therefore, we need a clear definition and a good understanding of various kinds of tests, as well as a good classification of the kinds of testing. These are the topics of Part 1 of the book.

Proper test coverage would require good test case design by applying suitable testing techniques and by following certain principles and best practices. These are the main topics of Part 2 and Part 3.

1.3 TRADITIONAL CLASSIFICATIONS OF SOFTWARE TESTING

Software testing normally starts with documenting what to test and how to test. The basic unit of testing is what's called a ***test case***. We are going to define test cases formally and to define a systematic way to classify test cases in the next chapter, but now let's first discuss the major traditional testing classifications used in the industry and introduce some commonly used terminologies in software testing.

There are various ways to classify software testing, depending on what are the testing goals or what aspects of the application are the focuses for testing.

The classifications presented here are based on software internal knowledge, development stage levels, test coverage, software design layers, and real-world situations, respectively.

1.3.1 Knowledge of Software Internal Structure

These types of testing are based on how much knowledge of the software implementation is being reflected or being used in testing. The following major categories are defined.

(1) Black Box Testing

A black box is a system that can be modeled in terms of its inputs and outputs only, the system itself is opaque.

Block box testing strategy relies on the abstract description of the software application such as functional specifications or requirements, with no concerns on how the software is implemented.

This is the common and basic form of software testing and is mandatory. Most of the techniques discussed in this book can be applied to this type of testing. The definition of the test case is based on the black box idea, which we will see in the next chapter. Black box testing can be applied at all development stages.

(2) White Box Testing

White box testing is a testing strategy that relies on the structure of the software and makes use of the knowledge of code implementation.

The white box testing method can also be used in all types of testing at various stages, but it's being used more in the early stages of the development cycle and in unit testing (see below on unit testing).

(3) Grey Box Testing

Grey box testing is a combination of black box testing and white box testing that relies partially on the structure of the software and also on the software requirements.

In a general sense, while white box testing requires certain knowledge of the software implementation, it also can be considered as black box testing at different levels of abstraction. Examples of abstraction levels are the implementation level, module integration level, and functional requirement level.

In this book, we will not use the above three terminologies in our discussions.

1.3.2 Development Stage Level

Based on the current stage of the development cycle, the following types of testing are defined.

(1) Unit Testing

Unit testing is the testing of the software implementation at the early stage of the development cycle, and is usually embedded in the software development process, and is usually done by software developers. The goal of unit testing is to verify that the software modules are implemented as designed. In test-driven development methodology, unit tests are written before or during the software module implementation. Chapter 9 is dedicated to unit testing.

(2) Integration Testing

Integration testing is the next testing type after unit testing, it's the testing of interactions of software modules. The goal is to test how components of the application behave when individual modules are combined. The whole Chapter 10 is about integration testing.

(3) System Testing

System testing is performed after integration testing, the goal is to test the software as a whole when all components are completed and included in the application, to verify that the application is designed according to various non-functional requirements.

(4) Acceptance Testing

Acceptance testing is at the last stage of the development cycle before the product is released. The purpose of the testing is to validate if the software requirements are in line with the business requirements and with the shareholders' intention and if it is ready to be released to customers.

This kind of classification based on the development stage level is the foundation of the test case classification to be presented in the next chapter.

1.3.3 Test Coverage

These types of testing are based on testing scope, how much testing should be covered for different testing goals.

(1) Smoke Testing

Smoke testing is a small subset of the whole testing suite for an application. The purpose of the test is to verify a new build and to ensure that no major issues exist. The subset is small so it can be executed very fast, and it should contain only the critical tests that failing of any of them is a showstopper.

(2) Sanity Testing

Sanity testing is a subset of the whole testing suite for the application or a subset of the test suite for a particular functionality of the application. The purpose of sanity test is to ensure that the application or any particular functionality of the application still works as expected after a minor change or after fixing one or more defects, to determine if it's fine to send the application to further testing or to release the application to production in certain cases.

(3) Regression Testing

Regression testing is normally the whole set of test suites for an application or system. The purpose of the regression testing is to ensure that the application is ready to release, after any minor or major changes to the application.

Most of all the regression testing should be automated and executed regularly through the development and release cycles via a continuous integration process, for example.

Regression testing is covered in Chapter 8.

1.3.4 Software Architectural Layers

These types of testing are based on the logic layers of the software under test.

(1) UI Testing

UI testing is to test the user interfaces of the application such as a web interface or a mobile interface. UI is how users perform their work with. UI testing is also referred to as ***frontend testing*** and ***GUI testing***. The main goal of UI testing is to verify application functionalities. Other areas of UI testing include testing the appearances of UI components, browser testing, etc.

(2) Backend Testing

Backend testing is the testing of the application without using UI, it's the testing of all the layers under UI, including databases, database processing, business logic, application APIs used by the frontend and 3rd parties, and any other layers necessary for the application to function.

(3) Database Testing

Database testing is the testing of the databases used in the system, such as testing of database schema, queries to the databases, and data quality in the database, etc.

1.3.5 Non-Functional Real-World Situations

These types of testing are special testing focusing on a specific aspect of the application affecting user experiences and application efficiencies under various conditions. The following is not a complete list of this kind of testing, but the most popular ones.

(1) Performance Testing

Performance testing verifies the real-time performance of the application in terms of responsiveness, capacity, and scalability. Benchmark testing, stress testing, and load testing are the main types of performance testing, where the application or system is tested with user session load and data load with specific system configurations (including hardware configuration). Chapter 11 covers performance testing in more detail.

(2) Security Testing

Security testing verifies the security requirements of an application against various threats, maintains system integrity and availability, and protects the system and its data. Other areas of security testing include confidentiality, authentication, authorization, and non-repudiation.

(3) Usability Testing

Usability testing verifies application usability requirements, which is about the end-user experiences, to check if the application meets the user's expectations to understand the application, to use it efficiently, and to accomplish their intended tasks.

(4) Compatibility Testing

Compatibility testing verifies if an application works properly in different environments, including operating systems, hardware, networks, databases, web browsers, etc., also verifies if it works with different versions of the same application and with different versions of other relevant software.

Browser testing is a special type of compatibility testing, which is commonly performed for web applications. The goal is to verify that the application works on specified web browsers.

There are a lot of other commonly discussed testing types, usually, you can tell the nature of them by their names. We are not going to list them here.

We've just briefly summarized common testing types; we are introducing a new way to classify test cases into fundamental types in the next chapter.

2 SOFTWARE TEST CASES

In this chapter, test cases are formally defined in section 2.1, and certain test case characteristics are derived in section 2.2, then the concept of test vectors is introduced in section 2.3. Lastly, in section 2.4, various testing is classified into specific categories, or fundamental types, based on various criteria. This is the first time this classification method is presented.

2.1 TEST CASE DEFINITIONS

We define the test case formally here, and all the characteristics can be inducted from the definitions.

Definition 1: A test case is a statement about software inputs and outputs.

A test case is a statement that, with certain input(s) to a software module at the current state, the output(s) is/are specified.

Here, the *inputs* can be variables, conditions, steps to execute, etc. The *software* can be a method/function in the implementation, a module, a class, a package, a component, a specific feature of an application, a subset of an application, a whole application, an integrated software system, a distributed software system, and so on. The *outputs* can be variable(s), message(s), new state(s) of the module under test (including error states), etc.

The execution of a test case is to process the statement, that is, given a set of input(s), verify that the output(s) is/are as specified or expected.

The process can be represented with a 'black box' with input(s) and output(s):

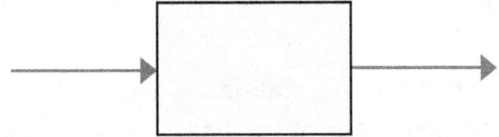

Figure 2.1: Black box representation of a test case

Based on the above test case definition, the execution result of a test case depends on the inputs, the current state, and the initial conditions of the software module.

We can write the test case result as a function of inputs, initial conditions, and the current state, including current events happening if relevant:

$$T = f(\Sigma, \Omega) \qquad (2\text{-}1)$$

where Σ is the input(s), and Ω is the initial condition, including initial state(s), initial data, current state(s), and current events, if applicable.

This function is different for different software modules, components, applications, or systems.

Let's look at a couple of test case examples.

Example 2.1: A Length Converter.

The software is a converter between the length measures of inch and centimeter, with two boxes on a web page. Here are a couple of test cases:

(a) Test case 1: Enter the number '1' in the inch box, verify the centimeter box presents the number '2.54'.
(b) Test case 2: Enter string 'abc' in the inch box, verify that an error message appears at the bottom of the input box in red and reads 'Only numbers are accepted.'

In the above test cases, the initial condition is that a web page with two boxes is displayed. The input for test case 1 is the number '1' to the inch box, and the output to be verified is the number '2.54' displays in the centimeter box. The input for test case 2 is 'abc', and the output is an error message in red under the input box.

Example 2.2: A Simple Web Page.

The software module to test is a simple web page.

(a) Test case 1: Verify that by clicking link *'link1'* on web page *'webpage1'* (an URL can be specified, for example), a new page is loaded with the title *'Title of link1'*.

In this example, the initial condition is that link *'link1'* is present on the page, and the input is a click to the link. The specified output to be verified is that a new page is displayed and has a specific title of *'Title of link1'*.

Definition 2: A test case is finite.

A test case is finite, it has a finite number of inputs and conditions, and can be executed within a finite time interval. This is similar to a finite state machine that has a limited or finite number of possible states. In other words, a test case is executable, and the underline module is testable. A test case execution should be done in polynomial time, and ideally, in constant time.

Consider this statement: Verify all swans are white.

According to our test case definition, the above statement is not a test case. Although 'all swans are white' is falsifiable (by observing a single black swan), it is not finite (at least in practice). The above statement is not likely to be resolved in a finite time interval.

Example 2.3: Logical XOR Gate

The **XOR gate** is a digital logic gate that implements an exclusive OR, that is, a *true* output results if one and only one of the inputs to the gate is *true*. If both inputs are *false* or both are *true*, a *false* output results.

The truth table representing the test cases for XOR is listed in Table 2.1. Both of the inputs and outputs are finite, each test case can be executed in finite time. Also, if all combinations of the inputs are included in the test cases, then the function as defined for the piece of software is tested fully.

Input A	Input B	Output A XOR B
0	0	0
0	1	1
1	0	1
1	1	0

Figure 2.2: A XOR gate

Table 2.1: Truth table for XOR gate

Definition 3: A Test case is encapsulating.

A test case is encapsulating, the actual implementation of the piece of software is hidden from the test. As long as the software API does not change, any change to the implementation is hidden from the execution of the tests. If a test case is to test the specific implementation, then any function being called within the implementation is hidden. There is a similar concept with information hiding supported using classes in most object-oriented programing languages.

This definition is important for regression testing which will be discussed in Chapter 8.

In this sense, all test cases are **black box** test cases.

Consider the XOR gate example again. In Boolean algebra, an XOR gate is defined as (A'B + AB'), and it can be expressed as (A+B)(A*B)' as well. The following two graphs show the two ways of implementation.

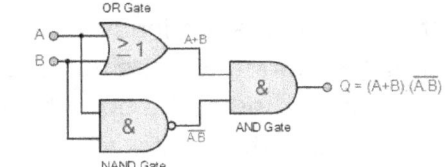

Figure 2.3: First XOR gate implementation

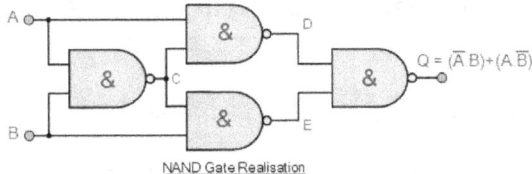

Figure 2.4: Second XOR gate implementation

From the point of view of a test case, the above two implementations are equivalent, or we can say that the implementations are transparent to the test. Both of the implementations have the same API, and the test cases (the ones represented by the truth table) are not specific to any specific implementation (unless the focus of the testing is to test the performance difference of the two implementations, for example, then they are different by requirement).

Definition 4: A test case is genuine.

A valid test case holds on the same software or any copy of it. The piece of software can be interpreted as an interface, which has a finite number of functionalities or behaviors. When the interface is defined, whether the piece of software is a method in a program with its proper signatures or an application with defined functionalities, the behaviors are defined.

Second, a test case holds on any implementation of the software, regardless of where and how it's implemented. For example, the same software can be run on different computers with different hardware and different operating systems, or with different cloud services, or on different devices (unless the features of the application being tested are device specific).

If test cases can be written for a software module, we say that the module is *testable*.

2.2 CHARACTERISTICS OF TEST CASES

From the definition of a test case, we can infer a few theorems.

2.2.1 A Test Case Is Deterministic

The execution of a test case produces defined outputs. The outputs are not fuzzy. For the same starting condition or state and the same inputs, the test case always produces the same outputs. The outputs are only determined by the starting condition or state and the inputs.

In other words, a software module has no 'free will', no randomness is involved in the development of future states of the software system.

Therefore, we have:

> ***Theorem 1: A test case is deterministic.***

From the definition, a test case is a statement that, with certain inputs to a software module at its current state, the outputs are specified. Since there is no ambiguity in the specification of the outputs, positive passing of the test case means that the same outputs are always produced for the same initial condition.

As you can see in the XOR gate example, for any test case, the output is determined only by the two inputs. All those test cases are deterministic.

You may have heard of the deterministic finite state machine and nondeterministic finite state machine in computing. Test case deterministic characteristic is a similar concept. We know even a nondeterministic finite state machine can be converted to a deterministic finite state machine. For this characteristic of test cases, determinism is stricter, that is, if a test case can be converted to a deterministic one, then it's deterministic.

In general, not only test cases of deterministic algorithms are deterministic, but also test cases for non-deterministic algorithms, as far as the expected behaviors are defined.

Let's look at two examples to illustrate the concept.

One way of implementing a non-deterministic algorithm is to use a random number generator, with random seeds for each execution. Let's assume it's non-deterministic, then for a feature of an application using the random number generator, what are the expected outputs? Let's say the expectation is that, given certain input X, the output can be 0, 1, 2, and 3, and the probability of each output value is 25%.

In this scenario, some of the test cases can be written as:

(a) Test case 1: "For input X, verify the output is in the set of [0, 1, 2, 3].
(b) Test case 2: Perform the above test 100 times, verify that each number in the set [0,1,2,3] appears between 23 and 27 times (assuming this precision is by design).
(c) Test case 3: Perform the above test 100 times again, verify no number is seen consecutively for more than three times (assuming this is also one of the requirements).

Another example is parallel computing involving threads.

Let's assume the following two threads execute once each time, and we need to test the result after each being run once.

```
Thread A:
    x = 0;
    if (y == 1)
        x++;
    x++;
Thread B:
    y = 0;
    if (x == 1)
        y++;
    y++;
```

Code Segment 2.1: Two threads in parallel computing

If the running order is A first then B, the output values are x = 2 and y = 1; while if the order is B first, then A, output values are x = 1 and y = 2. In production, there is no way to tell which one runs first. But in testing, we would like to cover the results for every order, with the following test cases:

(1) For thread running sequence AB, verify the expected result of x = 2 and y = 1.

(2) For thread running sequence BA, verify the expected result of x = 1 and y = 2.

With this approach, the non-deterministic feature is tested with deterministic test cases.

2.2.2 A Test Case is Reproducible

A valid test case is reproducible. In other words, no matter how many times you execute it, it holds, it's time independent (don't confuse it with a test that has time dependent inputs), it's repeatable.

We have:

> *Theorem 2: A test case is reproducible.*

A test case is reproducible, the test case holds at any time. Since a test case is deterministic, given the set of inputs specified in a test case, the same specified outputs will be produced after a test case execution.

From equation (2-1), the test case result is only a function of Σ (input(s)) and Ω (initial condition, initial data, current state(s) and/or events), therefore, it's not a function of time.

Written in mathematical form, the derivative of T with respect to time (t) is always zero:

$$\frac{\partial T}{\partial t} = 0 \qquad (2\text{-}2)$$

The plot in Figure 2.3 illustrates this characteristic.

Note, if a test case specifies that the output is a variable of time, but the output is specifically specified or formularized (the result is certain at a certain time), then this case is also reproducible and is too time independent.

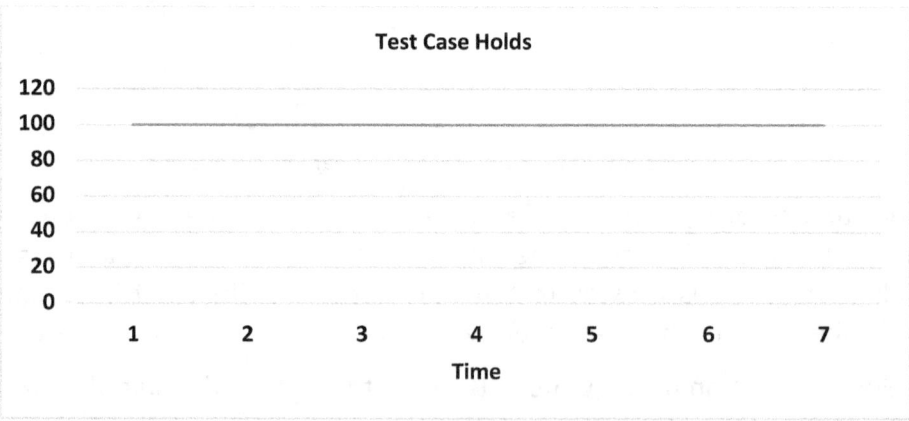

Figure 2.5: A test case is reproducible: it holds at any time

2.2.3 A Test Case is Atomic

Atom was thought to be the smallest unit of ordinary matter. Historically, there were various philosophies with the idea that matter is made up of discrete units, and the final indivisible unit is called 'atom' [with the advance of modern physics, we know that an atom consists of a nucleus and one or more electrons in various states; and a nucleus consists of protons and/or neutrons; and so on].

In computer sciences and computer software, atomicity describes a unitary action or object that is essentially indivisible, unchangeable, whole, and irreducible. In the world of databases, an atomic transaction is an indivisible and reducible series of database operations such that either all occur, or nothing occurs.

Similarly, a test case is atomic. A test case should contain only one or one set of related assertions with which only one specific scenario or usage pass is involved.

We have:

>   **Theorem 3. A test case is atomic.**

Atomicity is also a good principle to follow to reduce ambiguity and to quickly identify the defect if the test fails.

2.2.4 A Test Case is Independent

According to the definition of the test case in equation (2-1), the execution result of a test case depends on the inputs, the current state, and the initial conditions of the software module. Therefore, when a test case or a set of test cases are defined, they should not interfere with the input, or state, or initial conditions of other tests, or invalidate those for other tests.

We have:

>   **Theorem 4. A test case is independent.**

Expressed mathematically:

$$\frac{\partial T_i}{\partial T_j} = 0, \text{ for } i! = j \tag{2-3}$$

where i and j are test case numbers and are positive integers, and

$$0 < i \le N, 0 < j \le N,$$

where N is the total number of test cases in the test suite.

The derivative of a test case with respect to any other test case is zero, any test case is independent of all other test cases.

In practice, when writing automated tests, individual tests should be independent of each other. Here are the main reasons.

Firstly, since a test case is atomic, an automated test should reflect it and be implemented accordingly.

Secondly, test case independency guarantees test execution order independency and commutability. In common test frameworks, such as xUnit frameworks, tests in one test class are executed in random order, therefore, test case independency is essential to satisfy the deterministic property of a test case, and to produce the same results every time the tests are executed.

Thirdly, if artifacts are created as part of a test, or the state of the system is changed as a result of the test execution, cleanup should be done at the end of the test execution, to clean the artifacts created, and put the system back to the original state, so the initial conditions for other tests to be executed next are not changed, and those tests can be executed properly.

Last but not least, any subset of a test suite can be selected to run, the success of it also depends on individual test's independency.

2.2.5 Other Properties of Test Cases

Sometimes test cases are given other optional or auxiliary properties or tags, such as priority, category of testing (for example, smoke testing, sanity testing, etc.), automation flag, state (for example, draft, ready), and order of execution.

We will discuss some of those in part 3 of the book when regression testing is discussed.

Test case definitions are summarized in Table 2.2, and the test case characteristics we have discussed are summarized in Table 2.3.

	Test Case Definitions
1	Definition 1: A test case is a statement about software inputs and outputs.
2	Definition 2: A test case is finite.
3	Definition 3: A test case is encapsulating.
4	Definition 4: A test case is genuine.

Table 2.2: Summary of test case definitions

	Test Case Characteristics
1	Theorem 1: A test case is deterministic.
2	Theorem 2: A test case is reproducible.
3	Theorem 3. A test case is atomic.
4	Theorem 4. A test case is independent.

Table 2.3: Summary of test case characteristics

2.3 TEST VECTORS

According to the definition of the test case in equation (2-1), a test case has a set of inputs and a set of outputs.

Let's define the sets of inputs and outputs as ***test vectors***.

A test case can be described as:

$$Y = T(\Sigma) \tag{2-4}$$

with input vector $\Sigma = [x_1, x_2, ...]$ and output vector $Y = [y_1, y_2, ...]$.

For example, consider a login web page with two input fields: a username field, and a password field. In this case, the login system can be described as:

$$Y = L(\Sigma)$$

The function L takes input as a two-dimensional vector, and outputs a one-dimensional vector (scalar), where $Y = [y], y \in \{1, 0\}$, with 1 designating login successful, and 0 designating login failure, respectively, and $\Sigma = [x_1, x_2]$, $(x_1, x_2) \in \{string\}$, and x_1 is the username and x_2 is the password. Σ is the input vector and Y is the output vector.

To test the login page, a test case would specify both an input vector and an output vector.

For example, the following are two test cases:

    Test case 1: $\Sigma = [x_1, x_2]$ = [testuser001, P@sw0rdOn!]; $Y = [1]$.
    Test case 2: $\Sigma = [x_1, x_2]$ = [testuser002, &pA$$m0OdEr&]; $Y = [0]$.

The corresponding output vectors are specified as [1] and [0], which denotes login success for the 1st test case and login failure for the 2nd case.

Taking another example, consider a program to calculate the volume of a right rectangular prism, with three inputs, length L, width W, and height H, and one output value, the volume. The system can be described as:

$$Y = V(L, W, H)$$

With $Y = [y], y \in \{\mathcal{R}_{>=0}\}$ ($\mathcal{R}_{>=0}$ denotes non-negative real numbers), are the volume result values, the output vectors; and $(L, W, H) \in \{\mathcal{R}_{>=0}\}$, are the input values, the input vectors.

Or in general for the three-parameter case:

$$\Sigma = [x_1, x_2, x_3] = [L, W, H]; Y = [y].$$

A sample set of input vectors are: {[0, 0, 0], [1, 2, 3], [10, 5, 5]}, with corresponding output vectors in {[0], [6], [250]}. These constitute three test cases.

In the world of real software applications, test vector numbers are extremely large. Iterating over every permutation/combination would be extremely costly and are not practical.

If there are r number of parameters in a system under test, and there are n_i possible values for the ith parameter, then the total number of combinations (then test cases) would be:

$$N(Y) = \prod_{i=1}^{r} n_i \qquad (2\text{-}5)$$

Suppose there is a function taking two integers in the range of [-99, 99] as input parameters, then there are 199 possible input values for each parameter. How many input vectors are there?

According to the above equation, the number is 199*199 = 39601. Imagine the whole 32-bit integer range for each integer, the number of input vectors for two integers would practically be infinite.

Consider another type of combination. Statistically, the number of r combinations from a set with $n \geq r$ elements is:

$$C(n, r) = n!/((n-r)!\, r!) \qquad (2\text{-}6)$$

For example, how many ways are there to select 5 cards from a 52-card deck? From the formula:

$$C(52,5) = 52! / (47! * 5!) = 2598960.$$

Consider another example, suppose you need to pick two integers in the range of [-99,99], how many input vectors are there? Per the formula:

$$C(199,2) = 199! / (197! * 2!) = 19701.$$

You are right if you are thinking that not all of them are needed to be included in testing. We are introducing several techniques for selecting input vectors to generate test cases in the next few chapters.

2.4 CLASSIFICATION OF TEST CASES

There are various ways to classify test cases, depending on the factors of concern, as we have discussed in section 1.3 of Chapter 1. For example, depending on the testing scope and testing goal, smoke test, sanity test, and regression test are classified; depending on the degree of software implementation knowledge being used in the tests, black-box testing, grey-box testing, and white-box testing are classified; depending on testing complexity and testing requirements, unit test, integration test, performance test are classified.

The classification based on complexity and requirements are fundamental, and other classifications are just different arrangements or different ways of management of the fundamental types based on testing goals.

A software application deals with its software code units, functions, modules, interfaces, components, and interactions with other modules, and usually needs to work with other software applications, and is required to perform well under different environments and various production conditions.

The complexity of the tests for the software application should be aligned with the complexity of the application on which the tests are performed. Specifically, the more factors are involved, and the more complex the environments the application runs in, the more complex the tests are.

Based on these observations, we define the following four test case types: type 0 tests, type 1 tests, type 2 tests, and type 3 tests.

A. Type 0 Tests

Type 0 tests are tests that verify the implementation of program units such as methods or functions, modules, interfaces, and components of the software. There is no involvement with anything outside the software code components in this type of test. This type of test has been referred to as ***unit test***.

B. Type 1 Tests

Type 1 tests are tests that verify the functionalities of the software application and the integration of various pieces of the software that work together as a whole. This type of test is also referred to as ***integration test***.

C. Type 2 Tests

Type 2 tests are tests that verify the software requirements under real-world conditions with factors and variables beyond those with the software functionalities. For example, testing how the application performs when a large number of users are using the application at the same time. Some typical examples of type 2 tests are performance tests, security tests, and usability tests.

D. Type 3 Tests

Type 3 tests are tests that **validate** if the software requirements meet the needs of the customer and other identified stakeholders of the software. It concerns if the application is acceptable and suitable to use and if there is any potential adverse impact to customers/consumers. Type 3 tests are often referred to as *acceptance tests*.

We call testing with type 0 test cases type 0 testing, testing with type 1 test cases type 1 testing, and so on. Also, we may use 'test' or 'case' as a short form of 'test case'.

Type 0 tests are based on software implementation, type 1 and 2 tests are based on software requirements, and type 3 tests are based on user needs and if there is any discrepancy between the needs and the requirements.

This classification also illustrates various stages of the testing efforts and is also matching with the common sequences of testing along with software release. Type 0 tests are normally executed first (even before the whole application is built), followed by type 1 tests, and then type 2 tests, then type 3 tests in the last. In practice, different types of tests could be interleaved.

The more complex a test, the slower to execute it. Type 0 tests should execute the fastest since they are at a low level and have no or fewer dependencies.

Type 0 tests are usually implemented by software developers, type 1 tests are usually implemented and performed by either or both software developers and quality engineers, type 2 tests are normally executed by quality engineers, and type 3 tests are usually conducted by stockholders, such as product managers and customers.

The classification is summarized in Table 2.4.

As indicated earlier, types of testing also reflect stages of software development and release life cycles. Type 0 testing is done during the code development phase, type 1 testing is performed during the integration stage, type 2 testing is done when the whole system is assembled, and type 3 testing is done during the final stages of development processes before product release.

CHAPTER 2: SOFTWARE TEST CASES

	Type 0	Type 1	Type 2	Type 3
Validation of application acceptability				x
Verification of requirements in production			x	x
Verification of functionality requirements		x	x	x
Verification of individual code modules in implementation	x	x	x	x
	Unit tests	Integration tests		Acceptance tests

Table 2.4: Fundamental classification of test cases

The four types of tests are illustrated in Figure 2.6 in terms of complexity.

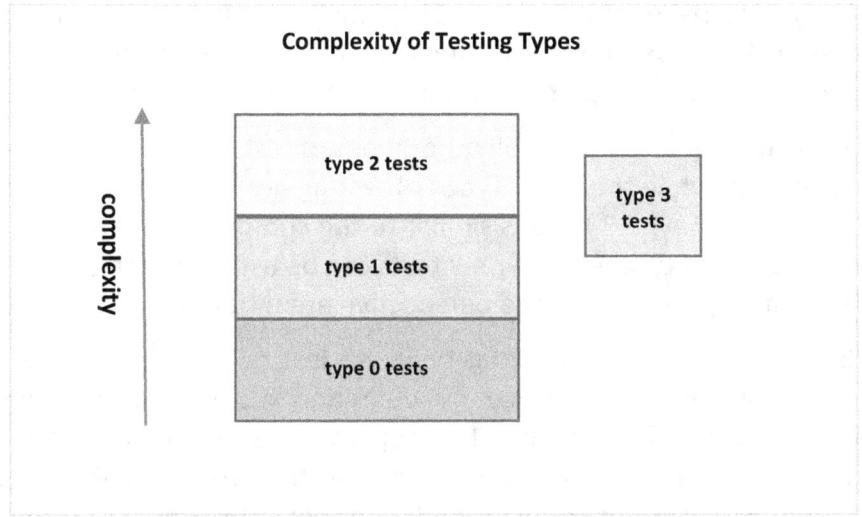

Figure 2.6: Illustration of the complexity of testing types

Type 0 testing is done along with software development at the implementation stage. Type 0 testing is part of a development process named test-driven development if the process is adopted. Type 0 tests are for the testing of the implementation of software units, and are usually written by software developers, and are embedded in the software development source control, release, and continuous integration processes.

Type 1 testing is closely coupled with software development. Functional modules of the application are tested individually along with other modules in the application interacting with the functionalities under test. Type 1 testing verifies that the functionalities meet the functional requirements.

Type 1 tests are usually the ones quality engineers spend most of their time on while working with software developers in an agile environment. The testing efforts are iterated through the development process.

Type 2 testing is often performed after type 1 testing and is also executed in parallel with type 1 testing in certain cases. Type 2 testing verifies that in various real-time scenarios the application meets the requirements under those circumstances. Type 2 testing is typically executed by quality engineers.

Type 3 testing is not to verify any functional or real-time requirements, but rather to validate that those software requirements and the design of the application meet the intended business usage of the application, to determine if there is any discrepancy between the stated purpose and what the application to be delivered can achieve. This type of testing is usually performed by stakeholders and sometimes by customers. A subset of the tests may also be executed by quality engineers in certain cases, to be included in the smoke test suite, for example, to validate the state of the application after certain changes, if the tests are well defined.

Type 3 testing is different from all other types of testing in that it is to *validate* the application, while the other types of testing are to *verify* the application. The complexity of type 3 tests is similar to the complexity of type 1 and type 2 tests. A subset of type 1 and type 2 tests can be used for type 3 testing, only that the testing purpose and the perspective are different.

Type 3 testing is not covered in this book, it's less relevant in terms of testing techniques and principles since by definition it's validation against the suitability of the software from the application shareholders perspective, rather than to verify if the software functionalities are as specified and if the application is robust in quality and can perform well in a real-world environment. Also, by definition, type 3 testing is not to be performed by software developers and quality engineers who are the intended audience of the book.

Table 2.5 lists the corresponding type numbers of certain common testing types.

A specific testing project for a particular testing purpose can contain different types of tests. For example, regression testing should include type 0, type 1, and type 2 tests. UI testing can be type 1 or type 2. Type 1 UI tests are the most common ones designed to verify UI functionalities and integrations with other services manifested on UI. Certain type 2 tests are performed on the UI as well, such as usability tests.

CHAPTER 2: SOFTWARE TEST CASES

A digit is assigned to a few types of performance tests: benchmark testing is classified as type 2.0; load testing is classified as type 2.1; stress testing is classified as type 2.2.

	Types
Unit testing	0
Integration testing	1
Functional testing	1
System testing	2
Acceptance testing	3
Performance testing	2
Benchmark testing	2.0
Load testing	2.1
Stress testing	2.2
Security testing	2
Usability testing	2
Compatibility testing	2
Browser testing	2
Internationalization testing	2
Database testing	0 to 2
Backend testing	0 to 2
UI testing	1 to 2
Smoke testing	0 to 2
Sanity testing	0 to 2
Regression testing	0 to 2
Black box testing	1 to 2
White box testing	0 to 2
Grey box testing	0 to 2

Table 2.5: Fundamental type classification of certain common testing types

Type 0 tests are discussed in more detail in Chapter 9, and type 1 tests in Chapter 10. Type 2 performance testing is discussed in Chapter 11.

EXERCISE PROBLEMS:

P2.1: Which of the following are test cases and which are not, based on the definitions in this chapter, and why?

(1) A bag contains 100 balls, 50 are red and 50 are blue. Randomly pick 50 balls out of the bag, keep a record of the number of red balls. Put the 50 balls back to the bag and repeat the same actions 99 times. You have a total of 100 records of the number of red balls. Do an average of the 100 numbers, verify that the average is between 22 and 28.

(2) Verify that the number of stars in the Milky Way Galaxy is 300 billion 200 million and 190,515.

(3) Open the calculator application on your mobile device, verify 2 plus 2 is 12.

(4) Go to google.com, enter search team: 'orange fruit', verify that the 3rd link in the result is www.myorangefruitsite.com.

P2.2: Write test cases for the following software module.

A door is controlled by one push button, if the door is open, push the button will close it, if the door is closed, push the button will open it, if the door is jammed, push the button will have no effect. Write test cases for this application. Discuss if the tests are finite, are encapsulating, are genuine, are deterministic, are reproducible, are atomic, and are independent.

P2.3: *Black Holes.

Black holes are the densest, most massive singular objects in the universe. The no-hair theorem states that, once it achieves a stable condition after formation, a black hole has only three independent physical properties: mass, charge, and angular momentum. An ***event horizon*** is a boundary in space-time beyond which events cannot affect an outside observer. At the event horizon, the escape velocity is equal to the speed of light. Since general relativity states that nothing can travel faster than the speed of light, nothing inside the event horizon can ever cross the boundary and escape beyond it, including light. Each black hole has its own event horizon.

Consider black hole as a software application, tests are needed to verify that a stable black hole with certain properties (mass, charge, and angular momentum) has a certain event horizon. In other words, given a set of values of mass, charge, and angular momentum, the size of the event horizon is defined. Is this system testable in this regard? If testable, in what sense the test cases are finite? are deterministic? are encapsulate? are reproducible?

P2.4: A web application has three input boxes for the day, month, and year, and produces the number of days since January 1, 1970. List 5 input vectors and 5 output vectors for this application.

P2.5: Classify the following tests into fundamental types.

(1) Verify that after a superuser, 'User_A', is signed in on a membership website, 'User_A' can see the address information of another user: 'User_B'.
(2) Verify after turning a web page with English (the default language for the site) into a different language, such as French, the form on the page displays properly.
(3) Verify under a fixed set of settings of environment variables, such as on the same browser and with the same kind of network connection, a specific web page loads between 1.5 and 2.0 seconds.
(4) A user logged on to a shopping website, verify the user can click on the shopping cart link and see the product items in the shopping cart.
(5) A Java method, *average (int a, int b)*, is written to calculate the average of two numbers, the following is a test for it:

```
@Test
public void testAverageOfTwoIntegersThreeAndFive () {
    assertEquals(4, average (3, 5));
}
```

PART TWO

Test Case Generation Techniques

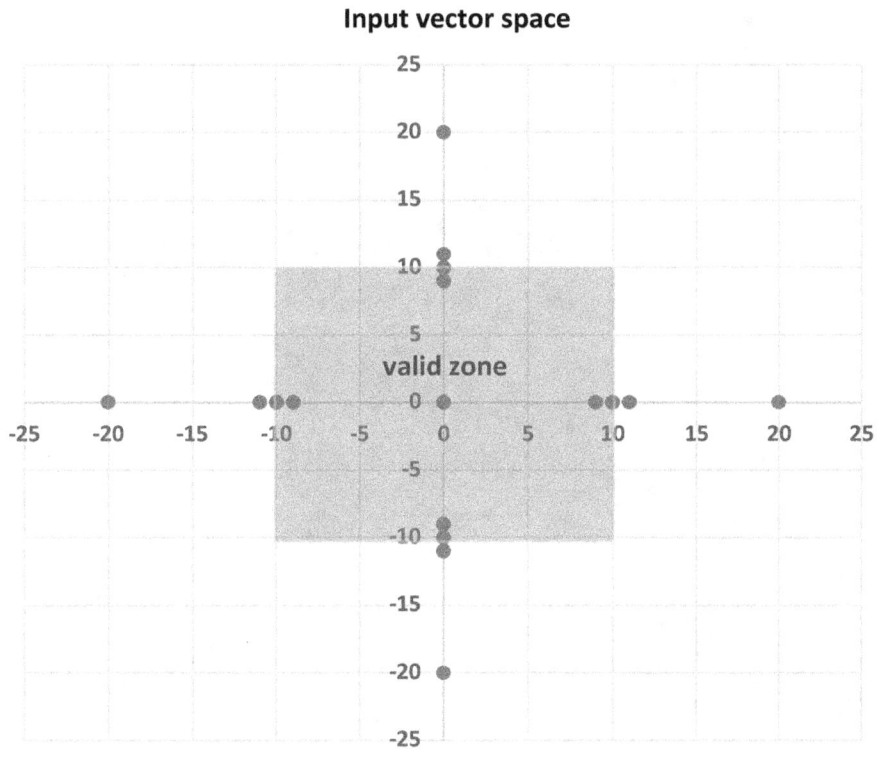

3 EQUIVALENCE PARTITIONING

Given that the number of input vectors is usually quite large, how to select a subset of the input vectors and still maintain proper testing coverage is essential in software testing. Equivalence partitioning is a simple way conceptually to reduce the number of tests for software applications and is the basic and most widely used technique in software testing.

3.1 EQUIVALENCE PARTITIONING

Mathematically, an equivalence class is a set that all the members of the set are in a given equivalence relation. For example, consider the set of all trees, and if an equivalence relation is defined as "are apple trees", then there is one particular equivalence class consisting of all apple trees.

More formally, an **equivalence relation** on a set X determines a partition of X. Given a set X and a set of n non-empty subsets $X_1, X_2, \ldots, X_n$, these subsets form a partition of X:

(1) iff $X_1 \cup X_2 \cup \ldots \cup X_n = X$
(2) $X_i \cap X_j = \{\}, \forall\, i, j \in \{1, \ldots, n\}, i \neq j$

The 1st condition ensures completeness of the subsets, and the 2nd condition ensures non-redundancy. Each subset is an equivalence class.

A partition of a set X is a set P of non-empty subsets of X for which each element x belongs to one and only one member of P. In other words, a partition P of X is a collection of nonempty, disjoint subsets of X such that each element of X belongs to a member of P, and $P = \{X_1, X_2, \ldots, X_n\}$.

For example, suppose there are 15 passengers on a bus, the set of people is:

X: {Abel(21), Bob(40), Carol(22), David(26), Emily(21), Frank(45), Henry(25), Iris(4), Jack(28), Ken(24), Lisa(48), May(8), Nancy(46), Owen(44), Peter(47)}

The number in the brackets indicates the age of the person. The passengers in the set are to be partitioned by age groups: 0 to 9, 10 to 19, 20 to 29, and so on.

The non-empty subsets are:

X_1 (age 0 to 9): {Iris, May}
X_2 (age 20 to 29): {Abel, Carol, David, Emily, Henry, Ken, Rick, Jack}
X_3 (age 40 to 49): {Bob, May, Frank, Lisa, Nancy}

Each person belongs to one and only one subset, all the 15 names are included in these sets, and there is no redundancy.

In software testing, an equivalence class is a subset of the input vectors (we also use 'input values' to refer to the same thing) such that if any value in a set is processed correctly (or incorrectly), then it is assumed that all other values in the set will be processed correctly (or incorrectly), the tests based on the values in the same set are expected to exhibit similar behaviors.

The input vectors are divided into equivalence class sets, and then one input vector is selected from each set. The total number of tests is reduced from the total number of input vectors to the number of equivalence class sets. There is no overlapping within the equivalence class sets, a specific input vector resides in one equivalence set.

For simplicity, instead of calling set P (the set of subsets of X) a partition, we call each subset, an equivalence class, a **partition**, so X_1 is a partition of X, and so on.

Let's look at an example.

Example 3.1: An Input Box for Integers 1 to 12 (Month Numbers)

The application is an input box that accepts an integer and returns a number representing a month in a year, 1 corresponds to January, 2 to February, and so on. Clearly, the valid numbers are from 1 to 12.

If only consider integer input values, there are three equivalence classes:

(i) Invalid input set 1: numbers less than 1: $\{x \mid x < 1\}$
(ii) Valid input set: numbers from 1 to 12: $\{x \mid 1 \leq x \leq 12\}$
(iii) Invalid input set 2: numbers greater than 12: $\{x \mid x > 12\}$

The following is an illustration of the three equivalence classes:

```
...-5 -4 -3 -2 -1 0 1 2 3 4 5 6 7 8 9 10 11 12 13 14 15 16 17 18...
------------------------|--------------------------------|-------------------------
      invalid set 1              valid set                 invalid set 2
```

Instead of testing every integer, we can just pick one number from each of the three sets, for example (the valid value is in bold):

{-2, **3**, 15}

Therefore, only three test cases are needed to cover all integer values.

Equivalence class partitioning relies on knowledge of the application, knowledge of software programming languages, and knowledge of computer science concepts. Often, it also relies on heuristics. In the above example, input values 1 through 12 can be handled the same way easily in any programing language. For example, the application could be implemented with the following Java code segment:

```java
public static int MonthNumber (int input) {
    int month = -1;
    if (input > 12 || input < 1) {
        System.out.println("month value should be between 1 and 12.");
    }
    else { month = input; }
    return month;
}
```

Code Segment 3.1: Java MonthNumber method for Example 3.1

Two or more values can be selected in each equivalence set for more confidence of coverage. For instance, selecting two values in each set:

{ -12, -2, **3, 11**, 15, 31}.

In general, the number of input values to select, hence the total number of test cases, can be written as:

$$N(Y) = an + c \qquad (3\text{-}1)$$

Where n is the number of equivalent sets of input vectors, and a is a small integer representing how many input vectors to choose from each set, and c is an integer representing the number of special cases to handle if any.

For instance, with the above example, if the following vectors are selected:

{-12, -2, 0, **3, 11**, 15, 31},

then $a = 2$, and $c = 1$. The vector [0] is added since '0' is considered special in computer programs where issues may exist.

Other special cases include the number of days in February in a leap year, the number of days in a non-leap year, number of months in the lunar calendar in a leap year.

When $a = 1$, and $c = 0$, we have:

$$N(Y) = n \tag{3-2}$$

The total number of test cases is the total number of equivalence partitioning sets. We call this scenario the **base case** *for* **equivalence partitioning**.

As we have mentioned, when it comes to what values to pick in each set, heuristics can be followed. For example, choose midpoints and boundary values to represent each set. In the above example, the following set of values could be selected:

{-99, -1, 0, **1, 6, 12**, 13, 101}.

We will discuss more on boundaries in section 3.3.

In equivalence partition technique, there are two main **principles** to follow:

(1) Each equivalence set should be atomic: every input vector leads to the same behavior.
(2) All equivalence sets applicable to the application should be included.

In Example 3.1, if the element is an input box on a web page, we have to consider other characters a user can type in the box from a computer keyboard, or any other device. Only integers between 1 and 12 are valid, but we know that there are non-integers and strings, including special characters you can type or paste into the input box.

Also, there are extreme conditions such as if the input is a huge number exceeding the maximum can be held in an integer (for a 32-bit integer, the range is from -2,147,483,648 to +2,147,483,647). The purpose of a test with an extreme value is to verify error handling with the value. In reality, there would be a maximum number of digits that can be put in the input box, in which case, the extreme value to select is the largest or smallest number the specified maximum number of digits is allowed.

Therefore, for an input box on a web page, we can amend the above partitions to the following sets:

(i) { integer x | x < -2,147,483,648}
(ii) { integer x | -2,147,483,648 ≤ x < 1}
(iii) { integer x | 1 ≤ x ≤ 12}
(iv) { integer x | 2,147,483,647 ≥ x > 12}

(v)   { integer x | x > 2,147,483,647}
(vi)   { real number x | x < 1.0}
(vii)   { real number x | 1.0 ≤ x ≤ 12.0}
(viii)   { real number x | x > 12.0}
(ix)   { x | x ∈ [a-zA-Z] }
(x)   { x | x ∈ [\t] }
(xi)   { x | x ∈ [!@#$%^&*()*\/;\-=[\\]\^_{|}<>~`] }
(xii)   { x | x ∈ [输入框] }

There are also other combinations or subsets of strings other than the last four partitions shown above, but since these are all invalid tests involving strings for a relatively simple application, further sub-partition is not necessary unless we have knowledge of the implementation in which those cases are treated differently.

Based on these partitions, if one vector is chosen from each of the partition sets, then a sample input vector set is shown below with total of 12 test cases:

     {-2147483649, -10 ,**6**, 20, 2147483648, 0.80, 3.01, 19.50, L, \t, #, 入}

The test cases with these input values are generated in Table 3.1.

Test cases	Input vectors	Expected result
1	-2147483649	invalid
2	-10	invalid
3	**6**	valid
4	20	invalid
5	2147483648	invalid
6	0.8	invalid
7	3.01	invalid
8	19.5	invalid
9	L	invalid
10	\t	invalid
11	#	invalid
12	入	invalid

Table 3.1: Test cases for Example 3.1

When generating and documenting test cases, the expected error messages or other behaviors should be specified for invalid cases, and the expected results should be specified for valid cases. For simplicity, sometimes we omit those details in this book.

This is an example of the base case equivalence partitioning technique ($a = 1$). We will see cases where a is 2 or more in the following sections.

3.2 LIMITATIONS OF BASE CASE EQUIVALENCE PARTITIONING

In certain cases, where the number of input vectors is not too large, partitioning can be combined with a brutal force approach, that is, every input vector in some of the equivalence sets can be selected for testing. The following example demonstrates the idea.

Example 3.2: A Season Printing Application

There are four valid seasons, 'Spring', 'Summer', 'Autumn', and 'Winter', each contains three months defined as:

Spring: months 3, 4, and 5;
Summer: months 6, 7, and 8;
Autumn: months 9, 10, and 11;
Winter: months 12, 1, and 2.

where month 1 represents January, month 2 represents February, and so on. The application takes a month number as an input and prints out the season.

The equivalence partitions are:

(i) $\{ x \mid x < 1 \}$
(ii) $\{ x \mid x \in [3,4,5] \}$
(iii) $\{ x \mid x \in [6,7,8] \}$
(iv) $\{ x \mid x \in [9,10,11] \}$
(v) $\{ x \mid x \in [12,1,2] \}$
(vi) $\{ x \mid x > 12 \}$

Selecting one value from each partition, we have a set of input vectors for testing:

{0, **3**, **6**, **9**, **12**, 15}.

There is a concern with the vector selection. Without any knowledge of the implementation, it's uncertain if all the values (3, 4, and 5) in set (ii) are treated the same way. For example, if the requirement was not met, instead of setting the seasons starting from month 3 for spring, it's set to start from 1, as seen in the following implementation with 'switch'.

CHAPTER 3: EQUIVALENCE PARTITIONING

```java
switch (month) {
case 1:
case 2:
case 3:
    out = "Spring";
    break;
}
```

Code Segment 3.2: Java code segment for Example 3.2

The defeat won't be discovered by the input values selected above. In this case, every number in partitions (ii) to (v) may have to be tested. In other words, if there is any unknown sub-partition, potential issues within the sub-partition may not be found.

Let's examine one more example to learn how a defect can be discovered with the base case equivalence partitioning technique, and more importantly, to illustrate what limitations base case equivalence partitioning has.

Example 3.3: A Program to Return Factorial of a Number

The requirement is to calculate factorials of numbers from 0 to 100.

The following code segment is an implementation of the program in Java:

```java
public static int Factorial (int n) {
    int c, fact = 1;
    if (n < 0)
        System.out.println ("The number should be non-negative.");
    else {
        for (c = 1; c <= n; c++)
            fact = fact*c;
    }
    return fact;
}
```

Code Segment 3.3: Initial Java implementation for Example 3.3

It's easy to come up with the following equivalence sets from the requirement:

(i)   { x | x < 0 }   : invalid set
(ii) { x | 0 ≤ x ≤ 100 }   : **valid set**
(iii) { x | x > 100 }   : invalid set

If we select one vector from each of the above sets and also include special cases of '0' and '1', then we have a set of test vectors:

{-5, **0**, **1**, **10**, 120}

All the test cases pass except the last one [120].

What's the expected result for vector 120? It should be similar to the expected result for vector -5, where a message is printed out to warn you of the limitations of the program. The above implementation failed to meet the requirement.

The following code segment shows an amendment aiming to meet the requirement.

```java
public static Integer Factorial (int n) {
    int c, fact = 1;
    if (n < 0)
        System.out.println("The number should be non-negative.");
    else if (n > 100) {
        System.out.println("The number should be no larger than 100.");
    } else {
        for (c = 1; c <= n; c++)
            fact = fact*c;
    }
    return fact;
}
```

Code Segment 3.4: Second Java implementation for Example 3.3

With this new implementation, all the test cases pass.

Can we declare that there is no defect in the program then? What will happen if you try input value 25?

The factorial of 25 is 25! = 15511210043330985984000000 ~ 1.55 x 10^{25}. It's much larger than a 4-byte 'int' can store. This defect is missed by the selected input vectors.

One way to handle this problem is to create subsets for valid set {x | 0 ≤ x ≤ 100} based on pieces of knowledge of the implementation. The other way is to include boundary values, the topic of the next section.

3.3: BOUNDARY VALUE PARTITIONING

Boundary is a concept in set theories. A boundary in a subset S is a set of elements or points within S, and these elements or points are close to the complement of S. It's the set of points such that every neighborhood of each of the points contains at least one point of S and at least one point not of S. A point or an element of the boundary of S is called a boundary point of S.

In our case, a boundary point is an input vector at the boundary of a partitioning set. Boundary partitioning testing is to include input vectors at the boundaries of each equivalence partition in the set of test cases.

When an equivalence partition set contains the same kind of linear elements, the boundary points would be the ones at both ends of the spectrum. For example, if only integers are in a set, then the smallest and the largest integers in this set are the boundaries.

Boundary partitioning testing only applies to cases where the input vectors have certain orders. If the set of input vectors contains discrete random values, such as string values with no clear orders, then boundary analysis is limited.

Let's go back to Example 3.1 from the last section, "An Input Box for Integers 1 to 12".

Examine the following partitions (only the subsets with integers are included to demonstrate the concept):

(i) { integer x | x < -2,147,483,648 }
(ii) { integer x | -2,147,483,648 ≤ x < 1}
(iii) { integer x | **1 ≤ x ≤ 12**}
(iv) { integer x | 2,147,483,647 ≥ x >12}
(v) { integer x | x > 2,147,483,647}

The boundary values in each of the partitions are listed below:

(i) {-2147483649}
(ii) {-2147483648, 0}
(iii) {1, 12}
(iv) {13, 2147483647}
(v) {2147483648}

We can construct the set of input vectors to consist of only boundary values:

{-3000000000, -2147483649,
-2147483648, 0,
1, 12,
13, 2147483647,
2147483648, 3000000000}.

For a partition having an open end, such as {integer x | x > 2,147,483,647}, the boundary is infinity, a relatively large value is selected, as we did with values '3000000000' and '-3000000000'.

The total number of test cases is twice the number of partitions ($a=2$, and $b=0$ in equation (3-1)).

It's advisable to include the values adjacent to the boundary values in a valid set as well, adding two more values in the valid set. For example, in set {integer x | 1 ≤ x ≤ 12}, the two boundary adjacent values are 2 (adjacent to the boundary value 1) and 11 (adjacent to boundary value 12). Even further, a mid-point in the valid set can also be included.

With this approach, we have a new set of input vectors to select:

{-3000000000, -2147483649,
-2147483648, 0,
1, 2, 6, 11, 12,
13, 2147483647,
2147483648, 3000000000}

The new set of input vectors produces a total of 13 test cases with 5 partitions.

This is a special case of equation (3-1), where 2 values are included for each of the invalid sets and 5 values are included for each of the valid sets.

The 5 valid values are:

min, min+1, midpoint, max-1, max;

where 'min' is the minimum possible valid value, 'min+1' is the value closest to 'min', 'midpoint' is the value at the center (or close to the center), 'max' is the maximum possible valid value, and 'max-1' is the valid value closest to 'max'.

the following plot illustrates the vector selections for the one-dimensional case on a line. The darker area represents the valid zone, the black dots represent the values selected in the valid partition and the circles represent the values selected in the two adjacent invalid partitions.

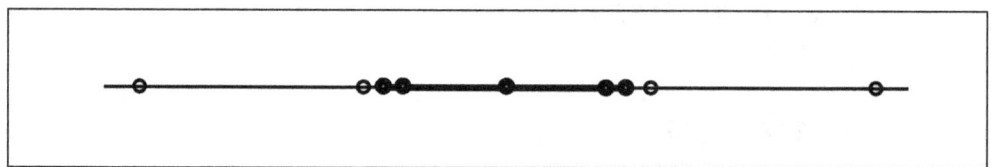

Figure 3.1: Illustration of boundary value selections

The two invalid values in each invalid zone normally would include one value close to the boundary and another further away from the boundary if the invalid zone is open on one side and include two boundary values if the invalid set has two boundaries.

In general, the following equation describes the number of input values to select:

$$N(Y) = au + bv + c \tag{3-3}$$

where u is the number of valid partition sets, and v is the number of invalid partition sets, a and b are the coefficients representing the number of vectors to select in each valid set and invalid set respectively, and c is a number representing any special cases. $N(Y)$ is the total number of input values to choose from. Normally more values are selected in a valid partition than in an invalid partition.

In the above example, $u = 1$, $v = 4$, $a = 5$, $b = 2$, and $c = 0$. Total number of input values to choose is $N = 5*1 + 2*4 = 13$.

When more than one value is selected in each partition, any special case is most likely covered, therefore we can set $c = 0$.

With this strategy, if there is only one input variable, the total number of input vectors to choose becomes:

$$N(Y) = 5u + 2v \tag{3-4}$$

We define this as the **standard case** for **equivalence partitioning**.

Let's look at another example.

Example 3.4: English Letter to Binary Code Conversion

An input box takes an English letter and outputs the binary code for the letter in another box on the UI. For example, the capital letter 'A' converts to 01000001, 'B' to 01000010, lower case 'a' to 01100001, etc. The valid input values are from A to Z and from a to z, only. Find the equivalence partitions and select input vectors in each partition for the standard case.

This is another linear (only one variable) input vector case. Based on ASCII character encoding sequence, we have the following equivalence partition sets:

(i) { x | x ∈ [space!'#$%&'()*+,-./] }
(ii) { x | x ∈ [0-9] }
(iii) { x | x ∈ [:;<=>?@] }
(iv) { x | x ∈ **[A-Z]** }
(v) { x | x ∈ [[^_`]]}
(vi) { x | x ∈ **[a-z]** }
(vii) { x | x ∈ [{|}~] }
(viii){ x | x ∈ [Ç-nbsp] }
(ix) { x | x ∈ [一-锓] }

The last set is a set of Unicode input vectors, part of a superset of ASCII to handle other languages such as CJK languages. Sets (iv) and (vi) are valid sets, all others are invalid sets.

There are 2 valid sets and 7 invalid sets, from equation (3-4) there should be total of 5*2 + 7*2 = 24 input vectors to select, with two boundary values in each invalid set, and 5 values in each valid set. The following set is a sample selection:

{ *space* / 0 9 : @ **A B M Y Z** [`a b n y z { ~ Ç *nbsp* — 锓 }.

In all the examples we have discussed so far, the valid input vectors are either numerical or alphabetical. If there is no clear sequence or order in the elements in an equivalence partition set, boundary value analysis is limited. For example, if a set contains colors such as {*red, orange, yellow, green, blue, violet*}, and there is no order of it, then boundary values are not defined, and the equivalence partitioning technique cannot be applied to it.

3.4 EQUIVALENCE PARTITIONING WITH MULTIPLE DIMENSIONS

So far, we have only considered cases involving only one parameter. It'll become very complicated if two or more parameters are involved. Simply speaking, all the permutations of the partition sets for each parameter should be included, minus any redundancies. The total number of test cases is then the number of elements in the set of Cartesian products of all the equivalence sets, excluding redundancies. We need a better strategy to handle multiple parameters.

Let's examine a case with two parameters first.

Example 3.5: Average of Two Integers

The program takes two integer parameters between -10 and 10 (inclusive) and return the average of the two values. The following is a Java implementation of the program:

```java
public static double AverageOfTwoNumbers (int x, int y) {
    double result = -1.00;
    if (x < -10 || x > 10 || y < -10 || y > 10)
        System.out.println("The inputs should be integers between -10 & 10.");
    else
        result = (x + y) / 2.0;
    return result;
}
```

Code Segment 3.5: Java implementation for Example 3.5

Below is the list of equivalence partition sets for both x and y, three sets for each variable:

(i) $\{x \mid x < 10\}$
(ii) $\{x \mid -10 \leq x \leq 10\}$
(iii) $\{x \mid x > 10\}$
(iv) $\{y \mid y < 10\}$
(v) $\{y \mid -10 \leq y \leq 10\}$
(vi) $\{y \mid y > 10\}$

For base case, one value from each partition is selected, for example:

x: {-20, **0**, 20}; y: {-99, **1**, 99}

To fully test the program, all permutations of value pairs in these two sets should be included:

(x,y): { [-20, -99], [-20, 1], [-20, 99],
[0, -99], [0, 1], [0, 99],
[20, -99], [20, 1], [20, 99] }

We define the scenario that all permutations of base case values from each partition must be included as the ***base worst case*** of equivalence partitioning.

In general, for base worst case, the total number of test cases is:

$$N(Y) = \prod_{i=1}^{r} n_i \qquad (3\text{-}5)$$

where n_i is the number of partitions for i^{th} parameter and r is the total number of parameters.

In the above example, $r = 2$, and each has three partitions ($n_x = 3$, and $n_y = 3$), the total number of test cases is 3 x 3 = 9.

In the same example, for each variable, if we adopt equation (3-4) ($N(Y) = 5u + 2v$) for standard case, then the total number of input values to choose is 9 for x and 9 for y ($u = 1$ and $v = 2$ for both x and y). For example, we can select (valid vectors are in bold):

x: {-99,-11,**-10,-9,0,9,10**,11,100}
y: {-101,-11,**-10,-9,0,9,10**,11,111}

A full set of input vectors for testing would include all permutations of the values in each of the above values, will a total number of 9*9 = 81 test cases:

(x,y): { [-99,-101], [-99, -11], ... [-11,-101], ... [100,111]}

We define the scenario that all permutations of standard case values from each partition must be included as the ***standard worst case*** of equivalence partitioning.

In general, the total number of test cases for the standard worst case is:

$$N(Y) = \prod_{i=1}^{r}(5u_i + 2v_i) \tag{3-6}$$

where u_i is the number of valid sets for the ith parameter, and v_i is the number of invalid partition sets for the ith parameter, and r is the total number of parameters.

The program for the average of two integers is an extremely simple one. For a real-world application, the number of tests for a worst-case scenario is much larger, and further reduction of the number is needed. We need better strategies to achieve this goal.

Now, let's try to examine the case visually. The input vector space is plotted in Figure 3.2 below, with x and y on each axis. Some points are marked with dots on the graph, which we will be discussing next.

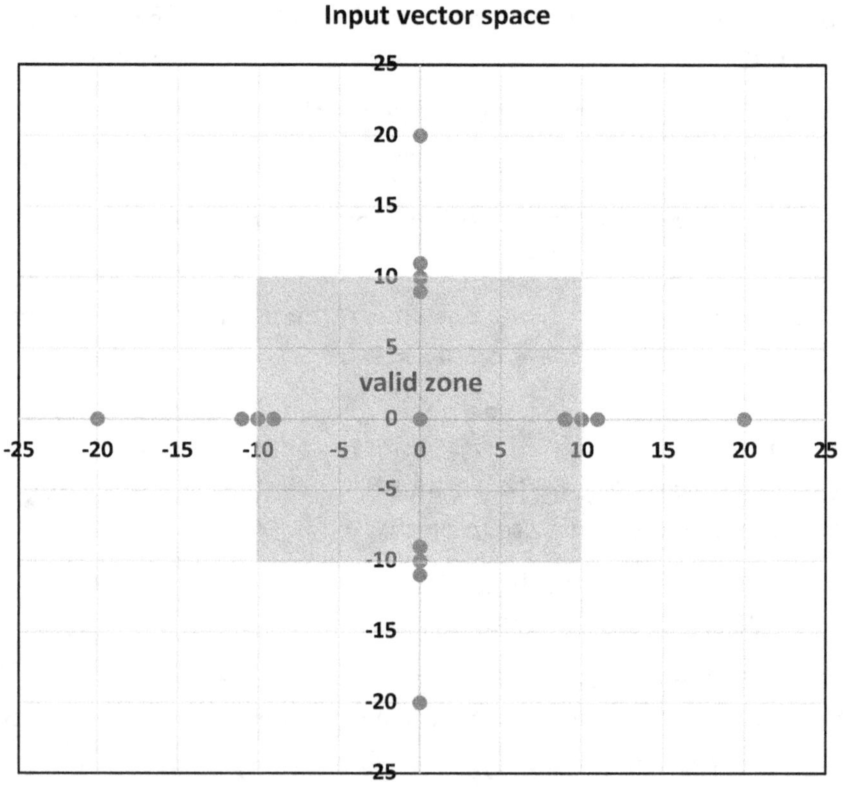

Figure 3.2: Input space for Example 3.5

It's clear that all valid values fall in the 'valid zone', a rectangle (a square in this case) with four corners at (-10, -10), (-10, 10), (10,10), and (10, -10), on the 2-dimensional space. All the rest space surrounding the valid zone is the invalid zone.

We can see on the plot that the valid zone has four edges. Instead of generating partitions for each variable, we could combine them, and identify partitions with the help of the graph. On this graph, boundary values on each side of the four edges are marked in dots. With some knowledge of the implementation (the Java code in Code Segment 3.5), we know that all the points in the valid zone should behave the same way, therefore, we can treat the valid zone as one partition.

On the vector space, all the points in the complement set of the valid zone set are invalid. With boundary analysis in mind, it's natural to divide the complement set into four partitions, corresponding to the number of edges.

Consider the following partitions (both x and y are integers):

(i) $\{x, y \mid -10 \leq x \leq 10, -10 \leq y \leq 10\}$
(ii) $\{x \mid x < -10\}$
(iii) $\{x \mid x > 10\}$
(iv) $\{y \mid y < -10\}$
(v) $\{y \mid y > 10\}$

Notice, the four invalid partitions are overlapping with each other if the absolute value of each parameter is over 10. We need to remove the overlaps.

To reduce redundancy with overlapping, the partitions are amended to:

(i) $\{x, y \mid -10 \leq x \leq 10, -10 \leq y \leq 10\}$
(ii) $\{x, y \mid x < -10, -10 < y < 10\}$
(iii) $\{x, y \mid x > 10, -10 < y < 10\}$
(iv) $\{x, y \mid y < -10, -10 < x < 10\}$
(v) $\{x, y \mid y > 10, -10 < x < 10\}$
(vi) $\{x, y \mid x < -10, y < -10\}$
(vii) $\{x, y \mid x > 10, y > 10\}$
(viii) $\{x, y \mid x < -10, y > 10\}$
(ix) $\{x, y \mid x > 10, y < -10\}$

These partitions are illustrated in Figure 3.3.

The last four partitions are the overlapping areas from the previous set of partitions and are marked as 'invalid zone O' (to be omitted) on the vector space.

CHAPTER 3: EQUIVALENCE PARTITIONING

Now let's examine these four zones marked as 'invalid zone O'. In these partitions, both variables are in their respected invalid zones individually, in other words, both x and y have invalid values.

In a software program, when one variable fails, the program will stop evaluating the second variable, and that makes the value of the second variable irrelevant.

In Code Segment 3.5, the evaluation is done by `if (x < -10 || x > 10 || y < -10 || y > 10)`. Clearly, when one condition satisfies it, the rest won't be evaluated. For example, if x > 10, then the next two conditions y < -10 and y > 10 are skipped to evaluate. Therefore, the four overlapping zones can be excluded from the set of equivalence partitions.

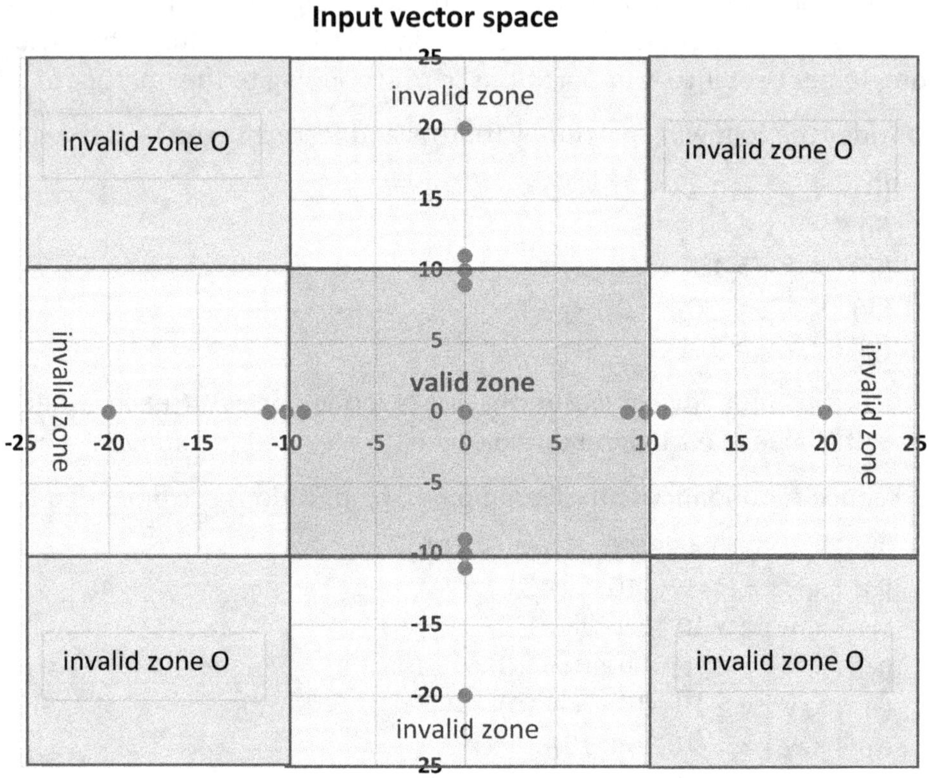

Figure 3.3: Input space for Example 3.5 with more specific invalid zones

This leaves us with the following 5 partitions:

(i)   { x, y | -10 ≤ x ≤ 10, -10 ≤ y ≤ 10}
(ii) { x, y | x < -10, -10 < y < 10}
(iii) { x, y | x > 10, -10 < y < 10}
(iv) { x, y | y < -10, -10 < x < 10}

(v) { x, y | y > 10, -10 < x < 10}

The two variables x and y are independent of each other, and there are four edges on the vector space surrounding the valid zone. We treat each of these four edges as one boundary. For the standard case of equivalence partitioning, we select one value on each edge and one value adjacent to the edge in the valid zone and select one value at the center of the valid zone. For the four invalid zones, we select two values as usual for each. The selected vectors are illustrated (not on the scale for certain values in the invalid zone) in dots on the vector space.

The total number of test cases is 4*2 + 1 + 4*2 = 17, a large reduction from 81 (the total number of cases for standard worst case).

Here is a sample selection of input vectors for each of the corresponding partitions:

(i) { [10, 0], [9, 1], [0, 9], [-1,10], [-10, 2], [-9,-2],[0, -10], [3,-9] ,[0,0] }
(ii) { [-11, 0], [-100, -2] }
(iii) { [11, 1], [99, 4] }
(iv) { [1, -11], [-1, -99] }
(v) { [0, 11], [5, 111] }

If we assume that the number of invalid zones is the same as the number of edges, then, the total number of input vectors are:

$$N(Y) = 4n + 1 \qquad (3\text{-}7)$$

where n is the number of edges. We define this scenario as the **standard case with edges** of equivalence partitioning.

We can also interpret this case as follows: four vectors are chosen with regards to each edge: two valid vectors and two invalid vectors, and one normal vector toward the center of the input space is chosen (basically there are only two partitions, one valid and one invalid).

With two parameters, the total number of edges is not necessarily four. The following example demonstrates a case with two parameters, but with only two edges.

Example 3.6: A Program Takes Two Integer Variables

A program takes two integer inputs, x, and y, the requirements are:

(1) $x \leq 10$
(2) $y \geq 5 - x$

The vector space is plotted in the graph in Figure 3.4.

Three partitions are identified:

(i) { x, y | x ≤ 10, y ≥ 5-x }
(ii) { x | x > 10 }
(iii) { x, y | y < 5-x, x ≤ 10 }

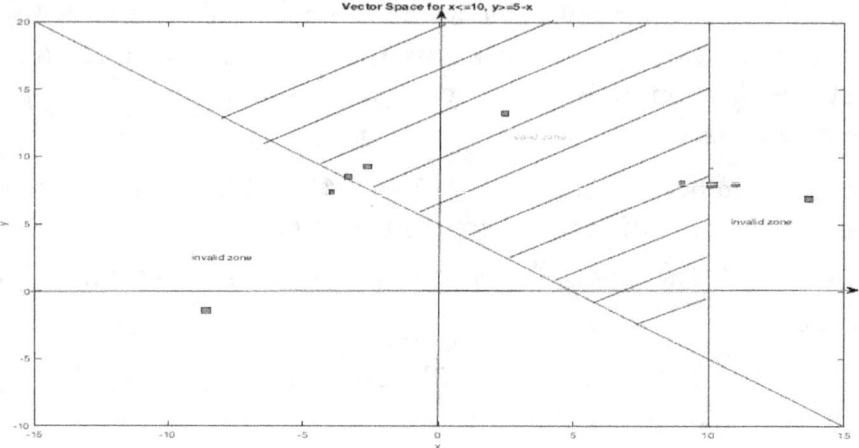

Figure 3.4: Vector space for Example 3.6

The valid partition (i) is the area with the stripes on the plot between two lines, and it's open towards the positive *y*-direction. The overlapping area of { x, y |y<5-x, x>10} is excluded as usual (both parameters have invalid values within this area). Note, we are not including the integer overflow partitions for simplicity (including those partitions won't add any value to the concepts we are demonstrating, but in a real situation, those partitions should be included).

On the above vector space, there are only two edges bordering the valid partition.

According to equation (3-7) for standard case with edges, the total number of test vectors to select is: 4 * 2 + 1 = 9. The small squares/rectangles in the above plot illustrate the selected test vectors. Here is a list of selections:

(i) { [3,12], [9,8], [10,8], [-2,8], [-3,8] }
(ii) { [11, 8], [14, 6] }
(iii) { [-4,8], [-9,-2] }

Now let's consider an example with three parameters.

Example 3.7: Area of a Triangle

Given three numbers as the lengths of the three sides of a triangle, calculate the area of the triangle. The length of each side is in the range of 1 and 100. Besides the length limit, the numbers should also satisfy that any of the numbers is no larger than the sum of the other two, otherwise, it's not a triangle.

The following is a Java implementation of the program.

```java
public static double TriangleArea (int x, int y, int z) {
    double hp = 0.0;
    double area = -1.0;
    if (x < 1 || x > 100 || y < 1 || y > 100 || z < 1 || z > 100) {
        System.out.println ("The sizes should be between 1 and 100.");
        return -1;
    } else if ( ( x >= y + z) || (y >= x + z) || ( z >= x + y) ) {
        System.out.println ("A side cannot be larger than the sum of the other 2.");
        return -1;
    } else {
        hp = (x + y + z) / 2.0;
        area = Math.sqrt ( hp * (hp - x) * (hp - y) * (hp - z) );
    }
    return area;
}
```

Code Segment 3.6: Java implementation for Example 3.7 triangle area

There are two requirements in this problem, one is that the range of valid values is between 1 and 100, the other is that any of the numbers is no larger than the sum of the other two numbers.

Let's consider the first requirement first. Since there are 3 variables, the input vector space has 3 dimensions, and the valid zone is a cube on the space with 6 surfaces.

The 8 corner vectors on the cube boundaries are:

[1,1,1], [1,1,100],
[1,100,1], [1,100,100],
[100,1,1], [100,1,100],
[100,100,1], [100,100,100].

If this is the only requirement, then we can divide the invalid zone into 6 partitions, each on one side of a surface, and remove the areas where 2 or 3 variables are all invalid. The partitions are:

(i) $\{x, y, z \mid x < y + z; y < x + z; z < x + y;$
     $1 \leq x \leq 100; 1 \leq y \leq 100; 1 \leq z \leq 100\}$
(ii) $\{x, y, z \mid x < 1; 1 \leq y \leq 100; 1 \leq z \leq 100\}$

(iii) {x, y, z | x > 100; 1 ≤ y ≤ 100; 1 ≤ z ≤ 100}
(iv) {x, y, z | y < 1; 1 ≤ x ≤ 100; 1 ≤ z ≤ 100}
(v) {x, y, z | y > 100; 1 ≤ x ≤ 100; 1 ≤ z ≤ 100}
(vi) {x, y, z | z < 1; 1 ≤ x ≤ 100; 1 ≤ y ≤ 100}
(vii) {x, y, z | z > 100; 1 ≤ x ≤ 100; 1 ≤ y ≤ 100}

The 1st one is the valid zone, and the rest are the invalid ones.

Now consider the second requirement, any number is no larger than the sum of the other two. It should be possible to plot the topology with a 3-dimensional Cartesian coordinates system, but let's just imagine that there is a chunk of the valid zone cube (which satisfies the first requirement) in which the input vectors do not satisfy the second requirement, and should be removed from the cube, and what's left with the valid zone is no longer a cube, and the boundaries are no longer the 6 regular square surfaces, but still are continuous surfaces, and these surfaces are the dividers of the invalid partitions and the valid partition in the vicinity of the cube.

These 5 corners would still be on the boundary: [1,1,1], [1,100,100], [100,1,100], [100,100,1], [100,100,100]; while these 3 won't: [1,1,100], [1,100,1], [100,1,1], and the missing area in the cube are around these 3 corners. In fact, 3 identical-in-shape chunks are removed from the cube and each chunk is a triangular pyramid. What's left in the valid zone is a prime with 6 surfaces. 3 of them are the cut-in-half squares of the cube at the far ends of the cube from the origin point [1,1,1]. Each of the other 3 surfaces is an equilateral triangle (all 3 sides are equal in length), which is the intersection of one of the three area, x = y + z; y = x + y; z = x + y, and the cube.

The 6 new surfaces are:

(1) {x, y, z | x = 100; 1 ≤ y ≤ 100; 1 ≤ z ≤ 100; y + z ≥ 100}
(2) {x, y, z | y = 100; 1 ≤ x ≤ 100; 1 ≤ z ≤ 100; x + z ≥ 100}
(3) {x, y, z | z = 100; 1 ≤ x ≤ 100; 1 ≤ y ≤ 100; x + y ≥ 100}
(4) {x, y, z | x = y + z; 1 ≤ x ≤ 100; 1 ≤ y ≤ 100; 1 ≤ z ≤ 100}
(5) {x, y, z | y = x + z; 1 ≤ x ≤ 100; 1 ≤ y ≤ 100; 1 ≤ z ≤ 100}
(6) {x, y, z | z = x + y; 1 ≤ x ≤ 100; 1 ≤ y ≤ 100; 1 ≤ z ≤ 100}

Similar to the two-dimension cases we have discussed in both Example 3.5 and Example 3.6, where four values are selected at each edge, we select 4 values around each of these 6 boundary surfaces, one on the boundary, one inside boundary in the valid zone, one outside boundary in the invalid zone, and one in the invalid zone further away from the boundary.

There are total of 6 surfaces, the total number of input vectors to select is 4*6 + 1 = 25.

Below is a list of input vector selections around the 6 surfaces:

(1) [**100, 75, 75**], [**99, 75, 75**], [101, 75, 75], [200, 75, 75]
(2) [**75, 100, 75**], [**75, 99, 75**], [75, 101, 75], [75, 200, 75]
(3) [**75, 75, 100**], [**75, 75, 99**], [75, 75, 101], [75, 75, 200]
(4) [**59, 30, 30**], [*60, 30, 30*], [61, 30, 30], [200, -10, 30]
(5) [**30, 59, 30**], [*30, 60, 30*], [30, 61, 30], [30, 200, -10]
(6) [**30, 30, 59**], [*30, 30, 60*], [30, 30, 61], [-10, 30, 200]

The values in **bold** indicate valid zone values, and the values in *italic* indicate boundary values. We also need one point close to the center of the cube, let's select [**50, 50, 50**].

In these vector selections, to demonstrate the idea, the same value such as 75 is used in multiple vectors. Variant values could also be selected, for example, [99, 75, 75] can be replaced by [99,80,50].

Test cases based on the above input vectors are listed in Table 3.2.

Test case	Input			Expected output
	x	y	z	
1	50	50	50	1082.53
2	100	75	75	2856.8
3	99	75	75	2789.1
4	101	75	75	Out of range
5	200	75	75	Out of range
6	75	100	75	2856.8
7	75	99	75	2789.1
8	75	101	75	Out of range
9	75	200	75	Out of range
10	75	75	100	2856.8
11	75	75	99	2789.1
12	75	75	101	Out of range
13	75	75	200	Out of range
14	59	30	30	160.90
15	60	30	30	Not a triangle
16	61	30	30	Not a triangle
17	200	-10	30	Out of range
18	30	59	30	160.90

19	30	60	30	Not a triangle
20	30	61	30	Not a triangle
21	30	200	-10	Out of range
22	30	30	59	160.90
23	30	30	60	Not a triangle
24	30	30	61	Not a triangle
25	-10	30	200	Out of range

Table 3.2: Test cases for Example 3.7

The total number of test cases for a case with three independent parameters is, in general, also satisfies equation (3-4), where n is the number of surfaces.

Note, the number of surfaces varies for different problems even with the same number of variables.

With the same partitioning strategy, we can extrapolate that, for a software module with multiple independent parameters, the total number of input vectors to select for the standard case of equivalence partitioning is:

$$N(Y) = 4n + 1 \qquad (3\text{-}8)$$

where n is **the number of faces in the hypergraph** of the independent variables.

As we have seen, for mathematically calculable parameters, the number of surfaces can be different even the number of parameters is the same, the number depends on the shape of the hyper graph.

A simple case is with a hypercube where the number of edges is fixed. For example, a cube with three parameters has six faces, a tesseract (the 4-dimensional analog of the cube) has eight faces, and a 5-cube has ten faces, and so on.

Furthermore, the number of tests can be further reduced based on knowledge of the application and its implementation.

In the triangle example, we know that each of the sides of the triangle is symmetric, and from the implementation, we also know that x, y and z are being treated the same way. Therefore, we can reduce the number of tests to 9. These 9 test cases are illustrated in Table 3.3.

Test case	x	y	z	Expected output
1	50	50	50	1082.53
2	100	75	75	2856.8
3	75	99	75	2789.1
4	75	75	101	Out of range
5	75	75	200	Out of range
6	59	30	30	160.90
7	30	60	30	Not a triangle
8	30	30	61	Not a triangle
9	-10	200	30	Out of range

Table 3.3: Reduced test case set for Example 3.7

3.5 CATEGORY PARTITIONING

The same kind of parameters is involved in the examples in the last section. In reality, a piece of software contains different kinds of parameters and has complex functional requirements. Even for an application with the same kind of parameters or with even a single parameter, there are often real-time environment dependences, such as the operating system the program is running on, the specific browser a web page is being loaded on.

One technique being used in practice to deal with applications with different kinds of parameters is called **category partition**, in which functional categories are identified based on requirements and the equivalence partitioning technique is applied in each of the functional categories independently.

Let's take a couple of examples to illustrate the concept.

Example 3.8: Password Creation Field on a Web Page

A password input box on a web page is used to create or update a password. Here are the requirements for this password module. The password string must contain:

(1) 8 to 20 characters.
(2) at least one upper case letter.
(3) at least one lower case letter.
(4) at least one number.
(5) at least one symbol in { *!@#$%* }.

So, 4 types of characters are accepted, upper case letters, lower case letters, numbers, and special characters. In regular expression, this can be represented by the following clause:

$$R = (?=^.\{8,20\}\$)(?=.*\backslash d)(?=.*[a\text{-}z]))?=.*[A\text{-}Z]0(?!.*\backslash s)[0\text{-}9a\text{-}zA\text{-}Z!@\#\$\%]*\$$$

Let' define R_1 as a password matching the requirements from (2) to (5):

$$R_1 = (?=.*\backslash d)(?=.*[a\text{-}z]))?=.*[A\text{-}Z]0(?!.*\backslash s)[0\text{-}9a\text{-}zA\text{-}Z!@\#\$\%]*\$$$

So, $R = (?=^.\{8,20\}\$)R_1$.

Now let's try to find equivalence partitions for this problem. There are different ways to approach the problem, but let's start by examining the requirements. From the requirements, we can infer that the following factors need to be considered:

(1) Length of the password string.
(2) Types of characters in the string.
(3) Position of different types of characters in the string.
(4) The number of characters in each type.
(5) Not-allowed characters.
(6) Special cases: e.g.: empty string, tab.

Each of the above items can be considered as one category, and the equivalence partitioning technique can be applied to each category.

We assume that if one condition is not met, the program will exist, so only one invalid value in each input vector is to be selected. That is, only selecting the input vectors in which only one of the parameters has an invalid value and the rest of the parameters take valid values.

Let's define a **one-error principle**:

For any invalid partition, any input vector to be selected must contain one and only one invalid parameter value.

Following the one-error principle, let's find the equivalence partitions for each of the 6 categories.

The first category, "(1) Length of the password string", is a linear case, we can easily come up with three partitions, one valid zone, and two invalid zones, one on each side of the valid zone. Based on the one-error principle, the input vectors to select in both of the invalid zones should meet the rest of the requirements – requirements (2) through (5). The size of the string is the parameter to test in this category.

For category (2), "Types of characters in the string", since there are four kinds of allowed characters, upper case, lower case, numerical, and special characters, constructing one valid partition and one invalid partition for each type should be a good approach. So, there are total of eight partitions for this category.

Come to category (3): "Position of different types of characters in the string". Let's define the position of a character in the password string as a parameter, then the position is a linear integer parameter with possible values of 1 to the length of the string. There are four partitions for this category, one for each type. We can combine these partitions with the four valid partitions in category (2) since for those valid partitions, there is no requirement on the position of a character for each type, a character can be at any position. Since five input vectors are to be selected in each of those four valid partitions, the same kind of characters in each of the five vectors can be arranged to put at different positions in the string. This way the requirement for category (3) is covered in those four partitions. For simplicity, only one character is inserted into the string to construct the input vectors for each character type. For example, when testing the 'number' type, only one number is placed in the string and the number is put at a different position for each of the five input vectors in a valid partition in category (2).

Category (4), "Number of characters in each type", is already covered by categories (1) and (2), since when a valid password is constructed, the length of the string must be equal to or greater than eight, more than one characters with at least one type are inevitable, given only four types are allowed.

Category (5) is "Not-allowed characters". There are a large variety of not-allowed characters, including not-allowed symbols (special characters), as we have seen in Example 3.3. For simplicity, let's just list one partition for all those not-allowed characters.

Category (6) is one partition with two special cases.

Based on the above arguments, we came up with the following partitions:

(a) { x | x ∈ [R] }
(b) { x | x ∈ [R_1]; length of x < 8 }
(c) { x | x ∈ [R_1]; length of x > 20 }
(d) { x | x ∈ [satisfies R except only one uppercase letter] }
(e) { x | x ∈ [satisfies R except only one lowercase letter] }
(f) { x | x ∈ [satisfies R except only one number] }
(g) { x | x ∈ [satisfies R except only one special character] }
(h) { x | x ∈ [satisfies R except no uppercase letter] }
(i) { x | x ∈ [satisfies R except no lowercase letter] }
(j) { x | x ∈ [satisfies R except no number] }

(k) { x | x ∈[satisfies R except no listed special character] }
(l) { x | x ∈[at least one character in $^\wedge R_1$; 8<= size of x <= 20] }
(m) { x | x ∈[\t] }

In partition (l) we denoted $^\wedge R_1$ as the complement of R_1.

The first three partitions are about the length of the string, the next four are about the positions of a character, the next four are about missing characters for each type of allowed characters, and the last two are about not-allowed characters and special cases.

There are total five valid partitions, and eight invalid partitions:

    valid partitions: (a), (d), (e), (f), (g);
    invalid partitions: (b), (c), (h), (i), (j), (k), (l), (m).

As we have seen that equivalence partitioning technique is better understood when a parameter can be linearly defined, or in other words, can be quantified in ordered numbers.

Let's now re-examine these partitions in a slightly different way.

The size of the password string, how many characters are there, is an easy one, the first three partitions cover this category. The position of a character in the string is another parameter as we have discussed for category (3).

We know that there are four types of allowed characters. The number of types of characters in a password string is a measurable quantity, so a parameter could be defined for it. This number can have values between 1 and 4.

For partition (l) on not-allowed characters, the number and the position of invalid characters are also measurable quantities. Let's use the number only for our discussion.

So, we have the following parameters plus a couple of special cases (think of $c = 2$ in equation (3-3) for special cases):

(a) Length of a valid string.
(b) Position of an allowed single character in the string, for each type.
(c) The number of types of characters (4 types are allowed).
(d) The number of invalid characters.

With this interpretation, the same equivalence partitions can be described slightly differently with these parameters:

(a) { x | x ∈[R] }
(b) { x | x ∈[R_1]; length of x < 8 }
(c) { x | x ∈[R_1]; length of x > 20 }
(d) { x | x ∈[R, except only 1 uppercase letter at different positions] }
(e) { x | x ∈[R, except only 1 lowercase letter at different positions] }
(f) { x | x ∈[R, except only 1 number at different positions] }
(g) { x | x ∈[R, except only 1 special character at different positions] }
(h) { x | x ∈[R, except no uppercase letter] }
(i) { x | x ∈[R, except no lowercase letter] }
(j) { x | x ∈[R, except no number] }
(k) { x | x ∈[R, except no listed special character] }
(l) { x | x ∈[at least one character in $^\wedge R_1$; 8 <= length of x <= 20] }
(m){ x | x ∈[\t] }

Next, let's generate input vectors for testing from these partitions.

Let's apply the standard equivalence partitioning technique first. Since each of the partitions is independent of each other, from equation (3-4), the total number of test cases is $5u + 2v$.

We could also separate them by categories by denoting u_i as the valid partitioning number for parameter i, and v_i as the invalid partitioning number for parameter i.

Then the total number of input vectors to select can be expressed as:

$$N(Y) = \sum_{i=1}^{r}(5u_i + 2v_i) \qquad (3\text{-}9)$$

where r is the number of categories.

Let's now select input vectors for these partitions. As usual, five values for each of the valid partitions are selected, two values for each of the invalid partitions are selected, with consideration of boundary conditions.

The following input vectors are carefully designed based on the above arguments:

(a) {ABcd123!, efgHIJ45@, MNO0909$xyz%Z#, 012345abadeUVWXY!@#, %$#@!fghij67890ACCCE }
(b) {012%abU, Aa0!}
(c) {%$#@!fghij67890ABCDEF, 1234567890ABCDEFGHijklmnop%$# }
(d) {A123abc!@#, 1Bxyz%$!789, ##66$eC888%%, fefefe7@7efefeYf, t8kn54t9%riojZ}
(e) {c343455TT%%, 3c43455TT%%, 4358dDD%$$#4, 343455TT%c%, 343455TT%%c}

(f) {0eoijfeog@AA, U1gjerpog$, foenr$#2YUYf, IUHIO%$#ffee3e, iuohgroooiuoH@!4}
(g) {%111222YYYaaa, 1$gdgkj878HHH, 4thigh@Yerj, jgd4UIHifsds!4, 56gkhJHJGddk%}
(h) {1234567abcd!@, qqqqqqq$#@}
(i) {AIHJIKH#%%435643, QQQQQQ99999}
(j) {!@ASDJDfgfgdfg, %%%%%%%%%%%%}
(k) {fjgoKJKLO34353, ojdoify58gioghir}
(l) {*ijg7543H@, O&fj64((k@g2}
(m) { *space*, \t }

The total number of input vectors is: 5 * 5 + 8 * 2 = 41.

In these input vectors, some other scenarios are also embedded. For example, a character shows multiple times at different locations. These scenarios could also be included in the partitions, depending on how the partition sets are generated.

The test cases generated with these input vectors are listed in Table 3.4.

The four parameters are listed in Table 3.4 as well. A minus sign on a position indicates counting backward from the last character. The values in bold indicate that the corresponding parameter is the one relevant to the specific test cases. For example, the values for 'Length' column are in bold for test cases 1 through 9, which are for partitions (a), (b), and (c), in which 'Length' is the parameter (8 ≤ length ≤ 20; length < 8; length > 20; respectively).

The empty cells in the position column indicate that position is not applicable for those cases.

Again, from the parameter values in the table, we can see that there is only one invalid value in each input vector, except in the last two special cases.

Is there any other approach to come up with partitions for this problem?

Remember we have identified four areas of parameters, let's denote them as:

(a) *l*: length of a valid string: [8-20]
(b) *p1, p2, p3, p4*: positions of an allowed single character for the four types: [1 to 20]
(c) *t*: number of types of characters: [1 to 4]
(d) *n*: number of invalid characters: [1 to 20]

We have a total of seven parameters: [*l, p1, p2, p3, p4, t, n*].

CHAPTER 3: EQUIVALENCE PARTITIONING

Test case	Input vector	Length	Position of allowed single character	Number of allowed types	Number & position of invalid characters	Expected result
1	ABcd123!	8		4	0	valid
2	efgHIJ45@	9		4	0	valid
3	MNO0909$xyz%Z#	14		4	0	valid
4	012345abadeUVWXY!@#	19		4	0	valid
5	%$#@!fghij67890ACCCE	20		4	0	valid
6	012%abU	7		4	0	invalid
7	Aa0!	4		4	0	invalid
8	%$#@!fghij67890ABCDEF	21		4	0	invalid
9	1234567890ABCDEFGHijklmnop%$#	24		4	0	invalid
10	A123abc!@#	10	1	4	0	valid
11	1Bxyz%$!789	11	2	4	0	valid
12	##66$eC888%%	12	7	4	0	valid
13	fefefe7@7efefeYf	16	15 (-2)	4	0	valid
14	t8kn54t9%riojZ	14	14 (-1)	4	0	valid
15	c343455TT%%	11	1	4	0	valid
16	3c43455TT%%	11	2	4	0	valid
17	4358dDD%$$#4	12	5	4	0	valid
18	343455TT%c%	11	10 (-2)	4	0	valid
19	343455TT%%c	11	11(-1)	4	0	valid
20	0eoijfeog@AA	12	1	4	0	valid
21	U1gjerpog$	10	2	4	0	valid
22	foenr$#2YUYf	12	8	4	0	valid
23	IUHIO%$#ffee3e	14	13 (-2)	4	0	valid
24	iuohgriuooooH@!4	15	16 (-1)	4	0	valid
25	%111222YYYaaa	13	1	4	0	valid
26	1$gdgkj878HHH	13	2	4	0	valid
27	4thigh@Yerj	11	7	4	0	valid
28	jgd4UIHifsds!4	14	13 (-2)	4	0	valid
29	56gkhJHJGddk%	13	14 (-1)	4	0	valid
30	1234567abcd!@	13		3	0	invalid
31	qqqqqqq$#@	10		2	0	invalid
32	AIHJIKH#%%435643	16		3	0	invalid
33	QQQQQQ99999	11		2	0	invalid
34	!@ASDJDfgfgdfg	14		3	0	invalid
35	%%%%%%%%%%%%%%%	15		1	0	invalid
36	fjgoKJKLO34353	14		3	0	invalid
37	ojdoify58gioghir	16		2	0	invalid
38	*ijg7543H@	10		5	1/1	invalid
39	O&fj64((k@g2	12		5	2/7,8	invalid
40	space	1		1	1/1	invalid
41	\t	1		1	1/1	invalid

Table 3.4: Test cases for Example 3.8

Let's try to construct the partitions with these parameters.

Notice, parameter n deals with invalid partitions, so only six parameters are having valid values. Partitions with n can be treated separately as a category partition. Furthermore, parameters $p1, p2, p3, p4$ cannot have invalid values, the values must be between 1 and 20, inclusive since position number cannot be negative; also, a value of 0 means no character of this type and is covered by parameter t (number of types) already; a position greater than 20 can only happen in certain invalid strings covered by parameter l.

Partitions with $p1, p2, p3, p4$ are also treated separately as category partitions.

As a result, we have the following categories to consider:

(1) Size of string and types of characters in the string: 2-dimensional partitioning with parameters l and t.
(2) Position of characters in each character set: parameters $p1, p2, p3, p4$.
(3) Not-allowed characters, and special cases.

Let's now try to generate test input vectors with these partitions.

Let's start with the first category with parameters l and t. Figure 3.4 is a plot of the input vector space for l and t, the x-axis is for l, and the y-axis is for t.

Since there is only one valid value for t (all 4 types of characters must present), the valid zone is a line (a collapsed rectangle) from point (8,4) to point (20,4) on the vector space.

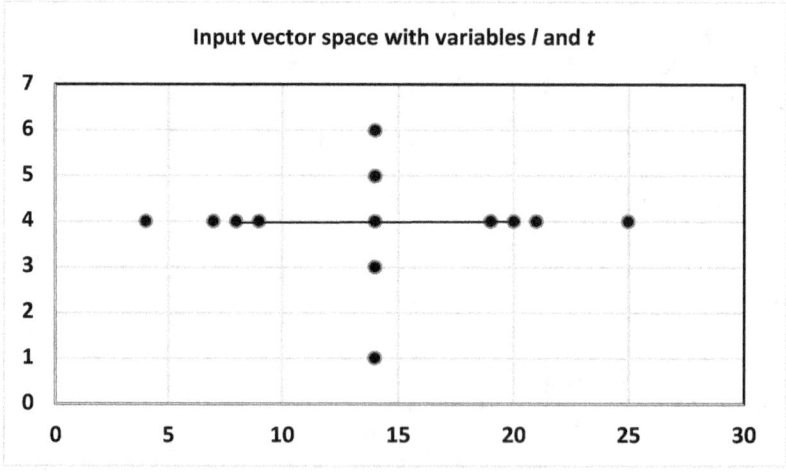

Figure 3.5: Input vector space with variables l and t for Example 3.8

The following are the equivalence partitions generated with these two parameters (l and t are both integers):

(i) $\{l, t \mid 8 \le l \le 20; t = 4\}$
(ii) $\{l, t \mid l < 8; ; t = 4\}$
(iii) $\{l, t \mid l > 20; ; t = 4\}$
(iv) $\{t \mid t > 4\}$
(v) $\{t \mid t < 4\}$

The valid zone has four edges, but since there is only one value in the valid set, the two edges parallel to the x-axis collapsed into one, and the boundary values are the same as the mid-value on this collapsed edge. Total three edges remain and two of them are two points, (8,4) and (20,4), on the vector space. Total number of test cases is 4*3 + 1 = 13. The selected input vectors are marked by dots on the plot.

Also, with regards to invalid zone (v) with $t < 4$, since there are requirements that each of the four types of characters should be in the input values, input vectors for missing each of the four types should be included.

Therefore, partition (v) should be split into four partitions:

(v) $\{t \mid t < 4$ & no uppercase letters $\}$
(vi) $\{t \mid t < 4$ & no lowercase letters $\}$
(vii) $\{t \mid t < 4$ & no numbers $\}$
(viii) $\{t \mid t < 4$ & no allowed special characters $\}$

Partitions (i), (ii), (iii), (iv) are exactly the same as partitions (a), (b), (c), and (l) we came up with initially on page 52, and partitions (v), (vi), (vii), and (viii) are the same as partitions (h), (i), (j), and (k). In Table 3.4, cases from 1 to 9, and 30 to 39 correspond to these partitions with l and t.

Partitions with $p1, p2, p3, p4$ are treated as separate category partitions, and the partitions are exactly the same as partitions (d), (e), (f), and (g) in the initial partitioning.

Also, the category "Not-allowed characters, and special cases" leads to the same partitions as (l) and (m).

To conclude, the same partitions are classified with this approach involving the seven parameters.

As a side note, when testing password fields, other requirements such as "the password can be toggled between hidden and show; or the password is encrypted" may not be explicitly specified, but should be considered in test case generation, which would be adding more partitions to the tests.

Let's take another example.

Example 3.9: An Order API

On an online shopping site, there is an application API that returns detailed information of product orders based on parameter values supplied to the API. For simplicity, assume there are 4 parameters: *start timestamp*, *end timestamp*, *type of order*, a *limit* on the maximum number of orders to return.

For example, if the *start timestamp* is Jan 1, 2021, and the *end timestamp* is Dec 31, 2021, the *type of order* is 'books', and the *limit* is 100, then the API returns details of the first 100 book orders from Jan 1, 2021, to Dec 31, 2021, such as order time, who made the order, shipping information, etc.

The requirements are:

(1) *start timestamp* and *end timestamp* are epoch time in seconds, in the range of 800,000,000 (5/8/1995) and 3,000,000,000 (1/23/2065).
(2) *start timestamp* should be less than or equal to the *end timestamp*.
(3) *type of order* is an integer in the set of {1, 2, 3, 4, 5, 6}, total of six types of orders (each number corresponds to a type of order, for instance, type 1 is for books, type 2 is for toys).
(4) *limit* is an integer between 1 and 1,000,000.
(5) product order information is returned in chronological order.
(6) the API parameter order (which parameter appears 1st in the API expression, and so on) does not matter.
(7) all parameters are required.

Let's define the four parameters as *start_time, end_time, order_type,* and *limit*.

The four parameters can serve as the initial categories for partitioning.

Let's name the API as api_order, and the API call is in the following form:

https://api_service_url/api_order?start_time=1000000000&end_time=1565733999&order_type=2&limit=100

where api_service_url is the URL of the API server. A question mark (?) after the API name starts the parameters, and the parameters with their values are separated by '&'.

Let's determine the equivalence partitions from the requirements.

CHAPTER 3: EQUIVALENCE PARTITIONING

First, *order_type* and *limit* are independently defined, but *start_time* and *end_time* are not. So, *start_time* and *end_time* can be handled together on a 2-dimensional vector space, and *order_type* and *limit* can be handled individually.

The 2-dimensional vector space for *start_time* and *end_time* contains a rectangle valid zone and four invalid zones.

Invalid partitions for *start_time* and *end_time* with the invalid types of inputs (non-integer) should also be included, as well as an empty string.

For *order_type*, 5 partitions are identified, one valid zone and 4 invalid zones. Same for parameter *limit*.

The following partitions are constructed:

(i) { start_time, end_time | 800,000,000 ≤ start_time ≤ 3,000,000,000; 800,000,000 ≤ end_time ≤ 3,000,000,000 ; start_time ≤ end_time }
(ii) { start_time | start_time < 800,000,000 }
(iii) { start_time | start_time > 3,000,000,000 }
(iv) { end_time | end_time < 800,000,000 }
(v) { end_time | end_time > 3,000,000,000 }
(vi) { start_time | start_time ∈ [string: at least one non-integer]}
(vii) { end_time | end_time ∈ [string: at least one non-integer]}
(viii) { start_time | start_time ∈ [empty string]}
(ix) { end_time | end_time ∈ [empty string]}
(x) { order_type | order_type ∈ [1, 2, 3, 4, 5, 6] }
(xi) { order_type | order_type < 1 }
(xii) { order_type | order_type > 6 }
(xiii) { order_type | order_type ∈ [string: at least one non-integer]}
(xiv) { order_type | order_type ∈ [empty string]}
(xv) { limit | 1 ≤ limit ≤ 1,000,000 }
(xvi) { limit | limit < 1 }
(xvii) { limit | limit > 1,000,000 }
(xviii) { limit | limit ∈ [string: at least one non-integer]}
(xix) { limit | limit ∈ [empty string]}

The number of input vectors for the first five partitions can be calculated via $4n + 1$ with total 17 cases ($n = 4$ [edges]), the rest can be calculated via equation (3-4) or equation (3-9), with a number of test cases of (5 * 2 + 2 * 12) = 34, which brings the total to 17 + 34 = 51 so far.

Again, we adopt the one-error principle. For example, when generating input vectors for parameter *start_time*, all the values for other parameters are valid in each input vector.

Other than the above partitions, we also need testing in the following categories:

(a) Parameter orders.
(b) Fewer parameters are present.
(c) One parameter appears more than once.

Now let's calculate the numbers of permutations for each of these categories.

Category (a): Parameter orders:

Since there are total of four parameters, the total number of permutations is: 4! = 24. Let's use numbers to represent the four parameters: *start_time* -> 1, *end_time* -> 2, *order_type* ->3, and *limit* -> 4.

The 24 permutations are:

{ [1234], [1243], [1324], [1342], [1423], [1432],
[2134], [2143], [2314], [2341], [2413], [2431],
[3124], [3143], [3214], [3241], [3412], [3421],
[4123], [4132], [4213], [4231], [4312], [4321] }

In each element in the above set, the number at each digit represents the parameter order. For example, [1243] means the first parameter (*start_time*) appears first in the API expression, the second parameter appears second, the fourth parameter appears at third position, and the third parameter appears at the end, as in the following API call:

https://api_service_url/api_order?start_time=1000000000&end_time=1565733999&limit=100&order_type=2

Category (b): Fewer parameters are present:

Since all parameters are required, we only need to test error conditions when the number of parameters is less than 4. The permutations needed are listed in the following set with parameter numbers 3, 2, 1, and 0, respectively.

{ [123], [124], [234],
[12], [13], [14], [23], [24], [34],
[1], [2], [3], [4],
[] }

Category (c): One parameter appears more than once:

There are 4 parameters, let select the following set with 4 input vectors one for each parameter repeating once:

{ [11234], [12234], [12334], [12344] }

These three categories add up 24 + 14 + 4 = 42 more cases, bringing the total to 51 + 42 = 93.

Now imagining modifying the 5th requirement to make all parameters optional, then valid scenarios with fewer parameters should also be included, which leads to an even larger total number of test cases.

There are 24 cases for 4 parameters in category (a). If the number of parameters n is larger, then the total number of input values to select ($n!$) would be much larger, and it would become impractical to include all permutations in the tests.

How about we assume that all we need to include are the ones that covering all the pairs of parameters? In other words, include all the order permutations for any two of the four parameters only:

[12],[21], [13], [31], [14],[41], [23],[32], [24], [42],[34],[43].

The following 5 vectors cover all the above pairs:

{ [1234], [4321], [1324], [3142], [4123] }

The test case number is reduced to 5 without sacrificing too much coverage. The reasons behind this will be discussed in the next chapter on another test case generation technique, namely combinatorial testing.

We'll omit to list the individual test cases for this example for now. An extended version of this example is presented in Chapter 12 as a case study.

3.6 EQUIVALENCE PARTITIONING WITH DEPENDENT VARIABLES

We have discussed the equivalence partitioning technique when the input variables are independent of each other. Can this technique be applied when there are dependencies in the input variables? In a case with dependent variables, the output values (expected results) depend on nonlinear value combinations of input variables. Simply put, an output value is calculated from the input values in a complex fashion. Let's take an example to illustrate the concept, and to learn if and to what extend the equivalence partitioning technique can be applied.

Example 3.10: Loan Rate under Different Conditions

A bank approves fixed mortgage loans with different interest rates based on the following two values:

(i) R: debt to income ratio of the applicant(s).
(ii) S: credit score of the applicant(s).

The debt-to-income ratio is a percentage calculated by the division of all the debts and the total raw income of the applicant(s). A credit score is a statistical number that evaluates a consumer's creditworthiness and is based on the person's credit history.

The requirement specifications are:

(a) if R > 40% or S < 600: reject application.
(b) if 20% < R ≤ 40% and 600 ≤ S < 700, interest rate is 5%.
(c) if 20% < R ≤ 40% and 750 > S ≥ 700, interest rate is 4.5%.
(d) if 20% < R ≤ 40% and S ≥ 750, interest rate is 4%.
(e) if R ≤ 20% and S ≥ 600, interest rate is 4%.

Valid values are between 0.0 and infinity for parameter R and are between 300 and 850 for S, inclusive. We omit the percentage (%) sign from now on for R, so a value of 20 means 20%.

The requirements provide natural partitions. let's generate a list of partitions first, and then determine how to choose input vectors.

To cover the whole vector space, we came up with 9 equivalence partitions:

(i) { R, S | R ∈ (20.0, 40.0], S ∈ [750, 850]}
(ii) { R, S | R ∈ (20.0, 40.0], S ∈ [700, 750)}
(iii) { R, S | R ∈ (20.0, 40.0], S ∈ [600, 700)}
(iv) { R, S | R ∈ [0.0, 20.0], S ∈ [600, 850]}
(v) { R, S | R ∈ (40.0, ∞), S ∈ [600, 850]}
(vi) { R, S | R ∈ (0.0, ∞), S ∈ [300, 600)}
(vii) { R, S | R ∈ (0.0, ∞), S ∈ (-∞, 300)}
(viii){ R, S | R ∈ (0.0, ∞), S ∈ (850, ∞)}
(ix) { R, S | R ∈ (-∞, 0.0), S ∈ (-∞, ∞)}

where R ∈ (20.0, 40.0] means 20.0 < R ≤ 40.0, and so on.

Partitions (i), (ii), (iii), and (iv) are valid partitions with specified interested rates, and are from requirements (b), (c), (d), and (e); next two partitions (v) and (vi) are also valid from requirement (a) but with a result of 'rejection'; the rest of 3 partitions are invalid ones. Since all the conditions are based on two variables, we can plot these equivalence partitions on a 2-dimensional space, as shown in Figure 3.6. Partition numbers are marked on the vector space. We can see that the whole 2-dimensional space is covered by the 9 partitions.

Since the partitions are well defined, it should be straightforward to generate input vectors, the only question is how to select input vectors given that each partition is surrounded by a different number of other partitions haphazardly.

Notice that the valid zones are adjacent to each other on the input space. In other words, they share edges. In earlier examples where the variables are independent, a valid zone is only adjacent to invalid zones. Consequently, to generate input vectors with variable dependencies, we need to come up with a strategy or set some rules.

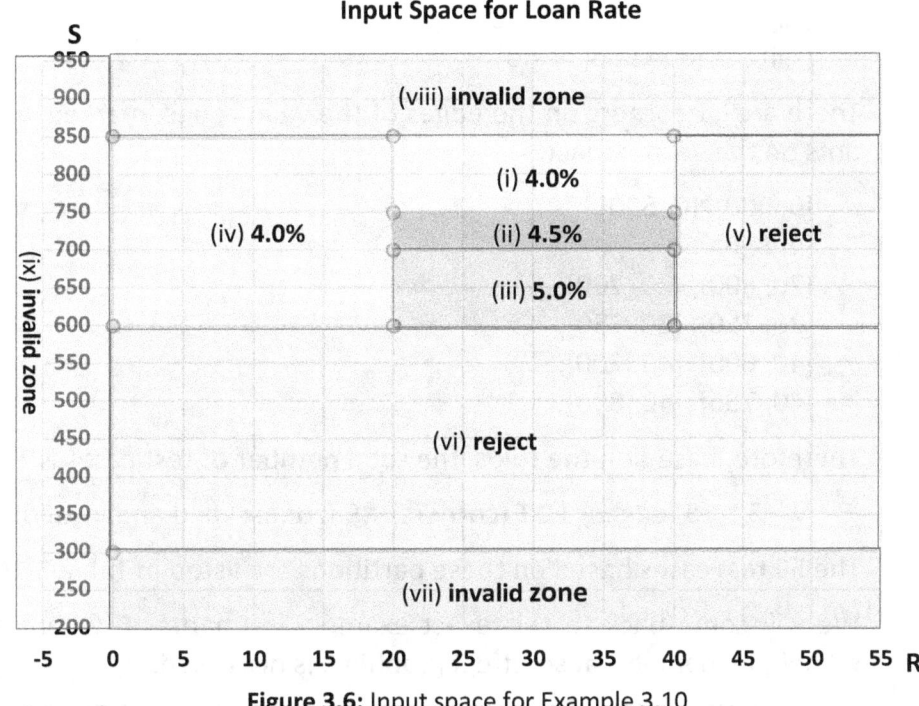

Figure 3.6: Input space for Example 3.10

We treat this case with the standard case of equivalence partitioning by adopting the following rules:

(a) for each edge within the valid zones, select one value on the edge, and one on each side of the edge close to the boundary.

(b) select the connector boundary values at each corner of every valid zone rectangle.
(c) select one regular value for each zone, both valid and invalid.

There are total 13 edges around the valid zones, the edges are:

(i) $S = 600, R \in [0, 20]$
(ii) $S = 850, R \in [0, 20]$
(iii) $S = 600, R \in [20, 40]$
(iv) $S = 700, R \in [20, 40]$
(v) $S = 750, R \in [20, 40]$
(vi) $S = 850, R \in [20, 40]$
(vii) $S \in [600, 700], R = 20$
(viii) $S \in [600, 700], R = 40$
(ix) $S \in [700, 750], R = 20$
(x) $S \in [700, 750], R = 40$
(xi) $S \in [750, 850], R = 20$
(xii) $S \in [750, 800], R = 40$
(xiii) $S \in [600, 850], R = 0$

There are 11 corners on the edges of the valid zones, marked with small dots on the vector space:

[0, 300], [0, 600],
[0, 850],
[20, 600], [20, 700],
[20, 750], [20, 850],
[40, 600], [40, 700],
[40, 750], [40, 850].

Therefore, based on the rules, the total number of test cases is:

$N = 3 * 13$ (edges) $+ 11$ (corners) $+ 9$ (zones: valid and invalid) $= 59$.

The 59 test cases based on these partitions are listed in Table 3.10.

We will come back to this exact example in Chapter 6 where another technique, namely cause-effect graphing, is discussed.

Test case	R (%)	S (credit score)	Expected rate (%)
1	15	599	reject
2	15	600	4.0
3	15	601	4.0
4	15	849	4.0
5	15	850	4.0
6	15	851	invalid

7	30	599	reject
8	30	600	5.0
9	30	601	5.0
10	30	699	5.0
11	30	700	4.5
12	30	701	4.5
13	30	749	4.5
14	30	750	4.0
15	30	751	4.0
16	30	849	4.0
17	30	850	4.0
18	30	851	invalid
19	19	650	4.0
20	20	650	4.0
21	21	650	4.0
22	39	650	5.0
23	40	650	5.0
24	41	650	reject
25	19	725	4.0
26	20	725	4.0
27	21	725	4.5
28	39	725	4.5
29	40	725	4.5
30	41	725	reject
31	-1	725	invalid
32	0	725	4.0
33	1	725	4.0
34	19	825	4.0
35	20	825	4.0
36	21	825	4.0
37	39	825	4.0
38	40	825	4.0
39	41	825	reject
40	0	300	reject
41	0	600	4.0
42	0	850	4.0
43	20	600	4.0
44	20	700	4.0
45	20	750	4.0
46	20	850	4.0
47	40	600	5.0
48	40	700	4.5
49	40	750	4.0
50	40	850	4.0
51	30	800	4.0
52	30	725	4.5

53	30	650	5.0
54	15	725	4.0
55	30	550	reject
56	45	725	reject
57	30	200	invalid
58	30	950	invalid
59	-10	600	Invalid

Table 3.5: Test cases for Example 3.10

The rules to use to generate input vectors may vary case by case, depending on how the partition zones are shaped and connected on the input vector space. The formula of the total number of test cases, equations (3-4) and (3-7), are not directly applicable.

3.7 SUMMARY OF EQUIVALENCE PARTITIONING TESTING

Equivalence partitioning technique can be applied to all types of tests, type 0, type 1, type 2, and type 3 tests, and are heavily used in type 1 integration and functional tests.

The maximum number of test cases for each case (independent input variables) discussed in this chapter is summarized in the following table:

	Max # of Test Cases	
base case	n	n: number of partitions
base worst case	$\prod_{i=1}^{r} n_i$	n_i number of partitions for ith parameter; r: number of parameters
standard case	$\sum_{i=1}^{r} (5u_i + 2v_i)$	u_i: number of valid partitions; v_i: number of invalid partitions
standard case with edges	$4n + 1$	n: number of faces
standard worst case	$\prod_{i=1}^{r} (5u_i + 2v_i)$	u_i: number of valid partitions; v_i: number of invalid partitions

Table 3.6: Number of test cases for different levels of equivalence partitioning

In real world scenarios, since the total number of test cases generated by equivalence partitioning is still very large, worst case scenarios are rarely being used, unless it's mission critical for certain part of the testing project.

Also, when the requirements become more complex, finding all the partitions become harder. Since the goal is to find a set of partitions that minimizes the number of test cases and in the meantime to cover as much as input vectors as possible, equivalence partitioning should be combined with other testing strategies.

EXERCISE PROBLEMS:

P3.1: Price Variable

A price at a product bidding site takes a dollar amount, here are the specifications:

(1) The value entered must be greater than 0 and less than 1,000,000.
(2) If the value is less than 10,000, take action A (reject).
(3) If the value is greater or equal to 10,000, take action B (accept).

Find equivalent partitions, select input vectors for each partition, and generate test cases for the following levels: (a) base case; (b) base worst case; (c) standard case.

P3.2: BMI Calculation

The formula for BMI is BMI = W/H^2 (kg/m^2), where W is a person's weight in kilograms and H^2 is their height in meters squared. For this program, there are two inputs, weight and height, and the output is the BMI.

The requirements are:

(1) The valid values for weight are between 1 and 200 kg, inclusive;
(2) The valid values for height are between 1 and 300 centimeters, inclusive.

Use equivalence partitioning technique, including boundary analysis, to generate test cases for both base case and standard case.

P3.3: The Game of Go Board

The game of Go is played on a 19 by 19 board, the valid values for the two coordinates are in the range of [1,19]. For example, the stone on the board to the right is at (D, 4) or (4,4) point.

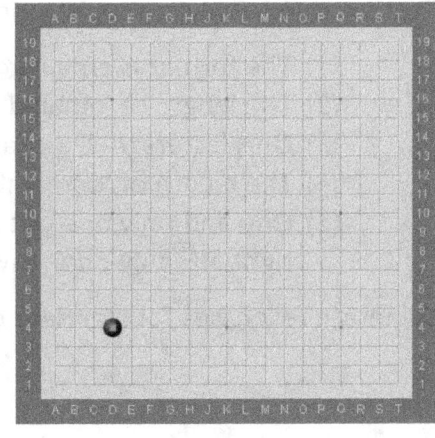

Find equivalent partitions for the application for points on the board, and list input vectors to select, including boundary analysis for standard case.

P3.4: Safe Add Program

The program takes two integers and computes the addition. The following is a sample implementation in Java. Use equivalence partitioning technique, including boundary analysis, to generate test cases for both base case and standard case.

```
public static int IntegerAddition (int a, int b) {
    int c = a + b;
    if ( a >= 0 && b >= 0 && c < 0 )
        System.out.println ("Result value overflow!\n");
    else if ( a < 0 && b < 0 && c >= 0 )
        System.out.println ("Result value overflow!\n");
    return c;
}
```

P3.5: Next Date Problem

A program takes three inputs: {year, month, day}, and produces the date of next day. For example: {2025, 6, 30} -> {2025-7-1}.

The following are the constraints:

    (1)   1900 ≤ year ≤ current year
    (2)   1 ≤ month ≤ 12
    (3)   1 ≤ day ≤ 31

Note, you need to take into considerations that some months have 31 days, some have 30 days, and February can have 28 or 29 days.

Generate test cases for standard case of equivalence partitioning.

P3.6: A Simplified Email Field

Test an email field on a registration form, the requirements are:

    (1) The format is emailId@domain.
    (2) The length of 'emailId' should be between 3 and 64.
    (3) Only letters (A-Z, a-z) and numbers (0-9) are accepted for 'emailId'.
    (4) The length of 'domain' should be between 5 and 64.
    (5) One and only one dot (.) in 'domain' is accepted, and it cannot be right after '@', nor any of the last two characters.

Generate test cases for standard case of equivalence partitioning.

4 COMBINATORIAL TESTING

As we have discussed earlier, the number of parameter permutations in a real-world situation is extremely large, and strategies to reduce the input vectors for testing are necessary. An example of the problem is the 'Language & Region' setting on a computer, as shown below.

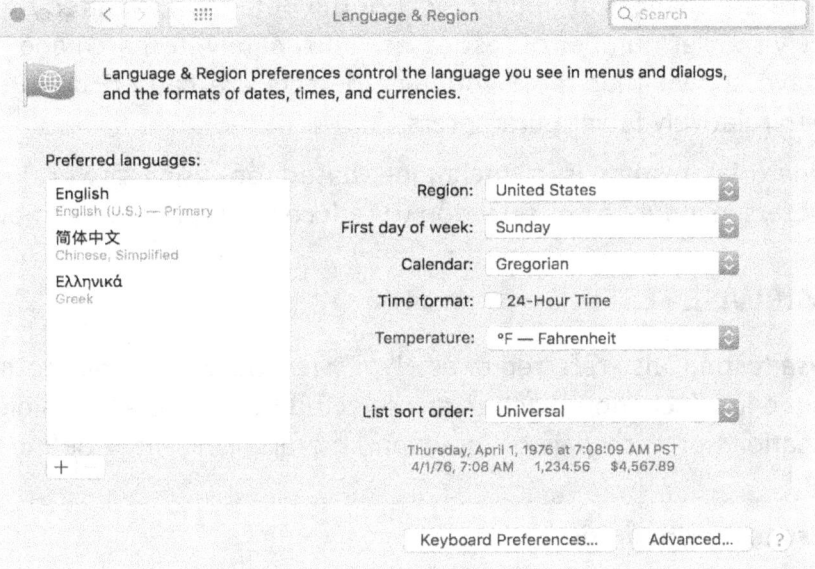

Just examine the dropdown lists to the right of the panel. There are total of five dropdowns or parameters, and let's say there are 200, 7, 10, 2, and 7 items respectively in each of the dropdown lists, then the total number of permutations is 200*7*10*2*7 = 196,000. Maybe when the region is 'Puerto Rico' and the temperature is 'Celsius', a defect will surface; or maybe when 'UK' is selected as the region, 'Monday' is selected as the First day of the week, and 'Fahrenheit' is selected as the Temperature, the system will crash.

To consider all the risks, you may want to test all the permutations, which is an unrealistic task. Reducing the number of permutations for testing is inevitable in this kind of scenario.

Although defects may surface when multiple parameters are involved, in most software applications, we can imagine that a defect happens only under one single condition, independent of any other conditions.

Take an example, an alignment defect on a web page is discovered on a specific version of a browser, regardless of the version of the operating system of the computer on which the page is viewed, or what kind of database is being used in the backend. In this case, if browser, operating system, and database are the three factors to consider, only one factor, browser, is related to the defect.

In certain cases, however, two or more conditions are do involved for a defect to surface.

As we have discussed earlier, trying to include all permutations in testing aiming to cover the whole input vector space is impractical. How can we maximize the chances of finding most of the defects in a limited time with a relatively smaller number of test cases? Fortunately, research and empirical data have shown that most software defects are caused by interactions between relatively fewer parameters.

Combinatorial testing is a technique based on using fewer interacting parameters in input vector selection to reduce the number of combinations.

4.1 PAIRWISE TESTING

Pairwise testing, also referred to as *all-pair testing*, is a combinatorial testing technique in which input vectors are selected to include all possible distinct combinations of each pair of input parameters. Let's now define pairwise testing.

Pairwise testing definition:

If there are n parameters: $\{p_1, p_2, \ldots, p_n\}$, and the number of input values for the parameters are r_i, for $i = 1$ to n, and the input values are:

$v_1(p_1), v_2(p_1), \ldots, v_{r_1}(p_1),$ (total number of values for p_1 is r_1)
$v_1(p_2), v_2(p_2), \ldots, v_{r_2}(p_2),$
....
$v_1(p_n), v_2(p_n), \ldots, v_{r_n}(p_n)$

then, all the pairs of input values should appear in the input vectors to select for testing:

$[v_1(p_1), v_1(p_2)], [v_1(p_1), v_2(p_2)], ..., [v_1(p_1), v_{r_2}(p_2)],$
$[v_2(p_1), v_1(p_2)], [v_2(p_1), v_2(p_2)], ..., [v_2(p_1), v_{r_2}(p_2)],$
... ...
$[v_1(p_1), v_1(p_n)], [v_1(p_1), v_2(p_n)], ..., [v_1(p_1), v_{r_2}(p_n)],$
$[v_1(p_2), v_1(p_3)], [v_1(p_2), v_2(p_3)], ..., [v_1(p_2), v_{r_3}(p_3)],$
... ...
... ...
$[v_{r_{n-1}}(p_{n-1}), v_1(p_n)], [v_{r_{n-1}}(p_{n-1}), v_2(p_n)], ..., [v_{r_{n-1}}(p_{n-1}), v_{r_n}(p_n)]$

This looks a bit messy, let's look at an example to understand the concept.

Example 4.1: A Panel with Three on/off Switches

Suppose we have an application with three on-off buttons on a panel. Let's denote the buttons as A, B, and C, and 'on' is represented by 1 and 'off' is by 0. All the possible permutations are listed in Table 4.1.

A	B	C
0	0	0
0	0	1
0	1	0
0	1	1
1	0	0
1	0	1
1	1	0
1	1	1

Table 4.1: All permutations of 3 parameters

There are total 3 parameters, each can have 2 values (n = 3, and r_i = 2, for i = 1 to 3). All the input value pairs are:

[A, B]: [0,0], [0,1], [1, 0], [1,1]
[B, C]: [0,0], [0,1], [1, 0], [1,1]
[C, A]: [0,0], [0,1], [1, 0], [1,1],

with total of 12 pair combinations.

With pairwise testing, only 4 test cases are needed, instead of all 8 combinations as listed in Table 4.1. The 4 pairwise cases are listed in Table 4.2.

Test case	A	B	C
1	0	0	0
2	0	1	1
3	1	1	0
4	1	0	1

Table 4.2: Pairwise test cases for Example 4.1

case 1 [0, 0, 0] includes pairs: [A, B] = [0, 0], [A, C] = [0, 0], [B, C] = [0, 0],
case 2 [0, 1, 1] includes pairs: [A, B] = [0, 1], [A, C] = [0, 1], [B, C] = [1, 1],
case 3 [1, 1, 0] includes pairs: [A, B] = [1, 1], [A, C] = [1, 0], [B, C] = [1, 0],
case 4 [1, 0, 1] includes pairs: [A, B] = [1, 0], [A, C] = [1, 1], [B, C] = [0, 1].

All the 12 pairs are covered in these 4 test cases.

What's the number of permutations with pairwise testing in general? There are a variety of theories on it, but for simplicity, let's assume that the maximum number of tests for pairwise testing is the product of the two largest element numbers in all the parameters involved. In other words, when each pair involving the two largest numbers are included, all the rest of the parameters that have an equal or smaller number of values should be covered.

For the above example, each parameter has 2 values to select, 1 and 0, so the max number of tests is 2*2 = 4.

Therefore, the max number of tests to select is:

$$N(Y) = r_m r_{m-1} \tag{4-1}$$

where r_m is the number of possible values for the parameter with the largest number of values, and r_{m-1} is the number of possible values for the parameter with the 2nd largest number of values. When there is a tie, choose any one of them. (See section 4.3 for a formal formula in orthogonal arrays for the number of tests for pairwise testing, as a special case).

Let's examine another example.

Example 4.2: A Custom Car Building Application

A car manufacturing company offers customers to customize a vehicle to buy. There are four steps in the process, and each step involves a selection of items. The four steps are to select model, feature tier, exterior color, and interior color. The number of selections for each step is listed in Table 4.3.

Parameters	# of selections	Selections
Model	4	A, B, C, D
Feature tier	3	Convenience, Premium, Executive
Exterior color	5	White, Black, Blue, Silver, Red
Interior color	2	Yellow, Grey

Table 4.3: Requirements for Example 4.2

The total number of permutations is 4*3*5*2 = 120. The maximum number to select for pairwise testing is 5*4 = 20 since 5 and 4 are the two largest possible values for parameters 'Exterior color' and 'Model'.

All the pairs are listed below (by starting from Exterior color which has 5 selections, and pairing with each value of the other four parameters):

[White, A], [White, B], [White, C], [White, D],
[Black, A], [Black, B], [Black, C], [Black, D],
[Blue, A], [Blue, B], [Blue, C], [Blue, D],
[Silver, A], [Silver, B], [Silver, C], [Silver, D],
[Red, A], [Red, B], [Red, C], [Red, D],
[White, Convenience], [White, Premium], [White, Executive],
[Black, Convenience], [Black, Premium], [Black, Executive],
[Blue, Convenience], [Blue, Premium], [Blue, Executive],
[Silver, Convenience], [Silver, Premium], [Silver, Executive],
[Red, Convenience], [Red, Premium], [Red, Executive],
[White, Yellow], [White, Grey],
[Black, Yellow], [Black, Grey],
[Blue, Yellow], [Blue, Grey],
[Silver, Yellow], [Silver, Grey],
[Red, Yellow], [Red, Grey],
[A, Convenience], [A, Premium], [A, Executive],
[B, Convenience], [B, Premium], [B, Executive],
[C, Convenience], [C, Premium], [C, Executive],
[D, Convenience], [D, Premium], [D, Executive],
[A, Yellow], [A, Grey],
[B, Yellow], [B, Grey],
[C, Yellow], [C, Grey],
[D, Yellow], [D, Grey],
[Convenience, Yellow], [Convenience, Grey],
[Premium, Yellow], [Premium, Grey],
[Executive, Yellow], [Executive, Grey].

Let's try to construct the 20 input vectors. We start by listing all the possible values of Exterior color in the first column in a table, which has the largest number of selections, then in the 2nd column, listing the values of the Model which has the 2nd largest number. Since there are 4 options for Model, the 1st column lists each of the selections in the Exterior color 4 times. Then in the 3rd column, Feature tier, for each row, fill the cell in the table in this fashion: White – A – Convenience; Black – B – Convenience; Blue – C – Convenience. That is, to find the rows with distinct values for both the 1st and the 2nd columns and fill the 3rd column with the 1st value (Convenience) first, then repeat the same process for the rest of the values for empty cells in the 3rd column.

Similarly, for the last column with Interior color, check if the cell value matches the pairs with 3rd column (Feature tier) first, then check the same with 2nd column (Model), and then with 1st column (Exterior color).

The result is shown in the table below. Examine the test cases, you will find that all pairs are included. The empty cells can be filled with values randomly since all pairs have been included.

Test case	Exterior color	Model	Feature tiers	Interior color
1	White	A	Convenience	Yellow
2	White	B	Premium	Grey
3	White	C	Executive	Grey
4	White	D		
6	Black	A		
6	Black	B	Convenience	
7	Black	C	Premium	Yellow
8	Black	D	Executive	Grey
9	Blue	A	Executive	Grey
10	Blue	B		
11	Blue	C	Convenience	
12	Blue	D	Premium	Yellow
13	Silver	A	Executive	
14	Silver	B	Premium	Yellow
15	Silver	C		
16	Silver	D	Convenience	Grey
17	Red	A	Premium	
18	Red	B	Executive	Yellow
19	Red	C	Convenience	
20	Red	D		Grey

Table 4.4: Pairwise test cases for Example 4.2

When the number of permutations is small, another way to construct the table is to list all permutations, then work backward from the bottom of the table (from the top is fine too), and examine each row, if all the pairs in the vector appear in other vectors, remove the row until no row is to be removed.

When the number of parameters and the number of options for the parameters is large, it's impractical to construct the table manually. There are simple programs (some are online) to generate input vectors for pairwise testing, which we are not going to cover in the book.

Besides combinatorial testing for application input vectors, the combination of configurations of an application is also a good candidate to apply this technique to.

Let's look at an example.

Example 4.3: A Web Application

A web application needs to be tested from UI on a set of browsers and a few operating systems, with a couple of database types, and with several different languages. The required configurations to test are listed in Table 4.5.

Parameters	# of selections	Selections
Browser	4	Chrome, FF(Firefox), Edge, Safari
OS	2	Windows, MacOS
DBMS	2	Mysql, Oracle
Language	3	English, Spanish, Chinese

Table 4.5: Configuration requirements for Example 4.3

The total number of permutations is 4*2*2*3 = 48, and with the pairwise technique, we can reduce the number of test cases to 4*3 = 12.

The configurations to select can be constructed by the method we've described in Example 4.2, or by listing all permutations and removing the ones not needed from either the bottom or top. The constructed test cases are listed in Table 4.6 (will leave the construction as an exercise for the reader).

Values need to be filled out in the empty cells, and the choice is arbitrary, but it's a good practice to add as much variety to the test cases as possible, such as by cycling through the possible values for the columns having missing cells.

Test case	Browser	OS	DBMS	Language
1	Chrome	Windows	Mysql	English
2	Chrome	MacOS	Oracle	Spanish
3	Chrome			Chinese
4	FF	MacOS		English
6	FF		Mysql	Spanish
6	FF	Windows	Oracle	Chinese
7	Edge		Mysql	Chinese
8	Edge	Windows	Oracle	English
9	Edge	MacOS		Spanish
10	Safari	Windows		Chinese
11	Safari	MacOS	Mysql	Spanish
12	Safari		Oracle	English

Table 4.6: Pairwise test cases for Example 4.3

If there are constraints with certain parameters, then the construction process would become more complicated. For example, if the combination of [Edge, MacOS] and [Safari, Windows] are not required for testing, then the rows with those combinations should be modified.

Simply removing the rows does not work since other pairs for other parameters may get removed too. In the above table, test case 9 contains three pairs: [Edge, MacOS], [Edge, Spanish], and [MacOS, Spanish]. within these 3 pairs, [MacOS, Spanish] has been covered by test case 2, but [Edge, Spanish] is not covered by any row, so we have to leave test case 9 in the table by changing 'MacOS' to 'Windows' in OS column to remove pair [Edge, MacOS]. Similarly test case 10 needs to be modified.

The filled test cases with this requirement are listed in Table 4.7.

Test case	Browser	OS	DBMS	Language
1	Chrome	Windows	Mysql	English
2	Chrome	MacOS	Oracle	Spanish
3	Chrome	Windows	Mysql	Chinese
4	FF	MacOS	Oracle	English
6	FF	Windows	Mysql	Spanish
6	FF	MacOS	Oracle	Chinese
7	Edge	Windows	Mysql	Chinese
8	Edge	Windows	Oracle	English
9	Edge	Windows	Mysql	Spanish
10	Safari	MacOS	Oracle	Chinese
11	Safari	MacOS	Mysql	Spanish
12	Safari	MacOS	Oracle	English

Table 4.7: Pairwise test cases when constraints are considered for Example 4.3

For the combination of configurations, the list of test cases can be further modified based on the following factors:

(a) Special requirements for certain configurations.
(b) Priority of certain parameters or configurations.
(c) Knowledge of interactions of certain parameters.
(d) Time constraint and/or cost constrain.

In Example 4.3, let's add the following three extra testing requirements:

(1) Test all combinations for Chrome browser when the language is English.
(2) Only test on Mysql DB for non-English languages due to cost constraints.
(3) Ignore Firefox & Safari browsers for non-English languages and Oracle DB.

The modified combinations are listed in Table 4.8 with these three extra requirements.

Since the number of cases is small, the list can be constructed with manual innervation. When the permutation number becomes larger, it may not be practical to construct the list manually.

Test case	Browser	OS	DBMS	Language
1	Chrome	Windows	Mysql	English
2	Chrome	Windows	Oracle	English
3	Chrome	MacOS	Mysql	English
4	Chrome	MacOS	Oracle	English
5	Chrome	MacOS	Mysql	Spanish
6	Chrome	MacOS	Mysql	Chinese
8	FF	Windows	Mysql	English
8	FF	MacOS	Oracle	English
10	Edge	Windows	Mysql	Chinese
11	Edge	Windows	Oracle	English
12	Edge	Windows	Mysql	Spanish
13	Safari	MacOS	Oracle	English

Table 4.8: Pairwise test cases with extra requirements for Example 4.3

4.2 LIMITATIONS OF PAIRWISE TESTING

While most defects of a software application are due to one parameter or two parameters interacting, there are sure cases where three or more parameters are involved for a defect or failure to surface. Consider the following example.

Example 4.4: A Weather Condition Coding Program

A weather condition coding application takes three parameters, 'sun', 'rain', and 'temperature', as inputs, and the output is a number code representing the condition.

The table below lists the coding definitions. For example, when it's sunny (sun = 1), raining (rain = 1), and the temperature is 20 degrees or higher, the expected code is 1.

sun	temperature	rain	result
1	≥ 20	1	1
1	≥ 20	0	2
1	< 20	1	3
1	< 20	0	4
0	≥ 20	1	5
0	≥ 20	0	6
0	< 20	1	7
0	< 20	0	8

Table 4.9: Requirement definitions for Example 4.4

All the requirements are covered in Table 4.9.

With the pairwise testing technique, the input vectors to select are listed in Table 4.10 (this is the same problem like that in Example 4.1).

Case	sun	temperature	rain	Expected coding
1	0	< 20	0	8
2	0	≥ 20	1	5
3	1	≥ 20	0	2
4	1	< 20	1	3

Table 4.10: Pairwise test cases for Example 4.4

Suppose the implementation is done with the code segment listed in Code Segment 4.1 using 'if' and 'else if' clauses to handle different conditions. During application development, the developer wrote one line of code for the condition in the 'if' clause, and copied the line and pasted to the rest of the 'else if' clauses, and then modified them to suit the rest of the conditions, but missed to change the '>='sign to '<' sign in (temperature >= 20) in the 'else if' clause when the code result is 7, and the error was not caught by the code reviewer.

```java
public static int WeatherCoding ( float temperature, int sun, int rain ) {
    int code = 0;
    if ( ( sun == 1) && (temperature >= 20) && (rain == 1) )
        code = 1;
    else if ( ( sun == 1) && (temperature >= 20) && (rain == 0) )
        code = 2;
    else if ( ( sun == 1) && (temperature < 20) && (rain == 1) )
        code = 3;
    else if ( ( sun == 1) && (temperature < 20) && (rain == 0) )
        code = 4;
    else if( ( sun == 0) && (temperature >= 20) && (rain == 1) )
        code = 5;
    else if ( ( sun == 0) && (temperature >= 20) && (rain == 0) )
        code = 6;
    else if ( ( sun == 0) && *(temperature >= 20)* && (rain == 1) )
        code = 7;
    else if ( ( sun == 0) && (temperature < 20) && (rain == 0))
        code = 8;
    else {
        //error handling
    }
    return code;
}
```

Code Segment 4.1: Java Implementation with the defect for Example 4.4

The program will fail with input vector [0, 18, 1], resulting in a color code of '0', instead of the expected result of '7'. But this case is not included in the input vectors in Table 4.10 selected with pairwise technique.

In the above example, pairwise testing failed to find the defect, and interactions with more parameters are needed (for this specific example, all permutations can be included in testing since the total number of permutations is small).

One solution to this problem is to use t-wise testing (or N-wise), which will be discussed next.

4.3 T-WISE TESTING

T-wise testing is an extension of pairwise testing. In *t*-wise testing, *t* number of parameters are included, where *t* is larger than 2. All possible discrete combinations of each *t*-tuple, *t-1* tuple, ..., 2-tuple, must be covered with *t*-wise testing. For instance, 3-wise testing should include all permutations of any three of the parameters, plus all pairs (pairwise is a subset of 3-wise). We will talk about a formal definition with orthogonal array in the next section and give a 3-wise testing example.

With t-wise testing, test coverage is much better, but there is a cost to it. Statistically, the number of test cases generated with t-wise testing increases exponentially with t, which makes it impractical and intractable when the number of parameters is large. So, t-wise testing is limited when t is larger, and should be planned carefully, and should be combined with other techniques in practice.

Here are a few areas that could be considered when deciding what t-wise testing to perform.

(1) knowledge of what parameters are likely interacting with each other.
(2) the severity of potential problems with certain combinations.
(3) the probability of real-time usage of certain combinations.
(4) permutations that defects are more likely to be found from historical testing data.

Other strategies to combine with t-wise testing include:

(1) prioritize t-wise test cases.
(2) further equivalence partitioning of input values for certain parameters.
(3) random testing.

The following list shows an example of strategies:

(a) use 3-wise, 4-wise, 5-wise, or even 6-wise testing for critical parameters, and use pairwise testing for less important parameters.
(b) use the equivalence partitioning technique to partition input values for certain applicable parameters before generating pairwise testing vectors.
(c) randomly test less important parameters.

Random selection is a good strategy in certain cases. There were studies comparing random testing with t-wise testing, with evidence that, when the number of test cases is very large, random testing is as close as effective as t-wise testing.

4.4 ORTHOGONAL ARRAYS

Mathematically, an orthogonal array is an array, normally expressed as a table (a two-dimensional array), where the entries are coming from a set of symbols arranged in such a way that for an integer t, for any selection of t columns of the array/table, all ordered t-tuples of the symbols appear the same number of times.

The number t is called the **strength** of the orthogonal array.

Formally, an orthogonal array:

$OA(\lambda, t, k, v)$, $(t \leq k)$,

is an N by k array, where

$$N = \lambda v^t \qquad (4\text{-}2)$$

and, in every N by t subarray, each t-tuple occurs exactly λ times. t is the strength of the coverage of interactions, k is the number of factors, and v is the number of possible values (levels) for each factor.

N is called the number of **runs**.

An example of OA (1,2,3,3), is shown in Table 4.11, with

  $t = 2$: 2-tuple (strength of 2);
  $k = 3$: 3 factors;
  $v = 3$: 3 possible values for each factor (1, 2, and 3);
  $\lambda = 1$: each 2-tuple appears once.

The number of runs is:

  $N = 1*3^2 = 9$.

1	1	1
1	2	2
1	3	3
2	2	3
2	3	1
2	1	2
3	3	2
3	1	3
3	2	1

Table 4.11: OA (1,2,3,3) array

Pick any 2 (strength) columns, for example, the 1st and the last (3rd), as shown in Table 4.12, we can see that all the 2-tuples appear once ($\lambda = 1$):

  11, 12, 13, 21, 22, 23, 31, 32, 33.

1	1
1	2
1	3
2	3
2	1
2	2
3	2
3	3
3	1

Table 4.12: 1st and 3rd columns in OA (1,2,3,3)

Numerical numbers are used to represent the values of the factors in the table for the OA (1,2,3,3) array, but the numbers could be replaced by any other entities. For instance, in Example 4.3, Brower type is a parameter, if it's a factor of an orthogonal array, then we can replace '1' by "Chrome', 'replace '2' by 'Firefox', and so on. Same for other parameters such as OS, replace '1' by 'Windows', replace '2' by 'or 'MacOS', etc.

Now let's apply orthogonal array to t-wise combinatorial testing.

For t-wise testing, test cases can be generated by finding the orthogonal array:

$$OA(1, t, k, v), \ (t \leq k), \tag{4-3}$$

where:
   (a) k is the number of parameters.
   (b) v is the maximum number of possible values for a single parameter.

λ is chosen to be 1 since no repeating is needed for the same t-tuple in software testing (each t-tuple occurs once). By definition of orthogonal array, each t-tuple occurs exactly λ times, and strictly $\lambda = 1$ can only be achieved if all parameters have the same number of values.

In software testing, if the parameters have a different number of possible values, then in the test cases generated from $OA(1, t, k, v)$, only the t-tuples involving the parameter(s) with the largest number of values appear once. In other words, the value of λ can be more than 1 for parameters with a smaller number of values.

In these cases, the definition of $OA(1, t, k, v)$ does not theoretically represent t-wise testing, we need to relax the condition that all t-tuples appear the same number of times. Therefore, we only require that the t-tuples involving the parameter(s) with the largest number of values occur only once.

Regardless of the value of λ, our goal is to find a suitable orthogonal array with the smallest number of rows.

The max number of rows for $OA(1, t, k, v)$, from (4-2), is:

$$N = v^t \qquad (4\text{-}4)$$

For example, for pairwise testing, $t = 2$, the max number of tests should be v^2.

In Example 4.1, there are 3 parameters, and each has 2 possible values, if to model it with $OA(1, \mathbf{2, 3, 2})$, then the number of test cases is $2^2 = 4$.

When the numbers of possible values for the parameters are not the same, and are spread out, the number of rows (test cases) is usually less than N.

Examine Examples 4.2 and 4.3 again, the number of tests was less than v^2, since the numbers of possible values for the parameters are not the same.

We can also conclude from this observation that a test suite generated solely based on an orthogonal array may contain extra test cases that may need to be removed.

Let's apply the orthogonal array technique to demonstrate test case construction with the following example.

Example 4.5: Visibility of Applications on a Web Page

Suppose there is a role-based access privilege to certain applications on a website. There are 4 items on a page, each can be hidden or visible depending on if the logged-in user has the corresponding roles to see each of them. For example, if the user has 3 roles for 3 of them, the user can see those 3 items (links leading to the applications) on the home page.

The goal of this exercise is to construct 3-wise test cases to test the visibility of applications on the home page.

We have:

(a) $t = 3$: For 3-wise testing.
(b) $k = 4$: There are 4 parameters, one for each role.
(c) $v = 2$: A user either has the role or does not have the role.

So, this problem can be represented by an $OA(1, 3, 4, 2)$ orthogonal array.

The total number of tests per (4-4) should be:

$v^t = 2^3 = 8$,

while the number of total combinations is 2*2*2*2 = 16.

An $OA(1, 3, 4, 2)$ array has 8 runs as listed in Table 4.13.

0	0	0	0
0	0	1	1
0	1	0	1
0	1	1	0
1	0	0	1
1	0	1	0
1	1	0	0
1	1	1	1

Table 4.13: OA (1, 3, 4, 2)

We can translate the array to test cases by replacing each column with each role, the 1st column is for 'role 1', and so on, and map '0' to 'has no role', and '1' to 'has role', as listed in Table 4.14.

Case	Role1	Role2	Role3	Role4	Expected Items
1	0	0	0	0	none
2	0	0	1	1	3,4
3	0	1	0	1	2,4
4	0	1	1	0	2,3
5	1	0	0	1	1,4
6	1	0	1	0	1,3
7	1	1	0	0	1,2
8	1	1	1	1	1,2,3,4

Table 4.14: 3-wise test cases for Example 4.4

Test case 1 is to verify the visibility of the items on the page when the user has none of the four roles, test case 2 is to verify the visibility of the items on the page when the user has role3 and role4, and so on.

The 3-wise test cases are neatly generated.

Let's have a quick comparison with pairwise testing for the same example.

For pairwise testing, the result is $OA(1, 2, 4, 2)$, with four test cases as listed in Table 4.15.

Case	Role1	Role2	Role3	Role4	Expected Items
1	1	1	1	1	1,2,3,4
2	1	0	0	0	1
3	0	0	1	0	3
4	0	1	0	1	2,4

Table 4.15: Pairwise test cases from OA (1,2,4,2)

The number of tests generated from pair-wise testing is half the number of tests generated from 3-wise testing. One interesting thing to notice is that the case with no role at all (case 1 in 3-wise suite) is not in the list of tests with pair-wise testing. You may feel uncomfortable not including it. If you do, that case may be included as a special case. This indicates, in a sense, that there are limitations with pairwise testing, and other testing techniques should be combined with pairwise or even t-wise testing in real-world situations.

When the number of parameters is large, finding a proper OA and constructing test cases are very complicated, especially when the number of possible values is diverse, and automated tools would be needed.

Pairwise, *t*-wise testing, and orthogonal array techniques apply to all types of tests with interactive parameters in a software application when combination permutations exist and are in quite large numbers. These techniques can yield a significant reduction in the number of test cases without compromising too much code/functional coverage.

But these techniques do have weaknesses, for example:
- (a) High-risk combinations may not be included.
- (b) Defects involving higher than *t* parameters may not be found, and increasing *t* is not practical.
- (c) Since test cases generated from these methods are not weighted, every case is considered equal, no priorities are given to test cases.

Therefore, these techniques should be combined with other methods or strategies in real-world situations.

EXERCISE PROBLEMS:

P4.1: Laptop Catalogs

An online e-commerce website sells laptops, with four categories to select. The selections are listed below.

Parameters	# of selections	Selections
Brand	6	A, B, C, D, E, F
RAM size (GB)	4	16, 32, 64, 128
Disk space (GB)	3	(1) 512 to 1023, (2) 1024 to 2047, (3) 2048 to 4095
OS	3	Windows, ChromeOS, MacOS

Construct input vectors using the pairwise testing technique.

P4.2: A System with 3-way Switches

A system has 5 switches, each has three states: On, Off, and Auto. Construct both pairwise and 3-wise test cases using orthogonal arrays.

5 DECISION TABLE TESTING

Decision table testing is another technique to handle combinations of input vectors, with consideration of various conditions leading to corresponding expected results. The technique is also referred to as decision tree testing if the input vectors and the results are expressed in a tree structure instead of a table. Sometimes it's also referred to as the cause-effect graphing technique, where a decision table can be constructed from drawing a cause-effect graph.

The applications or programs under test normally contain various *if*, *else if*, and *switch* clauses in the code implementation if using a high-level programing language.

Theoretically, this is also one kind of combination problem, where all permutations of scenarios under different conditions are listed.

5.1 DECISION TABLE

A decision table is a table that lists conditions/actions and expected results for an application.

The conditions/actions are listed in the 1st column of the table, and the permutations of each condition or action and the corresponding results are listed in the rest of the columns. Each of the condition permutation and result columns is referred to as a ***rule***, and each rule is a variant of the conditions.

The conditions can be either input vectors, or equivalence partitions, while the expected results can be either the output vectors or a set of functional units. In other words, the conditions and expected results can be abstract entities.

CHAPTER 5: DECISION TABLE TESTING

Let's look at an example to demonstrate this technique.

Example 5.1: Gym Fee Structure

A gym has the following fee structure:

(1) Paid annually: $500, membership level: Silver.
(2) Paid annually: $600, membership level: Gold.
(3) Paid monthly: $60, membership level: Silver.
(4) Paid monthly: $70, membership level: Gold.
(5) One-time usage: $30, membership: none.
(6) Senior discount (age ≥ 60): 20%.

The fee structure is implemented as a software application. To test this application, all the possible combinations or scenarios should be included.

The table below shows the decision table for this application.

	Rule 1	Rule 2	Rule 3	Rule 4	Rule 5	Rule 6	Rule 7	Rule 8	Rule 9	Rule 10
Yearly option 1	T					T				
Yearly option 2		T					T			
Monthly plan 1			T					T		
Monthly plan 2				T					T	
One-time					T					T
Senior person	F	F	F	F	F	T	T	T	T	T
Fee	500	600	60	70	30	400	480	48	56	24
Membership level	Silver	Gold	Silver	Gold	None	Silver	Gold	Silver	Gold	None

Table 5.1: Decision table for Example 5.1

1st column lists the various conditions to calculate the fees, the rest of the columns are rules, and each rule contains a permutation of the available values of all the conditions. In the table, 'T' means 'true' and 'F' means 'false,' for a particular condition. The cells that are left empty should be filled with 'F', they are omitted for easy reading. The bottom two rows list the resulting fee and membership level for each rule.

Since there are no interactions between the first five conditions with regards to membership level, if any one of them is 'true' all other four must be 'false' (this could be implemented as a dropdown list, one variable with five options),
the conditions can be defined as mutually exclusive Boolean expressions of the input vectors.

The total number of variants is 5 * 2 = 10, where the '2' comes from the 'T' or 'F' options for the last requirement (Senior person or not).

Each rule in the table is a test case, therefore there are 10 test cases to cover all the business scenarios.

5.2 DECISION TABLE CONSTRUCTION AND RULE COUNT

Let's look at a couple of more examples to learn how to construct a decision table.

Example 5.2: Chicken Feeding at a Farm

At a farm, chickens are fed in four areas, A, B, C, and D, with the following requirements:

(a) if the age of a chicken is greater than 6 months, then go to area A.
(b) if the age is less than or equal to 6 months, and weight is below 0.5 kg, and is an egg chicken, then go to area B;
(c) if the age is less than or equal to 6 months, weight is below 0.5 kg, and is not an egg chicken (meat chicken), go to area C;
(d) if the age is less than or equal to 6 months, and weight is above or equal to 0.5 kg, go to area D.

There are three Boolean variables or conditions:

(i) age > 6 months
(ii) weight < 0.5 kg
(iii) egg chicken

Let's start to construct the decision table from the requirement specification.

Form the first requirement, when 'age > 6 months' is true, the other two conditions are not evaluated, the cells are marked with '-' in Table 5.2 for the conditions that are irrelevant. This generates Rule1. There should be one rule for each of the next three requirements as well. Rule2 comes from the second requirement, Rule3 comes from the third requirement, and Rule4 comes from the last requirement. So, we have total of four rules as listed in Table 5.2.

	Rule1	Rule2	Rule3	Rule4
age > 6 months	T	F	F	F
weight < 0.5kg	-	T	T	F
egg chicken	-	T	F	-
Resulting Area	A	B	C	D

Table 5.2: Decision table for Example 5.2

The cells marked with '-' are referred to as ***do not care*** entries, since the values of those entries do not affect the expected results.

Since all the conditions are Boolean, for a complete test case set, each 'do not care' cell should be counted as two cases. If there are more than one 'do not care' condition in one rule, the rule should be expended to a total number of rules of:

$$N_d = 2^d \qquad (5\text{-}1)$$

where d is the number of 'do not care' conditions for that column. N_d is the **rule count** for the column.

Continuing with Example 5.2, the number of rules for each column with the consideration of 'do not care' conditions are listed in Table 5.3 in the row *'rule count'*.

	Rule1	*Rule2*	*Rule3*	*Rule4*
age > 6 months	T	F	F	F
weight < 0.5kg	-	T	T	F
egg chicken	-	T	F	-
rule count	*4*	*1*	*1*	*2*
Resulting Area	A	B	C	D

Table 5.3: Decision table for Example 5.2 with rule counts

If we construct the decision table from all the combinations of the conditions, we would have total of 8 rules rather than 4. The 8 rules are listed in Table 5.4.

Which table among these two to use in real testing is a choice that should be based on other factors, such as knowledge of the implementation, the priority of the cases, or time allocation, etc.

	Rule1	*Rule2*	*Rule3*	*Rule4*	*Rule5*	*Rule6*	*Rule7*	*Rule8*
age > 6 months	T	T	T	T	F	F	F	F
weight < 0.5kg	F	F	T	T	T	T	F	F
Egg chicken	F	T	F	T	T	F	T	F
Resulting Area	A	A	A	A	B	C	D	D

Table 5.4: Decision table for Example 5.2 with all combinations of conditions

If we can assume that only one case is needed for a rule with a don't care condition, then we can reduce the number of rules by collapsing the ones with common conditions and results if the table is constructed from all condition permutations. In Table 5.4, the first 4 rules can be collapsed into

CHAPTER 5: DECISION TABLE TESTING   95

one, and the last two can be collapsed into another, and the final decision table is the same as Table 5.3.

Here is a list of test cases based on the rules in Table 5.3.

Test case	Age (month)	Weight (kg)	Egg chicken	Expected Result
1	8	0.8	1	A
2	3	0.4	1	B
3	4	0.3	0	C
4	5	0.7	0	D

Table 5.5: Test cases for Example 5.2

The 'do not care' cells are filled with random possible values.

The condition requirements for an application can be represented by a tree structure, called a **decision tree**, to graphically illustrate the conditions and expected results. For instance, the following graph in Figure 5.1 is a flowchart decision tree for Example 5.2.

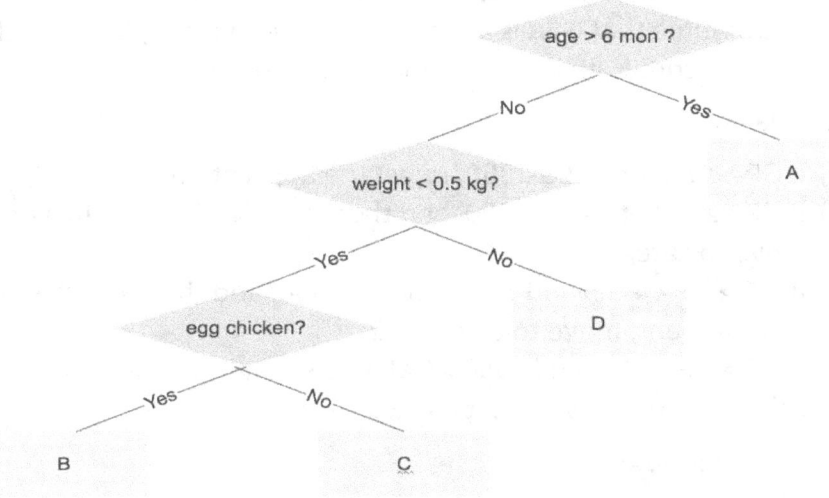

Figure 5.1: Decision tree for Example 5.2

The same decision table would be generated from the above graph.

When using a decision tree, be sure to traverse every path in the tree and visit every node in the tree when generating decision table conditions.

In general, when the conditions are mutually exclusive Boolean expressions, since each condition is a Boolean expression with two values, the maximum number of variants (then the number of test cases) is:

$$N = 2^n \tag{5-2}$$

where n is the total number of conditions.

Counting the number of rules is one way to examine if the decision table constructed from the requirements is complete or not. If the total count is smaller than the maximum number of rules calculated from equation (5-2), we know that the decision table is not complete and further revision is needed.

Let's look at another example to demonstrate how to construct a decision table in a different way, where non-Boolean conditions are present.

Example 5.3: College Admission Initial Categorization

A college admission office has an initial filtering program based on the following criteria. Three variables, 'GPA', 'SAT score', and 'if there is any significant achievement', are involved. GPA is the grade point average of all courses taken by a student in his/her high school years, SAT score is the test score from SAT standardized college entrance test, and a 'significant achievement' is a meaningful major accomplishment during the school years. Let's assume that GPA is a real value in the range [0, 5.0] (weighted GPA), and SAT score is an integer in the range [400, 1600].

The criteria are:

(1) If GPA ≤ 3.5 or SAT ≤ 1350, reject the application;
(2) If GPA ≥ 4.0 or SAT ≥ 1550, and there is a significant achievement, move to category 1;
(3) If 4.0 > GPA > 3.5 and 1550 > SAT > 1350, and there is a significant achievement, move to category 2;
(4) If 4.0 > GPA > 3.5 and 1550 > SAT > 1350, and there is no significant achievement, move to category 3.

The four categories are:

(1) 0: rejection.
(2) 1: 1st priority consideration with scholarship consideration.
(3) 2: 2nd priority consideration with no scholarship consideration.
(4) 3: 3rd priority consideration with no scholarship consideration.

There could be various ways to come up with Boolean conditions for this problem, for example, the following are three Boolean conditions based on the requirements:

(a) GPA > 3.5 && SAT > 1350
(b) Achievement == 1
(c) GPA ≥ 4.0 || SAT ≥ 1550

The actions or expected results are 0, 1, 2, or 3, each represents one category. Given that there are three conditions with Boolean values, the max number of variants is $2^3 = 8$.

Table 5.6 is the truth table for three Boolean conditions, and the decision table can be constructed from this truth table.

0	0	0
0	0	1
0	1	0
0	1	1
1	0	0
1	0	1
1	1	0
1	1	1

Table 5.6: Truth table for 3 Boolean conditions

We can construct the decision table by replacing 0 with F and 1 with T in the truth table, as shown in Table 5.7 (only showing the condition part, the result part is not shown).

GPA > 3.5 && SAT > 1350	F	F	F	F	T	T	T	T
Achievement == 1	F	F	T	T	F	F	T	T
GPA ≥ 4.0 || SAT ≥ 1550	F	T	F	T	F	T	F	T

Table 5.7: Condition part of the decision table for Example 5.3

We have to evaluate each variant since some of them may be conflicting with each other or are invalid and therefore need to be removed from the variant list. The conflicts or invalid rules should only be between condition (GPA > 3.5 && SAT > 1350) and condition (GPA ≥ 4.0 && SAT ≥ 1550), since both GPA and SAT score are involved in these two conditions.

The two variants, the 2nd one and the 4th one, marked in grey in the above table are invalid, since GPA cannot be greater or equal to 4.0 and at the same time, less than or equal to 3.5, similarly for SAT score, SAT ≥ 1550 and SAT ≤ 1350 are conflicts to each other.

These conflict conditions are often referred to as ***impossible*** conditions or ***can't happen*** conditions. Therefore, only the rest of the six rules are to remain.

The decision table is constructed below with the remaining 6 rules.

	Rule1	Rule2	Rule3	Rule4	Rule5	Rule6
GPA > 3.5 && SAT > 1350	F	F	T	T	T	T
Achievement == 1	F	T	F	F	T	T
GPA ≥4.0 || SAT ≥ 1550	F	F	F	T	F	T
Resulting Category	0	0	3	3	2	1

Table 5.8: Decision table for Example 5.3

We end up with six test cases for the application. Sample test cases based on this decision table are listed in Table 5.9.

Test case	GPA	SAT	Achievement	Expected Result
1	3.3	1320	0	0
2	3.5	1280	1	0
3	3.6	1400	0	3
4	4.0	1460	0	3
5	3.9	1540	0	2
6	4.1	1380	1	1

Table 5.9: Test cases for Example 5.3

Code segment 5.1 is a sample Java implementation based on the above conditions (treat this as an example of test-driven development).

```
//0: reject;
//1: 1st priority consideration with financial aid consideration.
//2: 2nd priority consideration with no financial aid consideration.
//3: 3rd priority consideration with no financial aid consideration.
public static int initialApplicationCatagorization (double gpa, int sat,
int achievement)
{ int result = 0;
  if (gpa > 3.5 && sat > 1350) {
     result = 3;
     if (achievement == 1) {
         result = 2;
         if (gpa >= 4.0 || sat >= 1550) {
             result = 1;
         }
     }
  }
  return result;
}
```

Code Segment 5.1: Implementation for Example 5.3: College admission categorization

There is a problem with this implementation. Notice, some of the input spaces for the variables are not included in the variants, such as when (3.5 < GPA < 4.0 && SAT > 1550) is true. The test cases we came up with do not cover the whole vector space completely, and the implementation in Code Segment 5.1 is flawed.

A better solution is to separate GPA and SAT scores. Let's improve the decision table by separating GPA and SAT scores in the conditions.

An easy way to separate them is with the following Boolean conditions:

   (a) GPA > 3.5
   (b) GPA ≥ 4.0
   (c) SAT > 1350
   (d) SAT ≥ 1550
   (e) Achievement == 1

With five conditions, to construct the decision table, we have to start with a truth table with $2^5 = 32$ entries, then examine the entries for invalid entries or can't happen conditions to further reduce the test case count.

Is there a better way to handle this problem? Notice that variable GPA appears in two of the above 5 conditions, and we could combine these two conditions and separate the Boolean conditions to deal with only one variable. Same for variable SAT. Conditions with one variable are no longer Boolean conditions but are non-Boolean conditions having multiple possible values.

A decision table with Boolean conditions is also referred to as **limited entry table**; a decision table contains non-Boolean conditions is also referred to as **extended entry table**.

A better solution to the college admission initial categorization problem is to use non-Boolean conditions for both GPA and SAT scores and to keep the Boolean condition for 'Achievement'. The non-Boolean conditions can now be expressed with value partitions.

The following are the new conditions to consider for the three variables:

   (a) GPA: value partitions:
      1: [0, 3.49];
      2: [3.50, 3.99];
      3: [4.0, 5.0].
   (b) SAT: value partitions:
      1: [400, 1350];
      2: [1360, 1540];
      3: [1550, 1600].
   (c) Achievement: Boolean [0, 1].

Let's construct the extended entry decision table with these conditions.

GPA and SAT scores are divided into equivalence partitions. We could include invalid zones as well, but since we are focusing on testing the business scenarios here, we are skipping those partitions in this example, and leave it as an exercise for the reader (as you can see, multiple testing techniques are being used).

The standard case of equivalence partitioning is normally applied to this kind of problem. For simplicity, we are adopting base case of equivalence partitioning here just to demonstrate test case generation with extended entry table, by selecting one value in each partition (but will try to use different values in different test cases for the same partition).

Since there are three partitions for each of the GPA and SAT conditions, and there are two values for the last Boolean condition, the total number of variants is 3 * 3 * 2 = 18. All the 18 variants are listed in the decision table in Table 5.10.

The condition cells are filled with partition numbers for both GPA and SAT, and 1 or 0 for Achievement. For example, a '1' in GPA means a value in partition [0, 3.49].

	1	2	3	4	5	6	7	8	9
GPA	1	1	1	2	2	2	3	3	3
SAT	1	2	3	1	2	3	1	2	3
Achievement	0	0	0	0	0	0	0	0	0
Category	0	0	0	0	3	3	0	3	3

	10	11	12	13	14	15	16	17	18
GPA	1	1	1	2	2	2	3	3	3
SAT	1	2	3	1	2	3	1	2	3
Achievement	1	1	1	1	1	1	1	1	1
Category	0	0	0	0	2	1	0	1	1

Table 5.10: Extended entry decision table for Example 5.3

Table 5.11 lists 18 test cases based on the extended entry decision table.

Notice an interesting fact with the 18 test cases, that the output vector distribution is not even, '0' appeared ten times, while '2' only showed one time. If a somewhat more even output vector distribution is desired or is required, you may add more input values, such as boundary values, for certain relevant partitions.

Test case	GPA	SAT	Achievement	Expected Result
1	2.7	1250	0	0
2	2.9	1360	0	0
3	3.1	1560	0	0
4	3.5	1260	0	0
5	3.6	1370	0	3
6	3.7	1570	0	3
7	4.0	1270	0	0
8	4.3	1380	0	3
9	4.5	1580	0	3
10	2.8	1280	1	0
11	3.0	1390	1	0
12	3.4	1590	1	0
13	3.5	1280	1	0
14	3.7	1390	1	2
15	3.9	1590	1	1
16	4.1	1350	1	0
17	4.4	1540	1	1
18	5.0	1600	1	1

Table 5.11: Test cases based on extended entry decision table for Example 5.3

Now let's try to collapse the decision table. From the requirements we can infer that if GPA ≤ 3.5 (GPA partition 1), or SAT ≤ 1350 (SAT partition 1), the result is a rejection, regardless of the value of *Achievement*, these are rules 1, 2, 3, 10, 11, and 12, and these rules can be collapsed into one rule. Similarly, rules 5 and 6 can be collapsed into one, rules 4, 7, 13, and 16 can be collapsed into one. Same for rules 8 and 9, rules 17 and 18. The table below shows these intermediate steps.

	1	2	3	4	5	6	7	8	9
GPA	1	1	1	2	2	2	3	3	3
SAT	1	2	3	1	2	3	1	2	3
Achievement	0	0	0	0	0	0	0	0	0
Category	0	0	0	0	3	3	0	3	3

	10	11	12	13	14	15	16	17	18
GPA	1	1	1	2	2	2	3	3	3
SAT	1	2	3	1	2	3	1	2	3
Achievement	1	1	1	1	1	1	1	1	1
Category	0	0	0	0	2	1	0	1	1

Table 5.12: Intermediate steps collapsing the extended decision table for Example 5.3

Table 5.13 is the collapsed decision table, don't care conditions are marked and rule counts are listed in the table as well.

	1	4	5	8	14	15	17
GPA	1	-	2	3	2	2	3
SAT	-	1	-	-	2	3	-
Achievement	-	-	0	0	1	1	1
rule count	6	4	2	2	1	1	2
Result category	0	0	3	3	2	1	1

Table 5.13: Collapsed decision table for Example 5.3 with rule counts

We know how many rules are collapsed for each rule with 'don't care' conditions, so we know the rule count for the collapsed rule. It's easy to see that a Boolean 'don't care' condition doubles the rule count, while a non-Boolean condition makes the rule count number bigger by a factor of the total possible values for the specific condition. Table 5.14 is the final decision table.

	1	2	3	4	5	6	7
GPA	1	-	2	3	2	2	3
SAT	-	1	-	-	2	3	-
Achievement	-	-	0	0	1	1	1
Result category	0	0	3	3	2	1	1

Table 5.14: Final extended decision table for Example 5.3

Sample test cases based on the final extended decision table are listed in Table 5.15.

Test case	GPA	SAT	Achievement	Expected Result
1	2.7	1250	0	0
2	3.5	1260	0	0
3	3.6	1370	0	3
4	4.3	1380	0	3
5	3.7	1390	1	2
6	3.9	1590	1	1
7	4.4	1540	1	1

Table 5.15: Test cases based on extended decision Table 5.14 for Example 5.3

If invalid partitions are also involved, the results would be in the 'impossible' category, and those variants should be added and not be removed by the collapsing. Specifying impossible actions/results is a good way to catch defects, which we will leave to the readers to explore them.

Another point to make is that what conditions should be used to construct the decision table for a specific application, and whether or to what extend equivalence partitioning is to be used together with the decision table technique, also depend on the UI implementation of the application. For example, if the variables for both GPA and SAT are implemented as dropdown lists with value choices, then the number of choices for a variable is the number of possible values for the variable; but if they are implemented as input boxes, then you will need to consider both boundary values and invalid values, and end up with adding more test cases.

In general, the maximum number of rules for an **extended entry decision table** is:

$$N = \prod_{i=1}^{r} v_i \qquad (5\text{-}3)$$

where r is the number of conditions, and v_i is the number of possible values for the ith condition.

Calculating rule counts using 'don't care' entries is a good way to find **inconsistency** or **redundancy** of conditions. For example, if a decision table constructed from the requirements contains more rules than the maximum number calculated by either equation (5-2) or (5-3), then there must be rules that are either redundant or inconsistent with other rules. Also, when the number of rules is less than what's expected, the decision table is incomplete, and needs revision.

In summary, there are two important ways to construct a decision table, one is from the requirements, the other is from all condition permutations. When the number of conditions is small, starting from all permutations is good, but if the number of conditions is too large, you may prefer to start from the requirements.

Similar to the equivalence partitioning method, the decision table technique is applicable when the order, in which the conditions are evaluated, does not affect the result.

The decision table technique is more appropriate for applications or modules where a lot of decision makings are involved, or there are logical relationships within the input variables (not fully dependent), or there are calculations to be made in a decision involving a subset of the input variables (as in example 5.3 where both GPA and SAT scores are calculated in a decision route), or the behaviors of the application are specified clearly to the conditions involved.

Comparing with the standard case of equivalence partitioning (with boundary values) technique, the decision table technique produces a smaller number of test cases. it's more efficient for applicable situations, but sometimes there may be test coverages concerns. Therefore, it's better to combine different techniques in testing whenever applicable.

5.3 CAUSE-EFFECT GRAPHING

Cause-effect graphing is another way to construct a decision table. The causes are the input conditions and the effects are the actions or expected results. The causes are identified and numbered, as well as the effects. Which causes lead to which effects are evaluated based on the requirement specification, and graphs are drawn to represent the cause-effect relationship, with certain conventions.

In a cause-effect graph, a node is drawn for each cause and each effect, a line from a cause to an effect indicates that the cause is a necessary condition for the effect. If a single effect has two or more causes, the logical relationship of the causes is annotated by symbols for logical AND (^) and logical OR (v) placed between the lines. A cause whose negation is necessary is shown by a logical not (~). A single cause may be necessary for many effects; a single effect may have many necessary causes. Sometimes, intermediate nodes may be used to simplify the graph and its construction.

Let's look at an example to demonstrate this technique.

Example 5.4: Loan Rate under Different Conditions

A bank approves fixed mortgage loans with different interest rates based on the following two values:

(i) R: debt to income ratio of the applicant(s).
(ii) S: credit score of the applicant(s).

Here are the requirement specifications:

(a) if $R > 40\%$ or $S < 600$: reject application.
(b) if $20\% < R \leq 40\%$ and $600 \leq S < 700$, interest rate is 5%.
(c) if $20\% < R \leq 40\%$ and $750 > S \geq 700$, interest rate is 4.5%.
(d) if $20\% < R \leq 40\%$ and $S \geq 750$, interest rate is 4%.
(e) if $R \leq 20\%$ and $S \geq 600$, interest rate is 4%.

Valid values are between 0.0 and infinity for parameter R, and are between 300 and 850 for S, inclusive.

This is the same application as that in Example 3.10, where equivalence partitioning technique was demonstrated with dependent variables. In that example, we came up with 59 test cases for the standard partitioning case.

Examine the requirements, we can infer that only two variables, R and S, determine the effects, and there are 3 sets of values for R, and 4 sets of values for S. Therefore, we have total of 7 distinct causes. The expected results are 5%, 4.5%, 4.0%, and reject, total 4 effects.

We marked the causes with unique numbers and effects with unique letters. The causes and effects are listed in both Tables 5.16 and 5.17.

	Causes
1	R ≤ 20%
2	20% < R ≤ 40%
3	R > 40%
4	S < 600
5	600 ≤ S < 700
6	750 > S ≥ 700
7	S ≥ 750

	Effects
a	rate 5.0%
b	rate 4.5%
c	rate 4.0%
d	reject

Table 5.16: Causes for Example 5.4   **Table 5.17:** Effects for Example 5.4

We plot the graph with causes on the left and effects on the right and connect the causes and effects according to the specification, as shown in Figure 5.2.

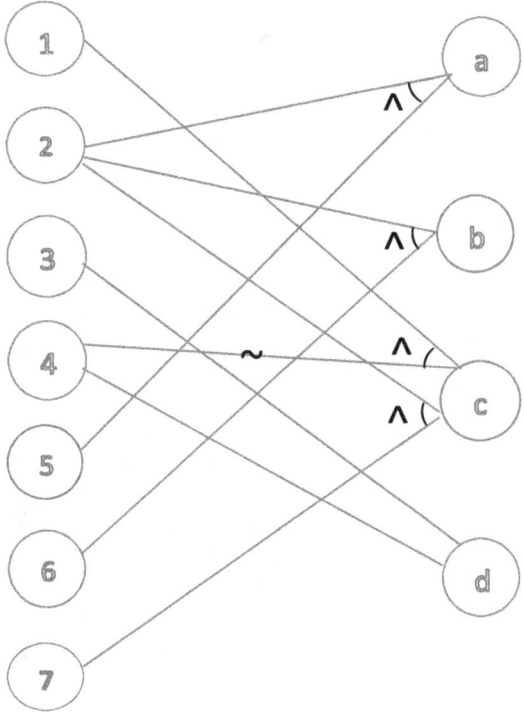

Figure 5.2: Cause-effect graph for Example 5.4: Loan rate under different conditions

The above cause-effect graph can also be separated into individual graphs as shown in Table 5.18.

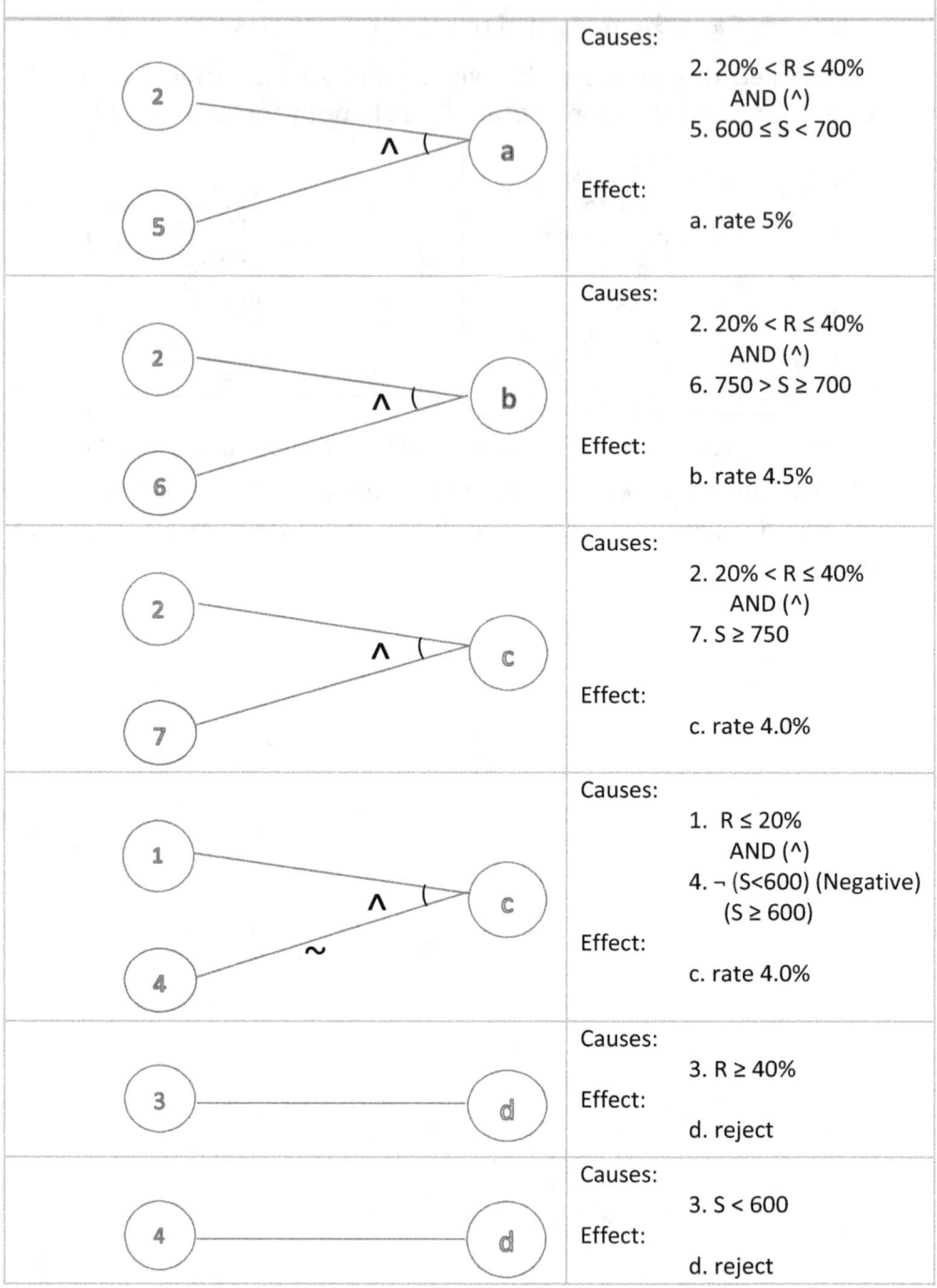

Table 5.18: Individual cause-effect graphs for Example 5.4

CHAPTER 5: DECISION TABLE TESTING

The next step is to construct the limited decision table (Boolean conditions) by going through all cause-effect relationships on the graph(s). The result is shown in Table 5.19.

		1	2	3	4	5	6	7	8
1	R ≤ 20%	0	0	0	1	1	1	0	0
2	20% < R ≤ 40%	1	1	1	0	0	0	0	0
3	R > 40%	0	0	0	0	0	0	1	0
4	S < 600	0	0	0	0	0	0	0	1
5	600 ≤ S < 700	1	0	0	1	0	0	0	0
6	750 > S ≥ 700	0	1	0	0	1	0	0	0
7	S ≥ 750	0	0	1	0	0	1	0	0
a	rate 5.0%	1							
b	rate 4.5%		1						
c	rate 4.0%			1	1	1	1		
d	reject							1	1

Table 5.19: Decision table based on cause-effect graphs for Example 5.4

A one ('1') in a cell indicates that the cause or effect is true, and a zero ('0') indicates that it is false. Note, the 4th individual graph involves negation, which means that any of the rest of the conditions concerning the same parameter should be true (we could have split that individual graph into multiples without using negation). Those are rules 4, 5, and 6 in Table 5.19.

The following table lists a set of sample test cases based on the decision table in Table 5.19.

Test case	R (%)	S	Expected result (%)
1	30	650	5.0
2	35	720	4.5
3	37	800	4.0
4	10	620	4.0
5	15	740	4.0
6	18	790	4.0
7	55	700 (don't care)	reject
8	25 (don't care)	500	reject

Table 5.20: Test cases for Example 5.4

The number of tests generated from this technique is much smaller than that from the equivalence partitioning technique as we have discussed in Example 3.10 for the same application. This is mainly that the boundary conditions are not considered, and invalid zones are not included. In real-world testing, different techniques should be combined to satisfy your specific testing goals.

This example is a very simple one, and you could come up with test cases from the requirements easily without using a cause-effect graph. However, for complex systems with more causes and effects, this technique is a good way to generate a decision table and to produce test cases.

This problem can also be solved by the extended decision table technique. We know that there are two variables, S and R, and there are 3 sets of values for S, and there are 4 sets of values for R, and the total number of rules should be 3 * 4 = 12. Will leave it as an exercise for the reader to come up with 'don't care' conditions and the final set of test cases (see exercise problem P5.4).

CHAPTER 5: DECISION TABLE TESTING

EXERCISE PROBLEMS:

P5.1: Movie Theater Ticket Pricing

A movie theater has the following ticket pricing formula:

(a) Regular price:
- (1) age <2: 0
- (2) age 2-12: $14
- (3) age 13-60: $20
- (4) age 60+: $16

(b) if before 12 noon:
- (1) age < 2: 0
- (2) age 2-12: $7
- (3) age 13-60: $10
- (4) age 60+: $8

Use the decision table technique to construct a decision table and generate test cases from it.

P5.2: Student Housing Arrangement

A school provides on-campus housing for certain groups of students. Depends on a few selections, a student is directed to a specific housing unit. Here are the specifications:

(1) single male domestic students, go to unit A.
(2) single female domestic students, go to unit B.
(3) single international students, go to unit C.
(4) students with families, go to unit D.

Use decision table technique to construct a decision table and generate test cases from it.

P5.3: NextMonth Function

A function NextMonth() takes a date as input, and outputs next month. For example, if the input is 'June 25, 2025', then NextMonth() returns 'July'; if the input is 'Dec 31, 2025', then the output is 'January'. The input can be any day of any year (say, between 1999 and 2099).

Use decision table technique to construct a decision table and generate test cases from it.

P5.4: Use extended decision table technique to generate test cases for Example 5.4: Loan Rate under Different Conditions.

6 STRUCTURAL TESTING

Structural testing technique is based on the structure of the implementation of a software, hence, it's a testing technique for type 0 tests, and is commonly used in unit test design in the early stages of software development. The concept can also be used in other types of tests with further abstraction (an example applying to use cases is discussed in section 6.7).

The structural testing technique is developed using graph theory, we will discuss some basic relevant graph concepts first, and then talk about several structural testing approaches.

Finite state machine model is also included toward the end of this chapter, since it's closely related to graphs.

6.1 CONTROL FLOW GRAPH

In graph theory, a graph is a set of elements in which some pairs of the elements are related in a certain manner. Each of the elements is called a vertex, a **node**, or a point (*node* will be used in this book), and each of the related pairs is called an **edge**.

A directed graph is a graph in which edges have orientations. We can write it as $G = (N, E)$, where N is a set of elements (nodes), and E is a set of ordered pairs, or direct edges (we will simply call them edges).

An edge (n_i, n_j) is considered to be directed from n_i to n_j, n_j is said to be a *direct successor* of n_i, and n_i is said to be a *direct predecessor* of n_j.

A **path** is a sequence of nodes $p = [n_0, n_1, ..., n_k]$ such that n_{i+1} is a successor of n_i for $i = 0, ..., k-1$. The length of the path is k (paths with just one node have

0 length). A subsequence of *p* is called a **subpath** of *p*. A path is called a **cycle** if a node appears more than once in a path. A path contains a cycle in one of its subpaths is also a cycle.

If a path leads from n_i to n_j then n_j is said to be a *successor* of n_i and *reachable* from n_i, and n_i is said to be a *predecessor* of n_j.

Now, let's define test graph, a representation of the software under test.

A **test graph** is a directed graph, it's a tuple:

$$G = (N, N_0, N_f, E) \qquad (6\text{-}1)$$

where:

(a) N is a non-empty set of nodes.
(b) $N_0 \subseteq N$ is a non-empty set of initial nodes.
(c) $N_f \subseteq N$ is a non-empty set of final nodes.
(d) $E \subseteq N \times N$ is a set of edges.

For $(n_i, n_j) \in E$, we say n_i is a predecessor of n_j and n_j is a successor of n_i.

A **test path** is a path $p = [n_0, n_1, ..., n_k]$ such that $n_0 \in N_0$ and $n_k \in N_f$. That is, *a test path starts with an initial node and ends with a final node.* A test path *p* **visits** node *n* if *n* is in *p*, a test path *p* **visits** edge *e* if *e* is in *p*.

The execution of a test case corresponds to a test path in the graph. One test case corresponds to one and only one test path, the execution of a test case goes *from an initial start node and ends at a final node*.

We define *path(t)* as the test pass executed by test *t*, and *path(T)* as the set of test paths executed by the set of test *T*.

Let's take an example to illustrate the definitions.

Example 6.1: Test Graph One

A graph is defined by:

(1) $N = \{1, 2, 3, 4, 5\}$
(2) $N_0 = \{1\}$
(3) $N_f = \{2, 5\}$
(4) $E = \{(1,2), (1, 3), (3, 4), \{4, 3\}, (3, 5)\}$

Figure 6.1 is the graph that satisfies the definition.

The following are some facts about certain paths of this graph:

(1) [3], length 0.
(2) [3,5], length 1.

(3) [3,5] is a subpath of [1,3,5].
(4) [3,4,3] is a cycle.
(5) [1,3,4,3,5] contains a cycle.

The following are three test paths:

[1,2],
[1,3,5],
[1,3,4,3,5].

The *test paths* start from the initial node 1 and end at a final node, 2 or 5.

Examine test path [1,3,4,3,5], it visits nodes 1, 3, 4, and 5, visits edges (1,3), (3,4), (4,3), and (3,5); it contains subpath [1,3,4], [3,4,3], [4,3,5], [1,3], [3,4], [4,3], and [3,5].

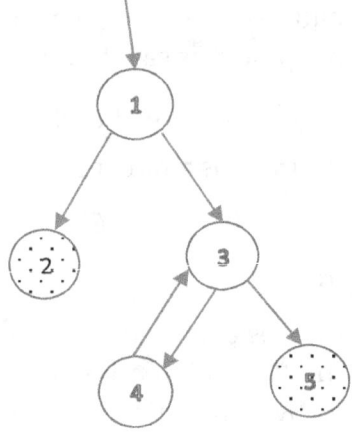

Figure 6.1: Graph for Example 6.1

Some paths may be included in multiple test cases, and some paths may not be included in any test case.

A node in a graph can be reached from another node if there is a sequence of edges from the 1st node to the 2nd node. There are two notions of reachability, one is syntactic reach, the other is semantic reach.

(a) A node *n* is **syntactically** reachable from node *m* if there exists a path from *m* to *n*.
(b) A node *n* is **semantically** reachable from node *m* if it's possible to execute a path from *m* to *n* with certain input.

We also define **reach(n)** as the set of nodes that can be syntactically reached from node *n*. In the above example, *reach(1) = {2,3,4,5}, reach(3) = {4,5}*.

Syntactic and semantic reaches are illustrated with Code Segment 6.1.

```
public static int numberReturn (int n, int m) {
    int result = 0;
    while (m > 0) {
        m--;
        if (n < 10) {
            result = n * n;
            break;
        }
        result = result + n * n;
    }
    return result;
}
```

Code Segment 6.1: An example to illustrate syntactic and semantic reaches

For example, in the above code, line result = result + n * n; is reachable syntactically, but reaching it semantically depends on the input value of *n*. If (n < 10) is true, then this line will not be reached, and only when (n < 10) evaluate to false, this line can be reached, semantically.

A *control flow graph (CFG)* is a test graph (a directed graph), an abstract representation of a piece of software source code.

In a control flow graph, the nodes represent **basic blocks**, which are sequences of instructions that always execute together in sequence; the edges represent **control flow** between basic blocks. The **entry node** corresponds to an entry point of the code segment under test; the **final nodes** correspond to exit points; the **decision nodes** represent choices in control flow, the choices are the results of a control statement, such as a '*for*' loop, a '*while*' loop, and an '*if*' statement.

Let's start by examining a few common control statements in high-level programming languages to illustrate the concepts and to learn how to construct a control flow graph.

Common Control Statements:

(1) For Loop: Consider the 'for' loop on the left side of Figure 6.2. The control flow graph to the right represents this loop. The node numbers represent lines/blocks in the code, noted with comments (after '//') in the code segment.

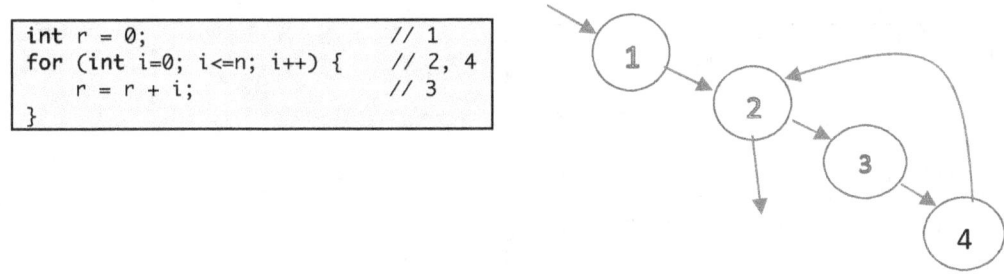

Figure 6.2: A 'for' loop and its control flow graph

(2) While Loop: Here is a 'while' loop and its control flow graph representation.

```
int r = 0;                  // 1
int i = 0;                  // 1
while ( i <= n) {           // 2
    r = r + i;              // 3
    i++;                    // 3
}
```

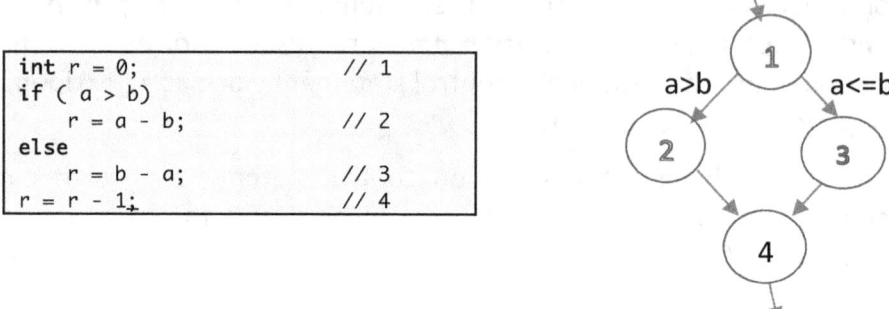

Figure 6.3: A 'while' loop and its control flow graph

(3) If Else: The following is an if-else code segment and its control flow graph representation.

```
int r = 0;          // 1
if ( a > b )
    r = a - b;      // 2
else
    r = b - a;      // 3
r = r - 1;          // 4
```

Figure 6.4: A 'if else' loop and its control flow graph

(4) Switch: The following is a switch code segment and its control flow graph representation.

```
int color = getColor();              //1
String colorString = "";             //1
switch (color) {
    case 1: colorString = "Blue";    //2
            break;
    case 2: colorString = "Yellow";  //3
            break;
    case 3: colorString = "Red";     //4
            break;
    default: colorString = "White";  //5
}
System.out.println(colorString);     //6
```

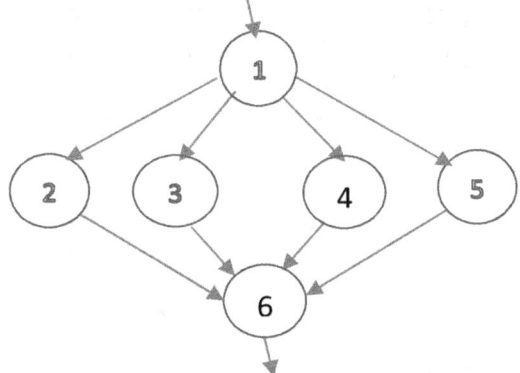

Figure 6.5: A 'switch' loop and its control flow graph

Now, let's work with an example to demonstrate how to construct a control flow graph, and how to generate test cases from the graph.

CHAPTER 6: STRUCTURAL TESTING

Example 6.2: A Function to Check Occurrence Count of a Character in a String

Code segment 6.2 is a Java method to count the occurrence of a character in a particular string. It contains a 'for' loop and two 'if' control statements.

```java
public static int characterCount (String c, String s) {
    if ((s == null) || (c == null)) {
        System.out.println("error: no input string.");
    }
    int count = 0;
    for (int i = 0; i < s.length(); i++) {
        if (s.charAt(i) == c.charAt(0) ) {
            count++; }
    }
    return count;
}
```

Code Segment 6.2: Occurrence count of a character in a string

First, we need to determine the basic blocks representing the nodes in the graph and to identify entry node(s), final node(s), and decision node(s), then we can construct the control flow graph by adding edges (control flows) to the nodes.

The basic blocks are listed in the table below, the entry node is '1', and final nodes are '2' and '8', and control nodes are '1', '4', and '5'.

1	if ((s == null) || c == null))
2	System.out.println(" error: no input string.");
3	int count = 0; int i = 0
4	i < s.length();
5	if (s.charAt(i) == c.charAt(0))
6	count++;
7	i++;
8	return count;

Table 6.1: basic blocks for Example 6.2

These basic blocks are represented by the nodes on the control flow graph, and the control flows are represented by the edges between nodes.

Here is the definition of this control flow graph as a test graph and is plotted in Figure 6.6 (not all basic blocks are marked on the graph).

(a) $N = \{1, 2, 3, 4, 5, 6, 7, 8\}$
(b) $N_0 = \{1\}$
(c) $N_f = \{2, 8\}$
(d) $E = \{(1,2), (1,3), (3,4), (4,5), (4,8), (5,6), (5,7), (6,7), (7,4)\}$

116   CHAPTER 6: STRUCTURAL TESTING

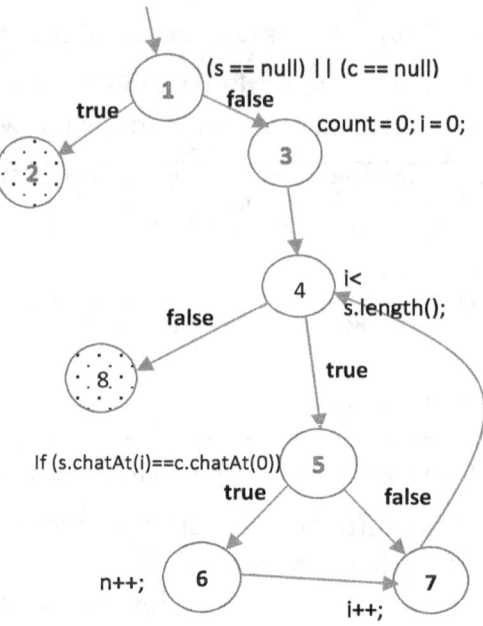

Figure 6.6: Graph for Example 6.2

We will come back to this example later in this chapter.

6.2 NODE AND EDGE COVERAGES

When using a test graph to model a software system, test coverage needs to be defined. Test coverage is defined with what's called a **test criterion**, a set of rules that impose requirements for test paths. That is, coverage criteria specify requirements as a set of test paths that must be covered.

Let's define C as the test criterion, and TR(C) as the test requirements, the execution of a test case t results in a test path path(t), then:

A set of test cases T **satisfies** C:

If and only if for every $r \in TR(C)$, there is $t \in T$ that tours r. (that is, r is a subpath of path(t)).

Simply speaking, for every test requirement, there is a test path that meets it.

Let's define two basic coverages, namely node coverage, and edge coverage.

Node Coverage (NC):

A test set T satisfies node coverage on graph G(N,E) if and only if for every syntactically reachable node n in N, there is some path p in path(T) such that p visits n.

In other words, each reachable node in G is included in the test paths of the test cases in set T, that is, TR(T) covers every reachable node in the test graph.

Node coverage is also referred to as **statement coverage**. Normally a statement is or is part of a node (a basic block).

Edge Coverage (EC):

TR(T) contains every reachable path of length up to 1 inclusive in graph G.

In node coverage (NC), the coverage is all nodes, that is, all length 0 paths; while in edge coverage (EC), by definition, it includes all paths of length 0 and 1. Therefore, EC contains NC (so EC is stronger).

Edge coverage is also referred to as **branch coverage**. A control statement would be branching out to different nodes.

Take a look at Example 6.1 again (See control flow graph in Figure 6.1):

    (1) $N = \{1, 2, 3, 4, 5\}$
    (2) $N_0 = \{1\}$
    (3) $N_f = \{2, 5\}$
    (4) $E = \{(1,2), (1, 3), (3, 4), \{4, 3\}, (3, 5)\}$

For node coverage, test requirements should include:

    $TR(NC) = \{1, 2, 3, 4, 5\}$.

For edge coverage, all edges should be included:

    $TR(EC) = TR(NC) \cup \{(1,2), (1, 3), (3, 4), \{4, 3\}, (3, 5)\}$.

The following two test paths satisfy both NC and EC (all nodes and all edges are covered):

    [1, 2], [1, 3, 4, 3, 5].

For any code segment, node coverage is never enough, and edge coverage is a necessary minimum for software testing.

Consider another example.

Example 6.3: Another Test Graph

    A CFG is defined as:

        (1) $N = \{1, 2, 3, 4\}$
        (2) $N_0 = \{1\}$
        (3) $N_f = \{4\}$
        (4) $E = \{(1,2), (1, 3), (2, 3), (3, 4)\}$

Figure 6.7 shows the CFG plot.

With this graph:

TR(NC) = {1, 2, 3, 4}, and
TR(EC) = {(1,2),(1,3),(2,3),(3,4)}.

Test path [1,2,3,4] satisfies NC, but it does not satisfy EC.

The following set of test paths satisfies both NC and EC:

{[1,3,4], [1,2,3,4]}

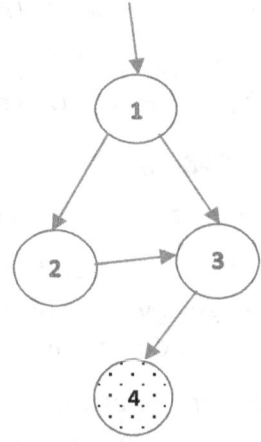

Figure 6.7: Graph for Example 6.3

Besides node coverage and edge coverage, there are other stronger coverage criteria, for example, **edge-pair coverage (*EPC*)**, which requires pairs of edges, that is, subpaths of length 2 to be covered. EPC subsumes both NC and EC. EPC covers all paths up to length 2, while EC covers up to length 1 and NC covers length 0 paths (nodes) only.

Edge Pair Coverage (EPC):

TR(T) contains every reachable path of length up to 2 inclusive in graph *G*.

In Example 6.3, EPC would require the following paths to be covered:

TR(EPC) = {(1,2,3), (2,3,4), (1,3,4)}

The test paths set {[1,3,4], [1,2,3,4]} satisfies EPC as well.

Beyond EPC, what if we increase the length to the maximum possible value, that is, to cover *all* paths in the tests? We define this scenario as:

Complete path coverage (CPC):

Complete path coverage requires all paths to be covered.

The number of paths could be infinite in a complete path coverage when the graph contains a loop for example. Therefore, in practice, a subset of the paths may have to be picked. There are various theories on the path approximation process, we are discussing one of them in the next section, *prime path coverage (PPC)*.

6.3 PRIME PATH COVERAGES

In this section we will be focusing on path coverage, primarily prime path coverage, and will also be discussing infeasible requirements, best effort touring, and cyclomatic complexity.

6.3.1 Prime Path Coverages

Let's define both simple path and prime path first.

A path $p = [n_0, n_1, ..., n_k]$ is a **simple path** if no node appears more than once, except possibly the 1st node and the last node. Note, a simple path has no internal loops (but may have a loop if the 1st node and the last node are the same node).

A simple path is a **prime path** if it's not a subpath of any other simple path.

Prime Path Coverage (PPC):

  TR(T) contains all prime paths in graph *G*.

PPC is an approximation and the set of prime paths is a subset of the set of complete path coverage paths.

EPC path set is not a subset of PPC path set, but EC path set is a subset of PPC.

To find the prime paths of a graph, first, we need to list all the simple paths, then pick the prime ones.

Take Example 6.1 again, the graph is shown in Figure 6.8.

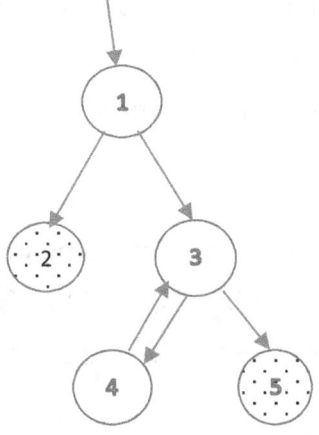

Figure 6.8: Graph for Example 6.1

Let's manually list both of the simple paths and prime paths, since it's a pretty simple graph.

Simple paths are (0 length paths are not included):

    [1,2], *[1,3]*, *[3,4]*, [4,3], *[3,5]*,
    [1,3,4], [1,3,5], [3,4,3], [4,3,5].

The simple paths in *italic* above are clearly subpaths of other simple paths, the rest are prime paths:

    [1,2], [1,3,4], [1,3,5], [3,4,3], [4,3,5].

PPC is a good way to handle loops in a graph. Prime paths have no internal loops, but test paths might have loops (remember a test path is from the initial node to an end node).

The following four test paths will cover the above 5 prime paths:

    [1,2], [1,3,5], [1,3,4,5], [1,3,4,3,5].

Now, let's work with an example to demonstrate how to produce prime paths and test paths systematically.

Example 6.4: A Function to Check Occurrence Count of a Character in a String

This is the same as Example 6.2, the CFG is plotted again in Figure 6.9, the definition of the test graph is:

  (a) $N = \{1, 2, 3, 4, 5, 6, 7, 8\}$
  (b) $N_0 = \{1\}$
  (c) $N_f = \{2, 8\}$
  (d) $E = \{(1,2), (1,3), (3,4), (4,5), (4,8), (5,6), (5,7), (6,7), (7,4)\}$

For **node coverage**, all the nodes should be visited:

    TR(NC) = {1, 2, 3, 4, 5, 6, 7}.

The following test paths would cover all the nodes:

    [1,2],
    [1,3,4,5,6,7,4,8]

For **edge coverage**, all the edges should be visited:

    TR(EC) = {(1,2), (1,3), (2,3), (3,4), (4,5), (4,8), (5,6), (5,7), (6,7), (7,4)}.

The following test paths would cover all the edges:

    [1,2],
    [1,3,4,5,7,4,5,6,7,8].

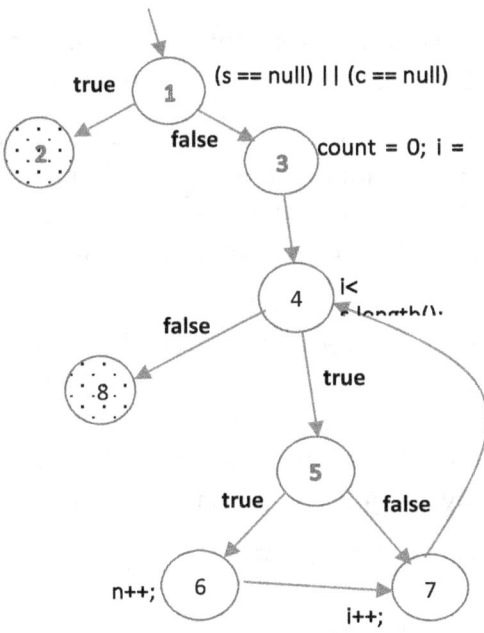

Figure 6.9: Graph for Example 6.4

Now, let's list all the **simple paths** with lengths greater than 0 in Table 6.2.

1	2	3	4	5
[1,2]!	[1,3,4]	[1,3,4,5]	[1,3,4,5,6]	[1,3,4,5,6,7]!
[1,3]	[3,4,5]	[1,3,4,8]!	[1,3,4,5,7]!	
[3,4]	[3,4,8]!	[3,4,5,6]	[3,4,5,6,7]	
[4,8]!	[4,5,6]	[3,4,5,7]	[4,5,6,7,4]*	
[4,5]	[4,5,7]	[4,5,6,7]	[5,6,7,4,5]*	
[5,6]	[5,6,7]	[4,5,7,4]*	[5,6,7,4,8]!	
[5,7]	[5,7,4]	[5,6,7,4]	[6,7,4,5,6]*	
[6,7]	[6,7,4]	[5,7,4,5]*	[7,4,5,6,7]*	
[7,4]	[7,4,5]	[5,7,4,8]!		
	[7,4,8]!	[6,7,4,5]		
		[6,7,4,8]!		
		[7,4,5,6]		
		[7,4,5,7]*		

Table 6.2: Simple paths for Example 6.4

The simple paths with length 1 are computed by adding the successor nodes for each node in the graph (length 0 paths). Similarly, the simple paths with length 2 and above can be computed by starting from every node and find all the paths with a certain length with no node appears twice except the 1st and the last. The exclamation mark at the end of a path tells that this path cannot be extended. A path that ends with a final node is not extended further. The asterisk at the end of a path tells that that pass cannot go any further since the 1st node and the last node are the same node.

If extending a path leads to a repeating node and thus making the path not simple, then the path cannot be extended further. For example, [1,3,4,5,7] cannot be extended further since the next node would be '4' that already exists in the path and it's not the 1st node. Table 6.2 lists all the simple paths we've found.

Since any simple paths that are not marked by either '!' or '*' can be extended and must be subpaths of other simple paths, therefore, they can be eliminated when computing prime paths. So only the simple paths marked with '!' and '*' are prime path candidates. Examine these paths, any paths that are covered by a higher length path are eliminated further.

Here is the final list of **prime paths:**

[1,2],
[1,3,4,8], [4,5,7,4], [5,7,4,8], [5,7,4,5], [7,4,5,7],
[1,3,4,5,7], [4,5,6,7,4], [5,6,7,4,5], [5,6,7,4,8], [6,7,4,5,6], [7,4,5,6,7],
[1,3,4,5,6,7].

For complex control flow graphs, the prime paths can be computed programmatically.

Now let's compute **test paths** from these prime paths. Here we present a heuristic way to construct the paths manually.

All the prime paths are listed in Table 6.3.

[1,2]
[1,3,4,8]
[4,5,7,4]
[5,7,4,8]
[5,7,4,5]
[7,4,5,7]
[1,3,4,5,7]
[4,5,6,7,4]
[5,6,7,4,5]
[5,6,7,4,8]
[6,7,4,5,6]
[7,4,5,6,7]
[1,3,4,5,6,7]

Table 6.3: Calculate test paths from prime paths

Remember, a test path is a path from an initial or entry node to a final node. The 1st prime path [1,2] and the 2nd prime path [1,3,4,8] are test paths, so they remain in the test path list without any change.

Next, let's examine the longest path [1,3,4,5,6,7]. The last node in the longest path [1,3,4,5,6,7] is '7', and let's find another prime path starting with '7', by looking from the bottom up, and we found [7,4,5,6,7]. So, we can construct one test path by appending the 2nd path to the 1st (keep one '7' at the connection point of the two paths), then add the shortest route to a final node, [7,4,8] in this case. So, we have a test path: [1,3,4,5,6,7,4,5,6,7,4,8].

Next, examine the list and check if any other prime paths are included in this test path, and mark them, so they can be excluded. We found: [4,5,6,7,4], [,5,6,7,4,5], [6,7,4,5,6], & [5,6,7,4,8].

Now examine the next length level, and notice [1,3,4,5,7] starts with the entry node, and similarly, find another one starting with the last node '7' in this path, [7,4,5,7], and add nodes to the final node. Now we have another test path: [1,3,4,5,7,4,5,7,4,8]. Examine the list again, all the rest of the paths are included in the test paths.

Therefore, we have the following 4 test paths satisfying prime path coverage:

[1,2],
[1,3,4,8],
[1,3,4,5,7,4,5,7,4,8],
[1,3,4,5,6,7,4,5,6,7,4,8].

Test cases generated with the above test paths are listed in Table 6.4.

Test Cases	Test Characters	Test Strings	Expected Results	Test Paths
1	"e"	null	error message	[1,2]
2	"e"	"" (empty string)	0	[1,3,4,8]
3	"e"	"mn"	0	[1,3,4,5,7,4,5,7,4,8]
4	"e"	"ee"	2	[1,3,4,5,6,7,4,5,6,7,4,8]

Table 6.4: Test cases for Example 6.4

Different ways of test path construction could produce different results.

Notice, all edges are covered by the above test paths (PPC subsumes EC).

For this specific example, you probably could come up with better test cases and better coverages by hand, or by using the equivalence partitioning technique or combinatorial technique. For example, test vectors [null, 'mn'], ['', ''], ['e', 'ae'], ['e', 'ea'], and ['e', 'aebec'] could be generated from other testing techniques. In practice, what technique(s) to use is a judgment based on experiences and other factors.

In general, for software programs with complex control logic, the control flow graph technique is a good way to come up with coverage paths systematically with the help of an automated path generator.

As you may have noticed, there is a compound Boolean condition if ((s == null) || c == null)) in Code Segment 6.2, and this piece of code is represented with one node in the CFG, only one condition in the Boolean expression is included in the test cases to satisfy NC, EC, and PPC. If there are nested compound Boolean expressions, then a lot of necessary test scenarios would be excluded. Handling compound Boolean expressions is the topic of section 6.4.

6.3.2 Infeasible Requirements and Best Effort Touring

There are situations where a test path is infeasible due to control conditions, for which a workaround is needed to compute test paths. There are other cases where a test requirement cannot be satisfied, such as if there are any unreachable code or logic contradictions. (It's usually undecidable if all test requirements are feasible or not, though). We define these cases as ***infeasible requirements.***

We introduce the best effort touring workaround to deal with infeasible requirements.

First, let's introduce a few terminologies.

Tour: Test path p is said to tour subpath q, if and only if q is a subpath of p.

Tour with Sidetrip: Test path p is said to tour subpath q with a sidetrip, if and only if every **edge** in q is also in p in the same order.

Tour with Detour: Test path p is said to tour subpath q with a detour, if and only if every **node** in q is also in p in the same order.

The concepts are illustrated by the graphs in Figure 6.10.

In these graphs, [1,2,3,4] is a tour, [1,2,5,6,2,3,4] is a tour with a sidetrip, and [1,2,5,6,3,4] is a tour with a detour.

In this specific example, the subpath [2,5,6,2] is a sidetrip to [1,2,3,4], it leaves at node 2 and returns at the same node, thus, every edge in subpath [1,2,3,4] is executed in the same order; while subpath [2,5,6,3] is a detour to [1,2,3,4], it leaves at node 2 but returns at node 4, the subsequent node in subpath [1,2,3,4], bypassing edge [3,4]. In other words, every node in subpath [1,2,3,4] is included in the tour with a detour in the same order, but every edge is not.

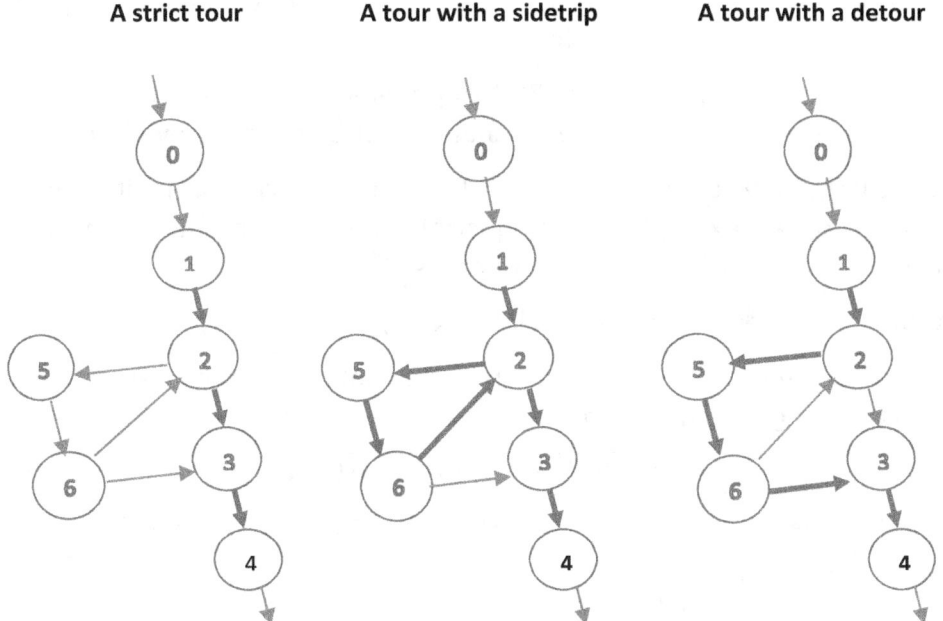

Figure 6.10: Tour, tour with sidetrip, and tour with detour examples

We can see that, if loop [2,5,6,2] is required and cannot be skipped, then any prime path with subpath [1,2,3,4] is infeasible. In other words, if you try to exercise path [1,2,3,4], when node [2] is reached, you cannot go to node [3] directly, but have to go through route [2,5,6,2] first, and end up with path [1,2,5,6,2,3,4] (with a sidetrip).

To deal with infeasible paths, we can relax prime path coverage to allow sidetrips. Allowing detours in test paths may change the tests drastically and is not practical. We will only consider sidetrips here.

If a test requirement can be met without a sidetrip, then using a sidetrip should be avoided. Only when a strict tour is not possible, a test requirement with sidetrip is considered.

Assume $TR_{tour}(T)$ is a set of test requirements such that all paths that must be covered in a graph can be directly toured and assume $TR_{sidetrips}(T)$ is a set of test requirements such that all the paths can be either directly toured or toured with sidetrips, we define the *best effort touring* as following:

Best Effort Touring:

A test set $TR(T)$ satisfies best effort touring, if:

(1) for every path p in $path(TR_{tour}(T))$, some paths in T tours p directly.

(2) for every path p in $path(TR_{sidetrips}(T))$, some paths in T tours p either directly or with a sidetrip.

The goal is to satisfy as many $TR(T)$ as possible without sidetrips, and only allow sidetrips for a subset of $TR(T)$ that cannot be satisfied by direct tours.

We are not going to cover more details on best effort touring, instead, let's just work on an example to demonstrate infeasible requirements and to construct the best effort touring test cases.

Example 6.5: Average of Integers in an Array

Code Segment 6.3 is a Java method that calculates the average value of all the integer elements in an array.

```java
public static float IntegerAverageInArray (int[] a) {
    if ( (a == null) || (a.length == 0) ) {
        System.out.println ("Input array is empty or not specified.");
    }
    float result = 0;
    for (int i = 0; i < a.length; i++) {
        result = result + a[i];
    }
    result = result / a.length;
    return result;
}
```

Code Segment 6.3: Java method to calculate the average in an integer array

Here are the basic blocks:

1	if ((a == null) || (a.length == 0))
2	System.out.println(("Input array is empty or not specified.");
3	float result = 0; i = 0;
4	i < a.length;
5	result = result + a[i]; i++:
6	result = result / a.length; **return** result;

Table 6.5: Basic blocks for Example 6.5

The definition of this control flow graph as a test graph is:

(1) $N = \{1, 2, 3, 4, 5, 6\}$
(2) $N_0 = \{1\}$
(3) $N_f = \{2, 6\}$
(4) $E = \{(1,2), (1,3), (3,4), (4,5), (4,6), (5,4)\}$

The graph is plotted in Figure 6.11.

CHAPTER 6: STRUCTURAL TESTING

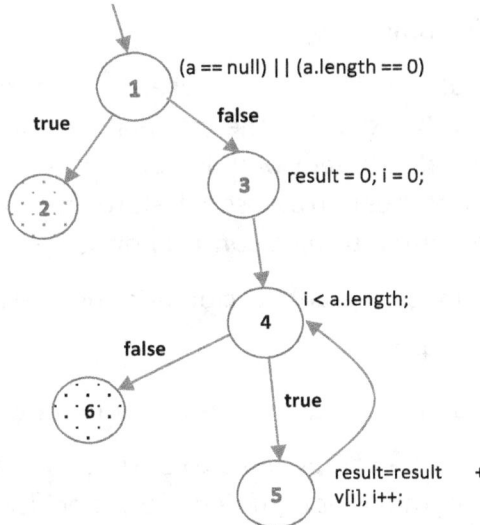

Figure 6.11: Graph for Example 6.5

All the simple paths for this problem are listed in Table 6.6, and the prime paths are listed in table 6.7.

1	2	3
[1,2]!	[1,3,4]	[1,3,4,5]
[1,3]	[3,4,5]	[1,3,4,6]!
[3,4]	[3,4,6]!	
[4,6]!	[4,5,4]*	
[4,5]	[5,4,6]!	
[5,4]		

Table 6.6: Simple paths for Example 6.5

1	[1,2]
2	[4,5,4]
3	[5,4,6]
4	[1,3,4,6]

Table 6.7: Prime paths for Example 6.5

The prime path [1,3,4,6] is infeasible since if the 'for' loop is reached, it will execute at least once. But it can be toured with test path [1,3,4,5,4,6], with sidetrip [4,5,4].

Test cases for best effort touring would include these two test paths:

[1,2], [1,3,4,5,4,6].

Prime paths 2, 3, and 4 are all covered by [1,3,4,5,4,6].

The following two test cases cover these two test paths:

a = {}, and a = {1}.

6.3.3 Cyclomatic Complexity

Cyclomatic complexity is a metric used to measure the complexity of a software program by counting the independent paths through the software source code. An independent path is defined as a path that has at least one edge that has not been traversed before in any other path. Cyclomatic complexity is computed using a control flow graph.

For a directly connected graph, cyclomatic complexity can be expressed as:

$$M = E - N + 2 \qquad (6\text{-}2)$$

where E is the number of edges, N is the number of nodes in the graph.

Cyclomatic complexity can be used to determine if the number of test cases for a software program is adequate or not, specifically:

(1) M is an upper bound for edge (branch) coverage.
(2) M is a lower bound of the number of paths in a graph.

There are 8 nodes, and 9 edges in Example 6.2 (a function to check the occurrence count of a character in a string), so the cyclomatic complexity is 9 − 8 + 2 = 3. The numbers of test cases to satisfy node coverage, edge coverage, and prime path coverage are 2, 2, 4, respectively. We can conclude for that example that node and edge coverages are not enough, while prime path coverage is better with 4 test cases, one larger than the cyclomatic complexity of that software piece.

In Example 6.5, a program to calculate the average of an integer array, there are 6 nodes and 6 edges, the cyclomatic complexity is 6 − 6 + 2 = 2, which equals to the number of the best effort touring test cases.

6.4 CONDITION COVERAGE

When a control flow graph contains compound Boolean expressions, each condition in an expression, and permutations of all individual conditions should be considered. We discuss a few condition coverage schemes in this section.

6.4.1 Basic Condition Coverage

The easiest way to cover a compound Boolean expression is to cover every individual condition within the compound expression. We define the coverage with this approach as *basic condition coverage*.

Basic condition coverage:

TR(T) satisfies basic condition coverage if and only if each basic condition evaluates to true in at least one test in T and evaluates to false in at least one test in T.

In Example 6.2, in the compound condition `if ((s == null) || (c == null))`, each of the two basic conditions `(s == null)` and `(c == null)` should be evaluated to both 'true' and 'false' in some of the test cases. Let's denote the two expressions as *a* and *b*, *a* is true means `(s == null)` is true and will be represented by '1'; and 'false' is represented by '0'. Similarly, *b* is true means `(c == null)` is true, and so on. The following two test vectors satisfy basic condition coverage:

(*a*, *b*): {[1,0], [0,1]},

which translate to sample test cases with input vectors for c and s: {[null, 'mn'], ['e', null]}.

Note, with the above two test cases, the compound expression evaluates to 'true' for both cases. In other words, basic condition coverage does not guarantee edge (branch) coverage. An extension to basic condition coverage is condition and edge coverage.

6.4.2 Condition and Edge (Branch) Coverage

Let's define condition and edge (branch) coverage.

Condition and edge (branch) coverage:

TR(T) satisfies condition and edge coverage if it satisfies both condition coverage and edge coverage.

Let's take an example with a compound Boolean expression.

Example 6.6: A Compound Boolean Expression

Consider expression: `if ( ((x < 0) && (y < 0)) || (z > 100 ) )`, or in its general form: ((*a* AND *b*) OR *c*), where *a*, *b*, and *c* represent the three basic conditions.

Basic condition coverage requires basic expressions *a*, *b*, and *c* to have both true and false values. The following 3 vectors satisfy basic condition coverage:

(*a*,*b*,*c*): { [0, 0, 1], [1, 0, 0], [0, 1, 1] }.

With these 3 vectors, all three basic conditions are evaluated once. The reason we have 3 test cases rather than 2 (for example [0, 0, 1] and [1, 1, 0]) is due to short-circuit evaluation of logic OR in high-level programming languages: if (*a* AND *b*) is evaluated to 'true', *c* won't be evaluated.

To satisfy edge coverage, the compound expression should evaluate to be both true and false. Let's examine the above 3 vectors satisfying basic condition coverage 1st. With [0, 0, 1], the whole compound expression evaluates to true; with [1, 0, 0], the whole compound expression evaluates to false. So, these 3 vectors satisfy both condition coverage and edge coverage, hence, they satisfy condition and edge coverage.

A set of test inputs for (*x, y, z*), the original variables in the expression, is:

(*x, y, z*): {[2, 2, 200], [-2, 2, 50], [2, -2, 200]}.

6.4.3 Compound Condition Coverage

Not all combinations of the Boolean test vectors are covered by condition and edge coverage. To cover all combinations, we define a *compound condition coverage* as below:

Compound Condition Coverage:

TR(T) satisfies compound condition coverage if and only if every combination of basic conditions is evaluated to be both true in at least one test in T and to false in at least one test in T.

If there are *n* basic conditions in a compound expression, then the total number of combinations is 2^n, which can grow exponentially when the number of basic conditions is big, although, due to short circuit and/or left to right evaluation order of logic expressions, the number of test cases can be decreased.

In practice, software developers should limit the number of basic conditions in a compound expression whenever possible with alternative design, to reduce potential defects and testing efforts.

CCC (compound condition coverage) ensures edge coverage.

In the compound condition `if ((s == null) || (c == null))` in Example 6.2, there are total $2^2 = 4$ combinations: [0,0], [0,1], [1,0], and [1,1]. Since when the 1st condition is true, the 2nd condition will not be evaluated, [1,1] is not needed. The rest three combinations satisfy compound condition coverage.

Now consider the expression in Example 6.6 in the form of ((*a* AND *b*) OR *c*). Compound condition coverage requires total of 7 cases, as listed in Table 6.8.

Test cases	a	b	c
1	1	1	-
2	1	0	1
3	1	0	0
4	0	1	1
5	0	1	0
6	0	0	1
7	0	0	0

Table 6.8: Compound coverage for Example 6.6

In test case 1, *c* is not evaluated, therefore the value of *c* does not affect the result of the expression, we denote the cell with a '-' (similar to the don't care condition in the decision table technique).

To generate input vectors for CCC, you can start from the first condition in the expression and work your way to the right one by one and make sure each condition evaluates to both *true* and *false,* and add a '-' if a condition is short-circuited. Alternatively, you can list all the combinations and collapse the ones with don't care conditions if the number of basic conditions is small.

Let's look at a few more examples.

Example 6.7: Compound Boolean Expression: (*a* OR *b* OR *c* OR *d*)

For Boolean expression (*a* OR *b* OR *c* OR *d*), the test cases required for compound condition coverage are listed in Table 6.9.

Test cases	a	b	c	d
1	1	-	-	-
2	0	1	-	-
3	0	0	1	-
4	0	0	0	1

Table 6.9: Compound coverage for Example 6.7

Example 6.8: Compound Boolean Expression: (*a* AND *b* AND *c* AND *d*)

For Boolean expression (*a* AND *b* AND *c* AND *d*), the test cases required for compound condition coverage are listed in Table 6.10.

Test cases	a	b	c	d
1	1	1	1	1
2	1	1	1	0
3	1	1	0	-
4	1	0	-	-
5	0	-	-	-

Table 6.10: Compound coverage for Example 6.8

Example 6.9: Compound Boolean Expression: ((((a AND b) OR c) AND d) OR e)

For Boolean expression ((((a AND b) OR c) AND d) OR e), the test cases required for compound condition coverage are listed in Table 6.11.

Test cases	a	b	c	d	e
1	1	1	-	1	-
2	1	1	-	0	1
3	1	1	-	0	0
4	1	0	1	1	-
5	1	0	1	0	1
6	1	0	1	0	0
7	1	0	0	1	-
8	1	0	0	0	1
9	1	0	0	0	0
10	0	1	1	1	-
11	0	1	1	0	1
12	0	1	1	0	0
13	0	1	0	1	-
14	0	1	0	0	1
15	0	1	0	0	0

Table 6.11: Compound coverage for Example 6.9

6.4.4 Modified Condition/Decision Coverage

The number of test cases could grow large with complex compound conditions. A compromise to compound condition coverage is *modified condition/decision coverage*, in which only important combinations of conditions are included.

Modified Condition/Decision Coverage (MCDC):

TR(T) satisfies modified condition/decision coverage if:

(1) Every decision takes all possible outcomes in at least one test in T.
(2) Every condition in a decision takes all possible outcomes in at least one test in T.
(3) Every condition in a decision is shown to independently affect the decision's outcome in at least one test in T.

For each basic condition C, two cases are needed to show that the outcome for each decision is independently affected. That is, for each basic condition C, there are two test cases in which the truth values of all evaluated conditions except C are the same, and the compound condition as a whole evaluates to true for one of those test cases and false for the other. Therefore,

CHAPTER 6: STRUCTURAL TESTING

MCDC (modified condition/decision coverage) can be satisfied with *n* + 1 test cases (minimum), where *n* is the number of variables in the expression.

Let's examine Example 6.6 and Example 6.9 with MCDC.

Example 6.6 With MCDC: Compound Boolean Expression ((*a* AND *b*) OR *c*)

We could start by listing the truth table for the expression, then eliminating the ones that are not contributing to MCDC. Since we have the list of 7 test cases for compound condition coverage, we can start from that list, and remove the ones that do not contribute to MCDC. Table 6.12 lists the 7 test cases. For the don't care condition in test case 1 we add a value 0 for *c*. The result of the whole expression is also shown in the last column.

Let's look backward at *c* first. If *c* is 1 (true), then the part before it, (*a* AND *b*), is 'masked', variables in that expression can have any value. Only when *c* is 0 the other two variables are exercised. So, all the test cases that *c* is 0 should remain in the list, these are cases 1, 3, 5, and 7. We mark these cases in grey in the table.

Test cases	a	b	c	Result
1	1	1	0	0
2	1	0	1	1
3	1	0	0	0
4	0	1	1	1
5	0	1	0	0
6	0	0	1	1
7	0	0	0	0

Table 6.12: MCDC construction for Example 6.6

Now let's look at the part (*a* AND *b*), since we already eliminated [1,1,1] for [*a,b,c*] in the above table due to the don't care condition, we now check the variables in (*a* AND *b*) itself. For an AND relationship, no condition is masked, all [1,1], [1,0], and [0,1] for *a* and *b* should be included. Cases 1, 3, and 5 have those three combinations covered.

Let's determine if these marked test cases satisfy MCDC criteria. As we have seen, for the AND conditions, all possible combinations [1,1], [1,0], and [0,1] are covered. For the OR conditions [one side is (*a* AND *b*), the other side is *c*], we need [0,0], [0,1], and [1,0] only, [1,1] is not needed for an OR relation. Test case 7 covers [0,0] ((*a* AND *b*) is 0, and *c* is 0), test case 1 covers [1,0]. [0,1] is not covered yet in the marked cases (cases 1, 3, 5, and 7). So, we need to add one more test to cover [0,1] for the OR relation. Let's pick test case 4.

Now, examine the last one, test case 7, not all the three conditions can independently affect the decision's outcome. For example, changing a from 0 to 1 won't change the outcome of the decision. Therefore, test case 7 can be eliminated. The rest of them (cases 1, 3, 4, and 5) satisfy the independently affecting decision criterion.

Table 6.13 lists the final list of test cases satisfying MCDC.

Test cases	a	b	c	Result
1	1	1	0	0
2	1	0	0	0
3	0	1	1	1
4	0	1	0	0

Table 6.13: MCDC test cases for Example 6.6

The total number of test cases is 4, which equals the minimum required number of test cases for MCDC with 3 conditions ($n + 1$: $3 + 1 = 4$).

The main steps we take to construct MCDC test cases from a complex condition are:

(1) Construct the Boolean expression for the complex condition.
(2) Identify input vectors, either from the requirements or from the truth table.
(3) Apply MCDC rules and eliminate masked input vectors.
(4) Examine if the remaining tests satisfy MCDC criteria.

As we have seen from the above example, here are the combinations to cover for 'OR' and 'AND' relationships respectively:

    A. OR: [0,0], [0,1], and [1,0]
    B. AND: [1,1], [0,1], and [1,0]

There are other relationships (or gates, e.g. XOR) for which MCDC can be applied, we will skip those in this book.

Let's follow these steps again to solve the problem in Example 6.9.

Example 6.9 with MCDC: Boolean Expression: ((((*a* AND *b*) OR *c*) AND *d*) OR *e*)

Let's start with the compound condition coverage test cases from Table 6.11. Again, fill the don't care conditions with 0s, and add the result column, see Table 6.14.

Let's define $E_2 = (((a \text{ AND } b) \text{ OR } c)$, and $E_1 = (E_2 \text{ AND } d) = (((a \text{ AND } b) \text{ OR } c) \text{ AND } d)$, therefore the whole Boolean expression is $(E_1 \text{ OR } e)$.

Test cases	a	b	c	d	e	result
1	1	1	0	1	0	1
2	1	1	0	0	1	1
3	1	1	0	0	0	0
4	1	0	1	1	0	0
5	1	0	1	0	1	1
6	1	0	1	0	0	0
7	1	0	0	1	0	0
8	1	0	0	0	1	1
9	1	0	0	0	0	0
10	0	1	1	1	0	0
11	0	1	1	0	1	1
12	0	1	1	0	0	0
13	0	1	0	1	0	0
14	0	1	0	0	1	1
15	0	1	0	0	0	0

Table 6.14: MCDC construction for Example 6.9

Again, let's look backward at e 1st, if e is 1 (true), then the expression before it, $E_1 = (((a \text{ AND } b) \text{ OR } c) \text{ AND } d)$, is 'masked', variables in that expression can have any value. So, all the test cases that e is 0 should remain in the list to start with, including cases [1,3,4,6,7,9,10,12,13,15]. We also need to include one test where e is 1, let's take case 2 for now. Now we have an initial list of cases to select from: [1,2,3,4,6,7,9,10,12,13,15].

Now let's look at $E_1 = (((a \text{ AND } b) \text{ OR } c) \text{ AND } d)$. Since we already eliminated [1,1] for [E_1,e] in the above table due to the don't care condition, we now need to check the conditions in E_1 itself. For an AND relationship, no condition is masked, we have to include [1,1], [1,0], and [0,1] for E_2 and d, where $E_2 = (((a \text{ AND } b) \text{ OR } c)$, and these are covered by test cases 1, 3, and 13, respectively, and these cases are all in the initial list.

Next look at $E_2 = (((a \text{ AND } b) \text{ OR } c)$. This is the same problem as Example 6.6, so we need to include the vectors from Table 6.13 for a, b, and c. Cases 1, 7, 10, 13 satisfy them, and they are in the initial list as well.

So far, we have test cases 1, 2, 3, 7, 10, and 13 that should be included. Now let's check if combinations [0,0], [0,1], and [1,0] are all included for

$[E_1, e]$ in $(E_1$ OR $e)$, the final expression. We can see that, test case 1 satisfies [1,0], test case 2 satisfies [0,1], and test case 3 satisfies [0,0].

We conclude, these 6 cases (1, 2, 3, 7, 10, and 13) satisfy MCDC criteria. The final list of the 6 cases, with total of 5 variables, is listed in Table 6.15.

Test cases	a	b	c	d	e	result
1	1	1	0	1	0	1
2	1	1	0	0	1	1
3	1	1	0	0	0	0
4	1	0	0	1	0	0
5	0	1	1	1	0	0
6	0	1	0	1	0	0

Table 6.15: MCDC test cases for Example 6.9

6.5 CALL GRAPH

When there are subroutine calls (procedures, functions, methods, units, etc.) within a subroutine, the individual subroutine call can be represented by a node in the control flow graph. In modern high-level programming languages like Java, C++, etc., the called subroutines can be from the same class/module/package or a different class/module/package.

The control flow graph with subroutine calls is named **call graph**. The subroutine itself, we will use 'method' to replace 'subroutine' for the rest of the section, is tested separately.

The call graph is a high-level abstraction of flows between methods in the application implementation. The structural coverages we have discussed in this chapter can be applied to the call graph. Node coverage requires that the method is executed at least once, while edge coverage requires that the method is called at least once.

Let's work on an example.

Example 6.10: A Program to Calculate Unit Pay for a Specific Situation

Code Segment 6.4 is an implementation in Java for a program to calculate the payment for a worker in a project. The amount of payment is based on worked hours, the month and year of the work were done, and the title code of the person.

A scale factor is calculated based on the person's title code, and the payment is proportional to worked hours, with a small adjustment for the number of days in a month.

CHAPTER 6: STRUCTURAL TESTING

The call graph is plotted in Figure 6.12.

```java
public class CallGraphExampleWorkerPayment {
  public static float paymenAmount (float workedHours, int month, long year,
                          int titleCode)
  {
     float result = 0;
     float factor = findFactor (titleCode, month, year);
     result = workedHours * factor * 1000 / daysInAMonth (month, year);
     return result;
  }
  public static int daysInAMonth (int month, long year) {
     int result = 0;
     if (month == 4 || month == 6 || month == 9 || month == 11)
         result = 30;
     else if (month == 2)
         result = (isLeap(year)) ? 29 : 28;
     else
         result = 31;
     return result;
  }
  public static boolean isLeap(long year) {
     return ((year & 3) == 0) && ((year % 100) != 0 || (year % 400) == 0);
  }
  private static float findFactor (int titleCode, int month, long year) {
     float factor = 1.0;
     if (titleCode == 1)
         factor = 2.0;
     else if (titleCode == 2)
         factor = 1.5;
     else
         factor = 1.0 * daysInAMonth (month, year) / 30;
     return factor;
  }
}
```

Code Segment 6.4: Java methods for Example 6.10

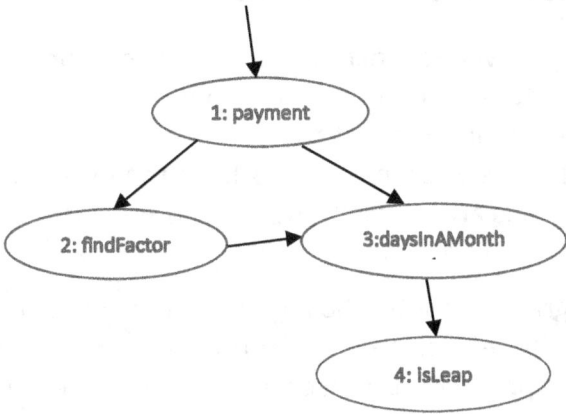

Figure 6.12: Call graph for Example 6.10

The graph has 4 nodes:

    {1, 2, 3, 4},

and 4 edges:

    {(1,2), (1,3), (2,3), (3,4)}.

The cyclomatic complexity of the graph is 4 − 4 + 2 = 2.

Test path [1,2,3,4] satisfies node coverage.

Two test paths are need for edge coverage:

    [1,3,4], and [1,2,3,4].

These two test paths also satisfy prime path coverage.

Table 6.16 lists the input vectors for the two test paths.

Test cases	workedHours	month	year	titleCode	result
1	20	2	2019	1	1429
2	40	2	2020	3	1333

Table 6.16: Edge coverage test cases for Example 6.10

There are limitations to using call graphs. For example, some of the methods in a class may not call each other. Other techniques would need to be used or explored to deal with method calls, such as finite state machine techniques.

Error handling is ignored in the above discussion since that's part of the lower level tests for the specific methods (see more on modularization principle in Chapter 7).

6.6 APPLICATION TO USE CASE TESTING

Use cases are high-level abstractions on how a software application is being used by end-users to perform real-world operations from end to end to serve the final purpose and interests of the end-users. Use cases usually involve a sequence of actions as a result of inputs from the users, the workflows of an application. Decisions are normally involved in specific steps in the sequence to branching out the workflows.

Similar to a call graph, a control flow graph can be used to represent the use case workflow, therefore, the control flow graph techniques we have discussed can be applied to use cases to generate high-level test cases.

We will demonstrate how CFG techniques are applied to use cases through an example.

CHAPTER 6: STRUCTURAL TESTING

Example 6.11: Online Ordering Process

Let's consider a simplified version of an online product ordering process starting from a shopping cart.

Here are the variables in the ordering process:

(1) Mailing address in the account saved or new.
(2) Payment type options.
(3) Credit card information: saved or new.
(4) Delivery options.

Based on the requirements and use cases, an activity graph is plotted in Figure 6.13.

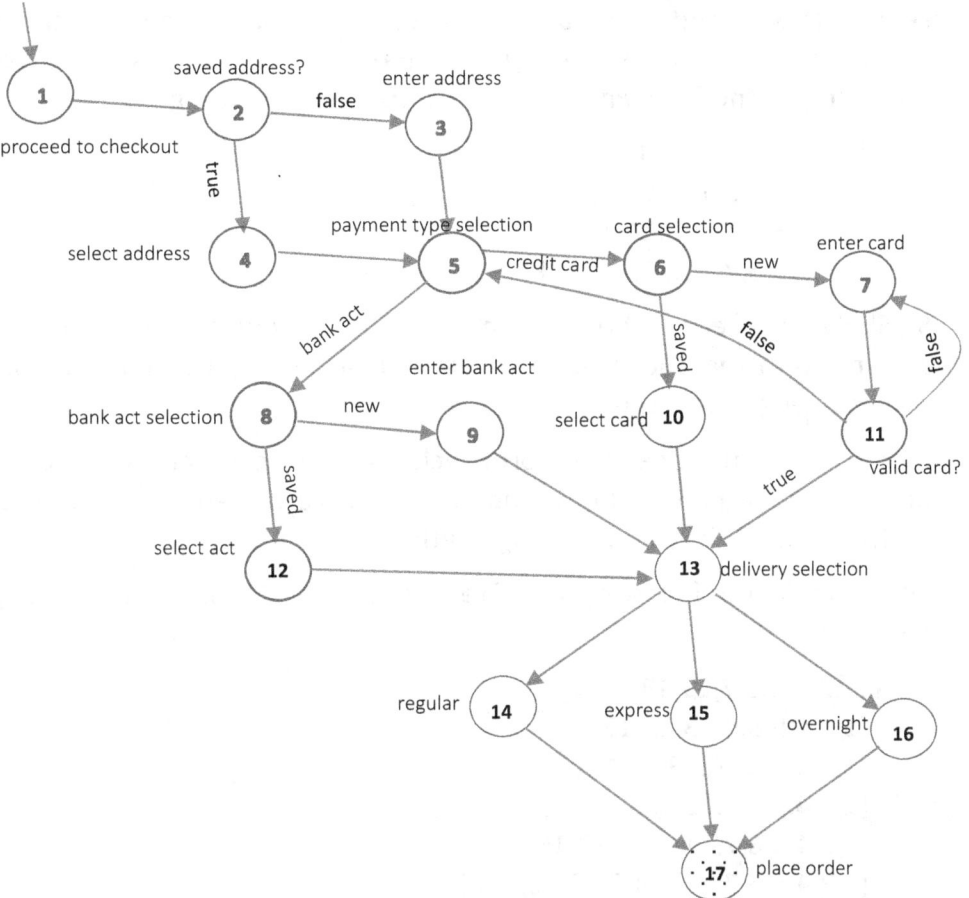

Figure 6.13: Activity graph for Example 6.11

We can treat this graph as a control flow graph and use the techniques we have learned in this chapter to generate test cases to cover this specific part of the ordering process.

The definition of this control flow graph as a test graph is:

(1) N = {1, 2, 3, 4, 5, 6, 7, 8, 9, 10, 11, 12, 13, 14, 15, 16, 17}
(2) N_0 = {1}
(3) N_f = {17}
(4) E = {[1,2],[2,3],[2,4],[3,5],[4,5],[5,6],[5,8],[6,7],[6,10], [7,11],[8,9],[8,12],[9,13],[10,13],[11,13],[11,5],[11,7], [12,13],[13,14],[13,15],[13,16],[14,17], [15,17], [16,17]}.

Depending on testing requirements, different coverage levels may be used, edge (branch) coverage is generally expected for use cases.

Let's start with node coverage. To cover all 17 nodes, we can manually construct some test cases and just to make sure all nodes are included. For example, the following test paths satisfy node coverage:

{ [1,2,3,5,6,7,11,13,16,17],
[1,2,4,5,8,9,13,15,17],
[1,2,3,5,6,10,13,14,17],
[1,2,4,5,6,7,12,13,14,17]}.

Similarly, to cover all 24 edges, we can manually construct the test cases, starting from the above node coverage test paths (node coverage is a subset of edge converge).

Only 2 edges, the ones that form cycles, are not covered by the above node coverage paths: [11,7], and [11,5], so we can add two more test paths on top of the node coverage paths.

For example, the following set of test paths (total 6 paths) satisfies edge coverage:

{ [1,2,3,5,6,7,11,13,16,17],
[1,2,4,5,8,9,13,15,17],
[1,2,3,5,6,10,13,14,17],
[1,2,4,5,6,7,12,13,14,17],
[1,2,4,5,6,7,11,7,11,13,15,17],
[1,2,4,5,6,7,11,5,8,9,13,16,17] }.

Note, in this graph, there are 17 nodes and 24 edges, the cyclomatic complexity of this graph is 24 - 17 + 2 = 9.

The total number of test paths we came up with for edge coverage is 6, a number smaller than the cyclomatic complexity. While cyclomatic complexity is a good indicator of test path adequacy for implementation-based control flow graphs, it may not be applicable to use cases. Another argument is that the independent parameters in this example, namely mailing address, payment types, and delivery options may not be strongly coupled, and a large number of permutations is not required in most cases.

If edge coverage is not enough, prime path coverage can be considered, which would require far more test paths than those for edge coverage (the number of prime paths exceeds 30 for this example). Calculating the prime paths manually for this problem is complex, and an automated program is recommended for it (P6.3 at the end of the chapter asks the reader to write a program to construct test paths from prime paths).

Also, based on domain knowledge and other factors, the testing requirements may be different. For example, some paths (permutations) with delivery options may be skipped if we know that the delivery option is isolated from saved addresses.

On the graph, some nodes represent a module, and there should be more use cases within those nodes, and those activities can be tested separately (modularization principle, see more in next chapter). For example, for the 'select address' node, multiple addresses exist, and there is also an address deletion functionality. Amending the above activity graph is also fine, but it would make the graph extremely complex.

6.7 FINITE STATE MACHINE MODEL

A finite state machine (FSM) is a mathematical computation model. We include FSM here (instead of a whole new chapter) since it's also a graph-based model, and CFG edge coverages can also be applied.

A finite state machine (FSM) is an abstract representation of behaviors exhibited by certain systems. A subset of software systems can be modeled by FSM.

A finite automaton FSM is defined by a 5-tuple:

$$\text{FSM} = (\Sigma, Q, q_0, q_f, \delta) \tag{6-3}$$

where
- Σ is the set of symbols representing inputs to M.
- Q is the set of states of M.

- $q_0 \in Q$ is the start state of M.
- $q_f \subseteq Q$ is the set of final states of M.
- $\delta: Q \times \Sigma \to Q$ is the transition function.

An FSM can be represented by a state transition diagram, a directed graph whose nodes correspond to the states of the machine and whose edges correspond to the state transitions. In the graph, each edge is labeled with the input and output associated with the transition.

The finite state machine model is used in automata-based programming. Object-oriented programming can be considered as a model of automata. But regardless of how the application is implemented, the finite state machine model can be used in software testing for situations where the application under test, or part of it, can be easily modeled by a finite state machine if application states and state transitions are clearly defined.

FSM model is a natural extension of the test case definition we presented in Chapter 2.

From the definition of the test case in Chapter 2, we know that the test case execution result is a function of initial conditions, inputs, and the current state, including current events happening, if relevant. From the test case definition (equation (2.1)), test cases can be modeled using FSM.

From equation (2-1) of the test case result definition: $T = f(\Sigma, \Omega)$, where Σ is the input(s), and Ω is the initial condition, the initial state and/or initial data of the system, and/or the current state(s) and or events. We can see that Q (the set of states) is a subset of Ω. Therefore, FSM can be used to module this subset of the system within Ω.

We will employ an example to demonstrate how to use the FSM model to generate test cases.

Example 6.12: Cat in a Black Box

A cat is confined in an opaque black box. There are three buttons on the black box, 'water', 'poison', and 'magic', and two lights that can be either on or off. See Figure 6.14 for an illustration of the situation.

Figure 6.14: Illustration for Example 6.12: Cat in a black box

After a button on the left is pushed, if the green light goes on, the cat is in the Alive state, and if the red light turns on, then the cat is in the Dead state. Only one button can be pushed down at a time.

Note, this is not Schrödinger's cat, that can be both alive and dead, in the context of quantum states. See P6.6 at the end of the chapter for Schrödinger's cat problem.

Model this application with a finite state machine, we have:

$$FSM = (\Sigma, Q, q_0, q_f, \delta)$$

where:

Σ = {Water, Poison, Magic}
Q = {Alive, Dead}
q_0 = {Alive}
q_f = {Alive, Dead}
$\delta: Q \times \Sigma \rightarrow Q$

where we assumed that the cat is alive initially.

Let's use the following abbreviation for the symbols: W: water, P: poison, M: magic potion. There are three possible input values. W, P, or M, and only one input is allowed at one time. There are two outputs: Alive or Dead.

The transition function δ is defined in Table 6.17.

input	initial state	output
W	Alive	Alive
W	Dead	Dead
P	Alive	Dead
P	Dead	Dead
M	Alive	Alive
M	Dead	Alive

Table 6.17: Transition function for Example 6.12

The state diagram is plotted in Figure 6.15.

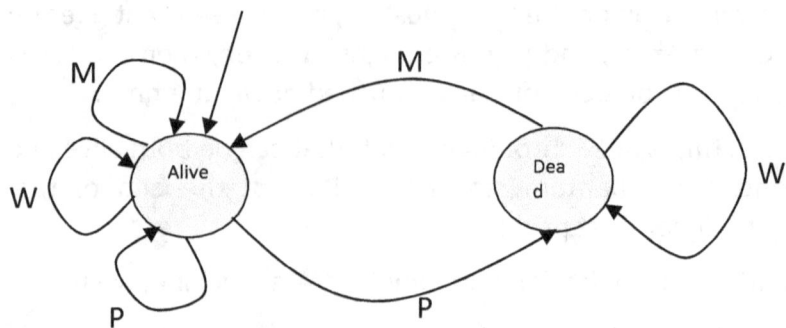

Figure 6.15: State transition diagram for Example 6.12

So, what test cases can be written for this example? It's pretty easy just by following the transition function. There are 6 possible ways to act, so there are 6 test cases.

The test cases converted from the transition table are listed in Table 6.18.

Cases	Description	Steps	Expected
1	Verify that if the cat is put in the black box alive, adding water to it, the cat would still be alive.	(1) put a live cat in the box. (2) push the 'water' button.	The green light is on.
2	Verify that if the cat is put in the black box dead, adding water to it, the cat would still be dead.	(1) put a dead cat in the box. (2) push the 'water' button.	The red light is on.
3	Verify that if the cat is put in the black box alive, adding poison to it, the cat would be dead.	(1) put a live cat in the box. (2) push the 'poison' button.	The red light is on.
4	Verify that if the cat is put in the black box dead, adding poison to it, the cat would still be dead.	(1) put a dead cat in the box. (2) push the 'poison' button.	The red light is on.
5	Verify that if the cat is put in the black box alive, adding magic to it, the cat would still be alive.	(1) put a live cat in the box. (2) push the 'magic' button.	The green light is on.
6	Verify that if the cat is put in the black box dead, adding magic to it, the cat would be alive.	(1) put a dead cat in the box. (2) push the 'magic' button.	The green light is on.

Table 6.18: Test cases generated from finite state machine for Example 6.12

The coverage of the tests generated from the transaction function is called **transaction coverage.** From what we have learned in control flow graph techniques, we know this is the same as edge coverage.

Is transaction coverage enough? That will depend on the specific system and the testing requirements. In this example, what if after 'magic' is applied, followed by 'poison', the cat is no longer dies? Then more nodes or edges on the graph need to be covered in one test path, so some form of path coverage may be needed. We will leave this to the reader for further analysis.

Note, the FSM model alone may not be enough to test the system. For example, what if both the red light and the green light are on due to some error conditions? The state that both lights are on is not part of the FSM, since no transaction function is defined to reach that state. Other techniques need to be applied to fully test the system.

Let's work on another example.

Example 6.13: A Simplified Alarm System

Consider an alarm system on an entry door to a building. If the alarm is set on when the door is opened the alarm would be triggered.

The alarm system can be at the following states:

(i) The door is open, not ready to arm: state A.
(ii) The door is closed, ready to arm: state B.
(iii) The system is in transit to be armed: state C.
(iv) The system is armed: state D.
(v) The door is opened, warning that alarm activation is pending: state E.
(vi) The alarm is activated: state F.

The actions and state changes are defined as:

1. When the alarm system is off, and the door is open, closing the door changes the state of the system from A to B.
2. When the system is off, the door is closed, opening the door changes the state from B to A.
3. When the system is off, the door is closed, clicking on the 'arm' button on the application (on a screen panel, for example) changes the state of the system from B to C.
4. If the system is in transit to be armed, clicking on the 'cancel' button within 1-minute changes the state from C to B.
5. If the system is in transit to be armed, wait for 1 minute, the state changes from C to D.
6. If the system is armed, opening the door, the state changes from D to E.
7. If the system is armed, and the door is opened, entering the correct passcode within 30 seconds, changes the state from E to A.

8. If the system is armed, and the door is opened, entering the wrong passcode within 30 seconds, the state remains at E.
9. If the system is armed, and the door is opened, no passcode is entered within 30 seconds, the state changes from E to F.
10. If the system is armed, and the door is opened, entering a wrong passcode within 30 seconds, the state changes from E to F.
11. If the alarm is activated, entering a correct passcode, changes the state from F to A.

There are 6 states for the system: A, B, C, D, E, and F.

The inputs (actions) are:

(a) Close the door.
(b) Open the door.
(c) Click on 'arm'.
(d) Click on 'cancel'.
(e) Wait for 1 minute.
(f) Enter correct passcode sequence.
(g) Enter incorrect passcode sequence.
(h) Wait for 30 seconds.

Let's label the inputs by letters, so the 1st input 'close the door' is labeled by 'a', 2nd input by 'b', and so on. The initial state is A. States C and E are 'transit' states that lasts 1 minute and 30 seconds respectively, therefore we assume that the rest of the states are all final states.

Model this application with a finite state machine, we have:

$$FSM = (\Sigma, Q, q_0, q_f, \delta)$$

where: $\Sigma = \{a, b, c, d, e, f, g, h\}$
$Q = \{A, B, C, D, E, F\}$
$q_0 = \{A\}$
$q_f = \{A, B, D, F\}$
$\delta: Q \times \Sigma \rightarrow Q$: see the action and state change list.

Since both of the states and the transitions are well defined, it's easy to generate the transition graph, as seen in Figure 6.16. The transaction numbers match those in the action list.

Since there are 11 transaction paths or edges on the graph, 11 test cases are needed for transaction coverage. The test cases generated from the 11 transactions are shown in Table 6.19.

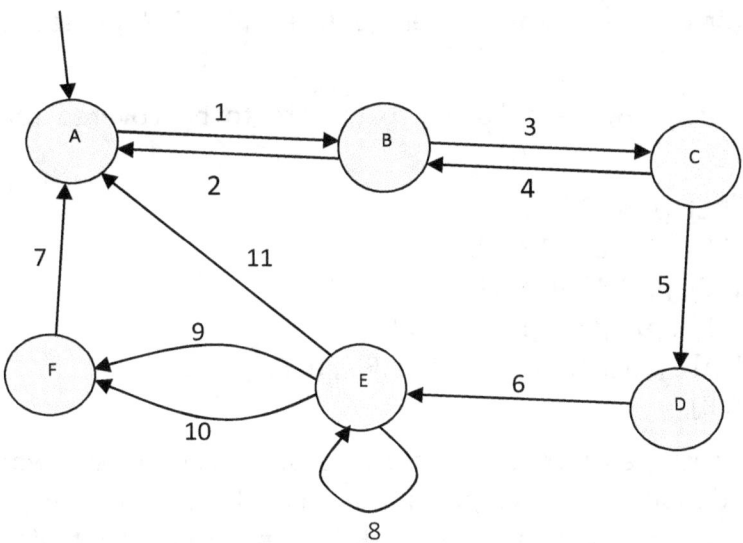

Figure 6.16: State transition diagram for Example 6.13: A simplified alarm system

Test cases	Input vectors	Start State	End State
1	a	A	B
2	b	B	A
3	c	B	C
4	d	C	B
5	e	C	D
6	b	D	E
7	f	E	A
8	g	E	E
9	h	E	F
10	g, h	E	F
11	f	F	A

Table 6.19: Test cases generated from FSM for Example 6.13

Note, in the FSM model, the final states are optional, in other words, the system under test can be at any possible states after one or more transactions. Therefore, path coverage is not applicable (where a test path is from a starting node to a final node).

Transaction (edge) coverage is a basic coverage as we have seen in control flow graph discussions.

Sometimes, transaction coverage is not enough. Let's work out edge-pair coverage (or transaction-pair coverage in terms of FSM) cases for Example 6.13.

Start from node A, the following paths are to be covered for edge-pair coverage:

[A,B,C], [A,B,A],
[B,C,D], [B,C,B], [B,A,B],
[C,D,E], [C,B,A], [C,B,C],
[D,E,F]$_9$, [D,E,F]$_{10}$, [D,E,E], [D,E,A],
[E,F,A]$_9$, [E,F,A]$_{10}$, [E,A,B], [E,E,F]$_9$, [E,E,F]$_{10}$, [E,E,E],
[F,A,B]

Total of 19 paths, each covers 2 transactions. Note, there are two edge-pairs for [D,E,F], denoted by subscript 9 and 10 since there are two edges from E to F with two actions 9 and 10. Same for [E,F,A] and [E,E,F]. The table for the test cases is skipped here, you can generate the cases on your own as an exercise.

FSM technique can be applied to both type 0 and type 1 tests, from unit testing to integration testing.

FSM is an easy-to-use technique for a stated application if the states are well defined and the transitions between states are easily specified. But it may not be suited for large systems in which the states and transitions are hard to manage.

CHAPTER 6: STRUCTURAL TESTING

EXERCISE PROBLEMS:

P6.1: A Method to Reverse a Number

The following code segment is an implementation in Java to reverse a number.

```java
public static int numberReversing (int n)
{
    int r = 0;
    while (n != 0) {
        int digit = n % 10;
        r = r * 10 + digit;
        n /= 10;
    }
    return r;
}
```

(1) Define a test graph for this method.
(2) Draw control flow graph.
(3) Identify TR(NC) and TR(EC), and construct test paths for both NC and TC.
(4) Construct simple paths and compute prime paths. identify TR(PPC).
(5) Construct test paths for PPC and write test cases for PPC.

P6.2: A Method to Determine if a Number is a Perfect Square

The following code segment is a sample implementation in Java to determine if a number is a perfect square.

```java
public static boolean isPerfectSquare (int n)
{
    int x = n % 10;
    if (x == 2 || x == 3 || x == 7 || x == 8) {
        return false;
    }
    for (int i = 0; i <= n / 2 + 1; i++) {
        if ((long) i * i == n) {
            return true;
        }
    }
    return false;
}
```

(1) Draw a control flow graph based on this piece of code.
(2) Identify TR(NC) and TR(EC), and construct test paths for both NC and TC.
(3) Construct simple paths and compute prime paths. identify TR(PPC).
(4) Construct test paths for PPC and generate test cases for PPC.
(5) Calculate Cyclomatic complexity for this graph and compare it with the number of test paths for PPC.

(6) Construct test paths for compound condition coverage for the compound Boolean condition in the code ((x == 2 || x == 3 || x == 7 || x == 8)) and generate test cases.

P6.3: Construct Test Paths from Prime Paths

Design and implement a program that will compute all prime paths in a graph, then derive test paths to tour the prime paths. The program will take a graph as input with a list of nodes, initial nodes, final nodes, and edges, and output a list of test paths.

P6.4: Compound Boolean Expression: $((((a$ OR $b)$ AND $c)$ OR $d)$ AND $e)$

For this Boolean expression, generate test vectors for the following requirements:

(1) Basic condition coverage.
(2) Condition and edge coverage.
(3) Compound condition coverage.
(4) Modified condition/decision coverage (MCDC).

P6.5: States of Water (H_2O)

Water can be at three states on the earth: solid, liquid, or gas. Let's denote them as S, L, and G, respectively. Transformation of states can happen under various conditions (inputs).

A software program is written to simulate water state changes through physical processes, with the following actions and effects:

(1) heating: S -> L; L -> G; S -> S; L -> L; G -> G.
(2) cooling: G -> L; L -> S; S -> S; L -> L; G -> G.
(3) precipitation: G -> L; G -> S.
(4) evaporation: L -> G.
(5) condensation: G -> L.
(6) deposition: G -> S.
(7) sublimation: S -> G.

Write down the finite state machine model for this system, plot the state transition diagram, and generate transaction coverage test cases from it.

P6.6*. Quantum Physics: Schrödinger's Cat.

Schrödinger's cat is a thought experiment. A cat is imagined as being enclosed in a box with a radioactive source and a poison that will be released when the source (unpredictably) emits radiation. If the poison is released the cat will be dead, but there is no way to tell if the poison is released or not without opening the box and check it. More formally, the cat is being considered (according to quantum mechanics) to be simultaneously both dead and alive until the box is opened, and the cat is observed. The probability of the radioactive source emitting radiation is p.

Can FSM be used for this system? Is the system testable? What test cases you can come up with for this system if it can be tested? Note, in automata theory, this is an example of a nondeterministic finite automaton.

PART THREE

Principles & Practices of Software Testing

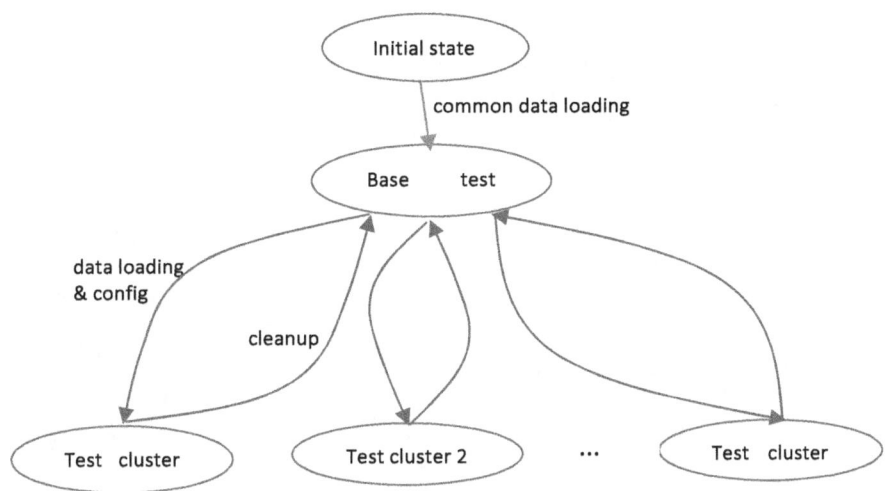

7 GENERAL PRINCIPLES OF TEST CASE DESIGN

We discuss test case design principles and best practices in this chapter. These principles apply to both manual and automated test designs, but we will discuss them in the context of automated tests by default.

Although, by definition, there is no requirement on how to write a test case, there are some practices that would make writing test cases and executing test cases more efficient and more manageable.

We have discussed several characteristics of test cases in Chapter 2, including atomic and independent characteristics. Atomicity and independency are two of the testing principles we will discuss first in this chapter followed by modularization and coverage principles.

These principles can be applied to all types of tests, from type 0 to type 3.

7.1 ATOMIC PRINCIPLE

We have learned from Chapter 2 that atomicity is one of the basic characteristics of test cases. It says that a test case should contain only one input vector or should contain only one specific scenario or one usage pass of an application. Atomicity ensures the isolation of test cases. One test case is an indivisible unit, it only has two states after execution, pass or fail. Test coverage is easily identified with atomic test cases, and any software defect is easily identified as well if a test case fails.

The test case generation techniques we have discussed in previous chapters are all designed to generate atomic test cases. Table 7.1 listed what is an atomic test case if the test case is generated by each of those techniques.

	Test case design technique	Atomic test case
1	equivalence partitioning	each input vector
2	combinatorial technique	each permutation of input vectors
3	decision table	each rule in the (collapsed) decision table
4	control flow graph; call graph; use case control flow graph	each test path
5	condition coverage	each test path with one condition permutation
6	finite state machine	each transaction path

Table 7.1: Atomic test case definition from common test case generation techniques

Let's examine a couple of examples from earlier chapters.

In Example 3.8, the 'password' field on a login form, we identified 13 equivalence partitions. Partitions (b) and (h) are:

(b) $\{ x \mid x \in [R_1]; \text{length of } x < 8 \}$

(h) $\{ x \mid x \in [\text{satisfies } R \text{ except no uppercase letter}] \}$

For partition (b), instead of having a test vector like '*Aa0!*' which satisfies (b), we can use vector '*1a0!*', which satisfies (b) and also partially satisfies partition (h). If the execution fails for the new vector, then without any knowledge of the implementation, the root cause of the defect is not identified immediately, since it could be either failed (b) or failed (h).

The one-error principle introduced on page 50 can also be considered as a direct consequence of the atomic principle, just as the above example hinted (vector '*1a0!*' violates the one-error principle).

In Example 6.13, a simplified alarm system, we applied the finite state machine model technique and generated 11 test cases for transaction coverage. The first 4 cases cover transactions [A,B], [B,A], [B.C], [C,B]. Instead of having these 4 atomic test cases, if we combine them together, and have one test case to cover paths [A,B,A,B,C,B], then if the test fails, either which transaction is at fault is not immediately determined, or the test exists without finishing all transactions, so not all the 4 atomic tests are executed. (if a 5-wise coverage is required, the above test case is a valid one, but the lower-wise pairs should also be part of the testing, including edges).

7.2 INDEPENDENCY PRINCIPLE

Another test case basic characteristic we have discussed in Chapter 2 is test case independency, it says that a test case is independent of any other test case. In other words, a test case is isolated from other test cases, test cases are commutable in execution. In other words, the order of test case execution is irrelevant to the successful run of all tests. Independency principle also requires that the execution and cleanup process of a test case will not change the state of the application under test, so as not to interfere with the execution of other test cases. The test case generation techniques we have discussed in previous chapters are all designed to generate independent test cases.

The following categories of test case independency are identified:

(1) order independency
(2) path independency
(3) state independency
(4) environment independency
(5) time independency

Let's examine them one by one.

7.2.1 Order Independency

Test cases in a test suite can be executed sequentially, randomly, or in parallel. The order of the test execution should not be an issue for the successful execution of a subset of the test cases, nor the testing results for all the test cases in the subset. For example, if there are 5 tests in a set, A, B, C, D, and E, then any order of execution such as ABCDEF, ABCDFE, ABCEDF, ... FEDCBA, should produce the same result for every individual test.

In the xUnit automation testing framework, e.g. Junit framework, individual tests in a test class are executed randomly by design by default (if no annotation like *@Step* is used, for example).

For state-less test cases, where the execution of a test case does not change the state of the application under test nor change any data in the system, such as content browsing on a website, execution order dependency can be easily achieved. The test cases in the examples we have discussed when presenting equivalence partitioning and decision table testing techniques are state-less test cases.

But for test cases with state changes, such as the examples we presented with finite state machine models, the test case design should include a starting state, and at the end of a test execution, the system should be set back to the starting state (this would require modifying the test paths for some of the test cases generated through FSM or a use case control flow graph). More details with regards to states are covered in the discussions on state independency.

7.2.2 Path Independency

Test path independency ensures that a subpath of any test path is not a test path. Sometimes it's also being referred to as linear independency. If a path has a new node in it then the path is linearly independent to all other linearly independent paths, since any path having a new node implies that it has a new edge. A subpath of any linearly independent path is not a linearly independent path.

If the control flow graph path coverage technique is used to generate test cases for an application, these test cases automatically satisfy test path independency.

For instance, in Example 6.4, a function to check the occurrence count of a character in a string, for prime path coverage the final test paths were: [1,2], [1,3,4,8], [1,3,4,5,7,4,5,7,4,8], [1,3,4,5,6,7,4,5,6,7,4,8], no test path contains any other test path as a subpath, and also, no test paths contain the same set of nodes.

Test path independency also enhances the atomicity of test cases. For example, if test path A contains another test path B, then a test execution failure in B would also cause A to fail, any defect that test path A is supposed to catch would be missed.

7.2.3 State Independency

State independency states that a test case can be executed successfully regardless of the current state of the application under test. A test case can be executed regardless of if any tests (include itself) were executed before it. It can also be considered as a manifestation of order independency. This requires that if any test would change the state of the application, including data, the state would need to be reset after the test; or at the start of a test case execution, the state of the application should be brought to the state the test case requires to begin with.

If an application or a module relevant to the testing is stateless, then state independency should be satisfied by default. For example, in Example 3.5, an average of two integers, any test can be executed regardless of if any other test was performed or not.

In Example 3.9, an order API, since the API only returns information in the database based on the input parameters, the result of any test case execution is independent of the execution of any other tests. But if there is an API that modified the data in a test, then any contamination by the test should be removed (as part of the test) before the next test case starts.

For certain web applications, for example, sessions, cookies, or tokens may be used on the client side. Before executing a test case, the current state of the application left from last the test execution would need to be reset to the required starting state of the test case, such as starting a new session.

In Example 6.12, a cat in a black box, the starting state of some tests is *Alive*, while the starting state of others is *Dead*. Thus, if the same cat is used for testing, then the cat should be at the starting state needed for a test. This can be done by executing certain transactions in the application, such as bringing a cat from *Dead* state to *Alive* state by using the magic potion.

7.2.4 Environment Independency

Environment independency ensures that a test case executes successfully under different testing environments. By the definition in Chapter 2, a test case is genuine, it holds on any instance of the application under test, and under any environments such as different browsers, or different backend data storages/databases.

For instance, if a SQL is used to query a database as part of a test, the SQL should be written in a fashion that succeeds on all applicable databases, such as MySQL and Oracle.

A test case could be specified that some aspects of it are environment dependent. For example, a GUI element on a web page may be rendered slightly differently on different browsers. Since that's part of the test case specification, the test case itself is still environment independent.

7.2.5 Time Independency

Another characteristic we've discussed in Chapter 2 is test case reproducibility, the test case holds at any time. In other words, a test case is time independent.

There are two aspects of time independency, one is that a test case holds any time on the application, the other is that the test case can be executed at any time.

The 1st one requires that a test case holds on different versions of an application if the feature or function under test is not supposed to be changed. This is essential to regression testing.

The 2nd one requires that a test case can be executed at any time of the year, of the month, of the day, of the hour, etc. This is important particularly to automated tests that could be launched at any time of the day. For example, if a test case is to verify properties of records added to a database table in the last 24 hours till the current time (the time the test case was executed), then the current time matters for the test (part of the input vector), and how the data are created (as part of the test) and how the test case is executed are also related to the time of the test execution. In this scenario, time independency ensures that the test case successfully runs and produces the same pass or fail result regardless of the test case execution time. An example of this scenario is presented in the case study in Chapter 13.

7.3 MODULARIZATION PRINCIPLE

7.3.1 Modularization Principle

Modularization is to break down test cases into reusable modules or sections, to better organize, classify, and categorize tests. This process may also reduce redundancy and increase test case maintainability (and pave the way to test automation).

Modularization for an application is based on various abstractions, such as different functionalities, how different functionalities interact with each other, and a lot of times how the workflow works within the application. It breaks down to the grouping of related pieces into different clusters that are loosely related to each other.

Let's discuss the concepts through a few examples.

Example 7.1: Function Calls

Consider the following functions:

```
Function A {
    Call function C;
    //Do some other work; }
Function B {
    Call function C;
    //Do some other work; }
Function C {
    Call Function X; // X is a build-in function in the programing language;
    //Do some other work; }
```

To write test cases for these functions, we first write tests for Function C, then write tests for both Function A and Function B. There is no need to include Function C specific tests in neither Function A nor Function B tests.

Testing of Function A includes testing of Function C, and when testing Function B, the tests for Function C are reused, there is no need to write tests for Function C again.

Note, when testing Function C, there is no need to test Function X, which is a build-in function in the programing language being used. Even more, for type 1 and type 2 tests, when a software application is tested, we don't care much about what programming language is being used to write the application, what we do care about are the functionality requirements and other requirements of the software.

Further down with the layers, what kind of hardware the application is running on is not a concern either. [The physics of how electrons and atoms work is not a concern when testing logic gates in the transistors and integrated circuits; the implementation of logic gates is not a concern when testing the compiler of a programming language, and so on].

Example 7.2: A Web Site with Common Breadcrumbs

This example involves testing a website. All the pages on the website have common breadcrumbs and a common navigation bar.

To test the pages on the website, the common breadcrumbs and navigation bar can be modularized, and there is no need to test the breadcrumbs and navigation bar on each page other than to check if they show up on the page. Furthermore, the UI appearance of certain modules on the web pages, such as forms, that come from the same template module, can be tested separately.

Writing modularized tests require an understanding of the application's branching and workflows, and the goal is to better categorize the tests and to create reusable modules.

For example, if a login module is being called by different modules in the application, each module requires different login credentials due to user role requirements (users have different roles are exposed to different functionalities), then the test cases for the login module should not be part of the testing of the current module, except reusing the part that is needed (to login).

Example 7.3: Shopping Site Workflow

At a shopping website, one simple workflow path contains the following steps:

(a) Login to the site.
(b) Find an item to buy.
(c) Put the item in the shopping cart.
(d) Start the checkout process.
(e) Add shipping address.
(f) Add payment type and payment information.
(g) Place the order.

Other paths may include fewer steps or more steps to reach the last part of placing the order, such as if the shipping address is already on file and can be selected, or the payment method is rejected.

Given the complexity of the possible scenarios, it's better to write each step above as a module and call the modules for each workflow path (assuming, for example, the same functionality for putting an item in the shopping cart exercises the same code segments in the implementation, no matter which page it initiated from).

Now let's discuss a hierarchical finite state machine model for test modularization.

7.3.2 Hierarchical Finite State Machine

A hierarchical finite state machine is an extension of FSM. No formal definition will be presented here, only the concept will be discussed.

In an FSM, a subset of states can be enclosed and form a **superstate.** A superstate can be represented as one node on the graph. The collapsed FSM with superstate(s) is a **hierarchical finite state machine** (HFSM). A superstate is a composite state that has common actions for the states inside it. The actions or transactions involving a superstate are referred to as **generalized transactions**.

An application under test can be modeled with a hierarchical finite state machine. Before testing starts, the application is at the initial state. In most cases, common testing data or sample data need to be loaded to the system before test execution, and we call the superstate after data loading 'base test state'. Then testing is divided into multiple modules or clusters depending on functionalities or other abstractions of the application.

Each cluster is a superstate in the HFSM graph, and each superstate itself is a separate FSM or HSFM. Each test cluster starts with a cluster base state, and cluster-specific data can also be loaded if needed. Each cluster spreads one or more superstates, such as test classes (sub-clusters are also possible). Each test class contains the final nodes of test cases.

The control graphs for this layered abstraction HFSM are illustrated in Figures 7.1, 7.2, and 7.3.

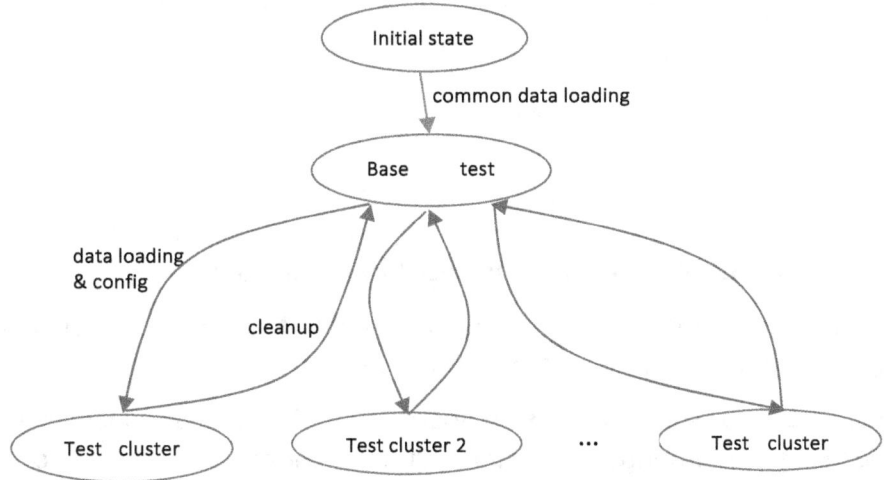

Figure 7.1: Graph for test modularization HFSM model

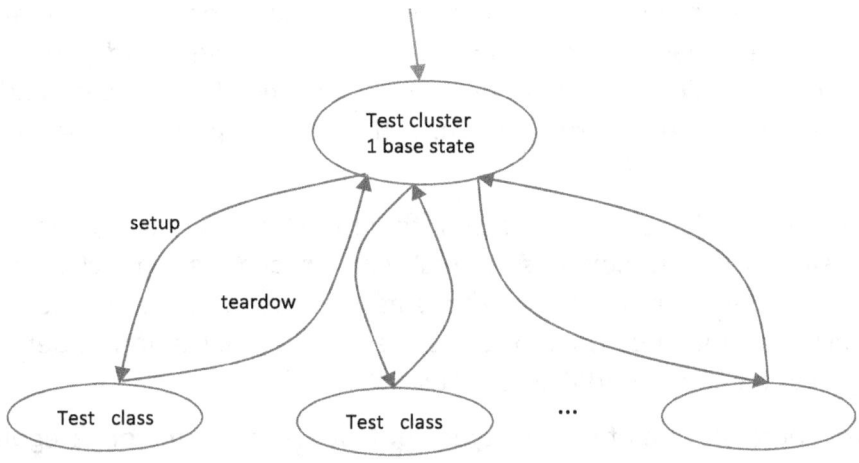

Figure 7.2: Graph for test modularization HFSM model: test clusters

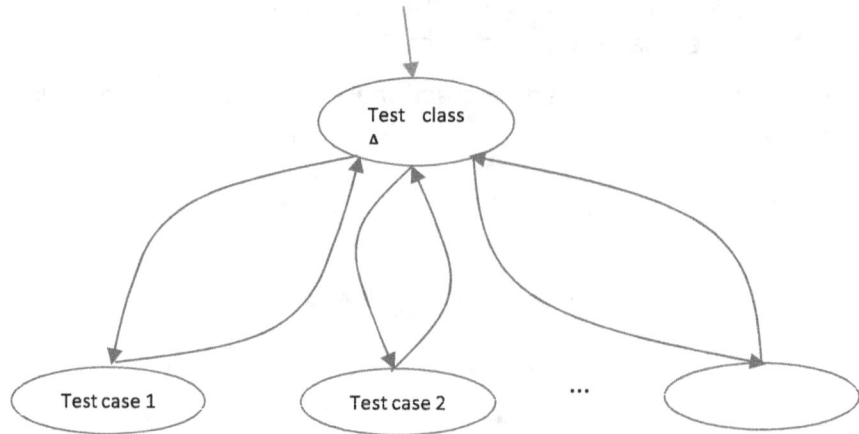

Figure 7.3: Graph for test modularization HFSM model: test classes

There is no restriction to the number of levels in the HFSM tree-structured graph, and the tree is not necessarily balanced.

Each superstate or super-node is an abstraction of some sort, such as a code module in the implementation, an individual functionality, a partition of input vectors, or a set of related test suites.

In these tree-like graphs, any edge going back to a parent node is an environment/data clean-up process and is required. In other words, an edge-pair coverage is required for any node pairs where the 2nd node is a child of the 1st node in the tree structure, in which the edges represent generalized transactions.

Modularization is reflected in most test automation frameworks. For instance, in tests using JUnit frameworks, a test cluster can be one class in a package/project, with individual methods as test cases. There can be class level or test level manipulations of the states of the application under test (including data creation, modification, deletion, etc.).

Manual test organization of various types of test cases and major categories in each testing type should also follow the modularization principle, and test suites can be classified with hierarchical representation. Major categories include functionalities and types of tests.

Table 7.2 shows an example of organizing test cases with different suites for a specific application feature.

Feature	Test type	1st level	2nd level	3rd level
Feature One	(A) type 1	(1) UI	(i) use cases	(a) permutations
				(b) error handling
			(ii) UI display	
		(2) backend	(i) API testing	
			(ii) DB testing	
		(3) upgrade		
	(B) type 2	(1) UI	(i) browser specific	
			(ii) usability testing	
		(2) Performance		

Table 7.2: An example of organizing test cases

If the content in the above table is represented by a tree structure, then the leaf nodes are the test suites containing the test cases.

Analogy of HFSM Approach with the Study of the Visible Universe:

Let's now take an analogy of the hierarchical approach with the content of the visible universe.

The Universe consists of billions of galaxies, and the galaxies are not uniformly distributed in the Universe, most of them are drawn together in clusters, each consists up to several thousand galaxies. Those clusters and additional isolated galaxies in turn form even larger structures called superclusters. While within each galaxy, a typical one contains billions of stars along with other components, and the stars are not uniformly distributed either but form various star clusters.

With this hierarchical view, the researches in astronomy and related fields are also done in a modularized way. For example, a study of the large-scale structure of the Universe won't care about any individual stars in a particular galaxy.

7.4 TEST COVERAGE PRINCIPLE

Test coverage is usually referred to as the measurement of what percentage of the requirements are exercised with the identified test cases for the software application under test. Sometimes percentage of coverage is misleading, since test cases may not be uniformly distributed or not weighted for different features or aspects of the application; also, the test cases may not fully cover the requirements if the requirements are not fully specified or not able to be fully specified. Therefore, listing what's covered rather than a percentage is a better idea.

The test coverage principle states that all requirements should be covered by the set of test cases. It seems obvious, but in practice, it's not always observed. How test cases are generated plays an essential role.

Test coverage measurement may be different for different types of tests, so in practice, it's recommended to separate the measurements for different types of tests. For instance, for a type 2 test, it's better to list what's being covered. For example, what browsers are covered for what areas, what scenarios are used in performance testing.

For type 0 tests, code coverage is often used instead of test coverage. Code coverage measures the degree to which the source code is exercised with a particular set of test cases. The structural testing techniques we have discussed in Chapter 7 provide various coverage criteria for type 0 tests.

The following table lists the recommended test coverages for test cases generated with the techniques we have discussed in Part 2 of the book. In practice, more than one technique is applied in generating test cases, and the coverage should be combined accordingly.

	Test case design techniques	Test coverage requirements
1	equivalence partitioning	standard case of partitioning
2	combinatorial technique	pair-wise testing
3	decision table	all rules in a decision table
4	control flow graph; call graph; use case cfg	edge or prime path coverage
5	condition coverage	modified condition/decision coverage
6	finite state machine	transaction coverage (edge coverage)

Table 7.3: Recommended test coverages for common test case generation techniques

In practice, test coverage requirements should be based on the nature of the application, and how critical certain functionalities are. Different modules of the application may have different test coverage requirements.

Another aspect of test coverage is to reduce redundancy in testing. A certain degree of redundancy is a good thing in some cases, but too much redundancy increases maintenance cost and takes more resources and time to execute without adding value to the testing effort. For example, if a change is made in the application, multiple redundant tests affected by the change need to be changed.

A good approach to reduce redundancy is to follow the modularization principle, especially in automated testing. For example, if specific functionality is tested by a set of type 0 tests or by a set of type 1 integration API tests, then there is no need to repeat the same tests in the type 1 GUI test suite.

EXERCISE PROBLEMS:

P7.1: Answer the following questions based on the discussions in this chapter.

(1) Explain the atomic principle.
(2) Explain the independency principle.
(3) What are the five categories of independencies? Explain each of them.
(4) Explain the modularization principle. Give an example of testing utilizing the modularization principle.
(5) What's the HFSM model? And how it's applied to software testing?
(6) Give an example of manual testing using the modularization principle.
(7) Explain the test coverage principle.

8 REGRESSION TESTING

8.1 REGRESSION TESTING

Regression testing is to run all or a selected portion of the whole test suite for a software application after a change is made. The purpose of regression testing is to ensure that the software still functions after the change and to determine if there is any defect or side effect in the existing functionalities or with any aspect of the performance of the application caused by the change. A deviation, defect, or side effect is called a ***regression***.

Let's look at an example. In Example 4.5, visibility of applications on a web page, there were 4 roles, and based on the roles a user has, the user can see different items on a page. We came up with 8 test cases with 3-wise testing in Table 5.12. Test cases 1, 2, 7, and 8 from that table are listed in Table 8.1.

Case	Role1	Role2	Role3	Role4	Expected Items	Actual result	Actual after fix #8
1	0	0	0	0	none	none	1,2,3,4
2	0	0	1	1	3,4	3,4	3,4
7	1	1	0	0	1,2	1,2	1,2
8	1	1	1	1	1,2,3,4	1,2,3	1,2,3,4

Table 8.1: Selected 3-wise test cases for Example 4.5

Suppose a defect is found with test case #8, instead of showing items 1, 2, 3, and 4, it shows 1, 2, and 3 only. A fix is made for this defect, and the result of test case #8 is as expected after the fix. But this fix breaks another scenario covered with case #1, that is, when all roles do not exist, no item should be seen, but now all items are shown. The last two columns in Table 8.1 show the actual results of the test cases before and after this fix.

As we can see, if only the failed test (#8) is executed after the fix, and no regression testing is done to re-run all the tests, then the newly introduced defect won't be caught. The new defect is a regression.

Regression testing needs to be done after the initial fix. Also, since a new defect is found, after fixing the new defect, regression testing should be performed again, until all tests included in the regression test set pass.

The whole test suite set for regression includes type 0 unit tests, type 1 integration and functional tests, and certain type 2 tests such as a subset of the performance tests.

Automated unit tests are usually closely integrated with the software product build process and are always executed whenever the product build is done. Type 1 integration and functional tests are usually automated and are part of a continuous integration process. A change in the code (include branch merging) triggers a new build followed by the execution of the integration test suite.

New feature additions, feature enhancements, and important defect fixes are all considered major changes. Other changes that may need regression tests are configuration changes, infrastructural changes including 3rd party software changes. The following list shows the common changes requiring regression testing:

(1) new features.
(2) feature enhancements.
(3) functional defect fixes.
(4) fixes of type 2 test failures such as fixes of issues in performance, security, and usability.
(5) configuration changes.
(6) code source control branch merges.
(7) upgrades of 3rd party or open-source software dependencies.

If new features or new enhancements are added to the system, or defects are fixed for which there were no tests existed (either manual or automated ones), then new tests need to be added. So, the integration test suite set increases in size with time.

Reducing the size of the regression test set is needed by constantly examine the test cases and remove obsolete ones and reduce redundancies (as we have discussed in the test coverage principle in the last chapter).

The frequency and scope of regression testing can be different, depending on the complexity of the software application, the scope of the changes, and the scope of the product release.

On one hand, for example, if there is an enhancement to add certain elements on a page for a web application, and there are no backend changes with this enhancement, then regression testing can be limited to the tests that are relevant to the page; on another if there are multiple changes or defect fixes to an application, and the whole application needs to be built as a whole, then a full regression, that is, rerunning all tests, is expected.

In general, a software product with long release cycles would require full regression running numerous times before release, while a short-cycled product release (e.g. daily) would not require a full regression but a selected subset of all test cases.

If not all the tests are to be re-run for regression testing, then test case selection and prioritization are needed. We will discuss these two aspects in the following two sections.

8.2 REGRESSION TEST SELECTION

If a subset of the whole test suite is desired to use for regression testing, then there are certain general principles and practices to follow for test selection.

Here is a list of major strategies or techniques for selecting regression test cases:

(1) Predefined test sets.
(2) Strategic test sets.
(3) Prioritized test sets.
(4) Random test sets.

In practice, multiple techniques from the above list can be used to generate the final list of test sets for regression testing. Let's examine these techniques one by one.

8.2.1 Predefined Test Sets

Predefined test sets are test suites defined to serve particular purposes or categorized by different aspects of the application such as software architectural layers.

Examples of predefined test sets include smoke test suite, sanity test suite, API test suite, UI test suite, performance benchmarking test suite, database test suite, I18N test suite, etc. These test sets are candidates to be included in the regression testing suite (super suite).

8.2.2 Strategic Test Sets

Strategic test sets are test sets that are classified based on testing strategies suitable for a specific testing project, including but not limited to the following ones:

(1) Test sets for the functionalities affected by the change.
   (a) include all tests in those areas.
   (b) include a subset of all tests in those areas.
(2) Test sets for business-critical functionalities.
(3) Test sets for functionalities affecting a large number of users.
(4) A set of tests (a core set) that must be included for any release.
(5) A set of tests that frequently failed in the past.

If the modularization principle is followed, test cases in different functionalities are usually clustered in different test packages or classes in automated test suites. The same is true for manual test cases.

The above classification can also be done by tagging either the automated tests or the manual tests in the management tools used. See the tagging example in section 8.2.5.

8.2.3 Prioritized Test Sets

Another technique is to prioritize all the test cases according to certain criteria and include in the regression test the test cases having a priority higher than a certain value or execute the test cases in priority order.

Prioritization of tests is similar to strategic classification, and a test case can be classified with both. The difference is that strategic test classification has meaningful names for annotation, and strategic sets are selected for a specific regression testing based on the specific situation; while with prioritization of test sets, tests are executed based on priorities, and lower priority tests may not get executed due to time constraints or resource availability.

Prioritization can be done in various ways, and each deals with different aspects of the application. The 1st rule is based on test case types, the lower the type, the higher the priority. For example, type 0 unit tests should have the highest priority and should be running every time. Type 0 tests run much faster than type 1 tests, usually, they are automated and are closed correlated with the product code and they are part of the product build process and can't be separated from it.

For type 1 and type 2 tests, prioritization is often based on other factors such as the risk of failures and business impact. The following table lists some of the common factors to consider and an example of a typical priority assignment:

Factors	Typical priorities
High business impact and critical functionalities	P0
Core features and functionalities	P0
Functionalities that are more visible to end-users	P1
Functionalities that affect a large number of users	P1
Functionalities that have undergone more and recent changes	P2
Test cases that have frequent defects in the past	P2
Web UI usability tests	P3
The rest of the regression test suite	P3

Table 8.2: A sample test case priority assignment

P0 tests have higher priority than P1 tests, P1 tests have higher priority than P2 tests, and so on. This is just a sample priority assignment; the priorities can be quite different under different situations.

The priorities of the test cases in the regression test suite should be constantly examined and modified. For example, certain tests that having frequent defects discovered in the past may no longer be the case anymore.

Various techniques or criteria could be used to prioritize regression test cases. In section 8.3 we will present a simple weighted technique to calculate test case priorities.

8.2.4 Random Test Sets

Random test case selection is sometimes used in cases where there are strict time constraints and regression testing is not critical for the specific project and a sanity type of testing or even ad hoc testing would be adequate.

Statistically speaking, random testing is not too far off from targeted testing when the application under test is a 'black box' to the tester. But for most of the business-critical applications, random testing should not be favored in any case, to minimize the probability of releasing the application with major product defects.

8.2.5 Test Sets Annotation

Automated test case selection can be done through annotation. For example, in the xUnit test framework, the following code skeleton segment in Code Segment 8.1 illustrates test tagging with annotations.

In this example, test case testCase1() is classified as a sanity test, as a P2 test, as a frequently failed test (tag: Freq_failed), and as an Oracle DB test; test case testCase2() is classified as a 'Critical' test, as a P0 test, and as a 'Smoke' test; and case testCase3() is classified as a P1 test and as a 'Large_num_users' tests. Test cases can be run based on specific tags.

```java
public class AnExampleTestClass ()
{
    @Test
    @Tag("Sanity")
    @Tag("P2")
    @Tag("Freq_failed")
    @Category(OracleTests.class)
    void testCase1() {
    }
    @Test
    @Tag("Critical")
    @Tag("P0")
    @Tag("Smoke")
    void testCase2() {
    }
    @Test
    @Tag("P1")
    @Tag("Large_num_users")
    void testCase3() {
    }
}
```

Code Segment 8.1: Tagging of test cases

In this tagging example, 4 sets of categories are used:

(1) **Predefined scopes**: Smoke, Sanity.
(2) **Predefined categories**: OracleTest.class.
(3) **Strategic types**: Freq_failed, Large_num_users.
(4) **Priorities**: P0, P1, P2.

One test case can be annotated in multiple categories. Test case selection based on annotation should be done with only one category, or the fewer categories the better if not one, to avoid selecting the same test multiple times. A better strategy is to use as less as annotations as possible for each test to avoid redundancy.

8.3 WEIGHTED PRIORITIZATION

We've just talked about prioritization based on factors such as the risk of failures, business impact, and testing types, and listed a sample priority assignment in Table 8.2. In this section, we present a simple method to calculate test case priorities based on weights concerning several major factors.

The following major factors are identified:

(1) Business requirements
(2) Changes and updates
(3) Frequent defect areas
(4) Testing time and cost

The business requirements would include high business impact and critical functionalities, core features, more visible features, used by a large number of users features, etc.; Changes and updates would include areas that have undergone more or recent changes, defect fixes or updates; Frequent defect areas are areas that more defects were found, and where more severe defects were found; Time and cost refers to the time and cost needed to execute a test.

Each of the above major categories is given a weight. Each test is assigned a number that corresponds to the ranking in each of the factors. The final priority is determined by a weighted sum of all the factors.

Let's f_i represents the weight of factor i, w_i represents the weight of a test case in factor i, then the priority of the test case is defined as:

$$P = \sum_{i=1}^{n} f_i w_i \qquad (8\text{-}1)$$

where n is the total number of factors. We have identified 4 factors above, so $n = 4$ in our case.

Based on the value of P for a test case, human-friendly terms such as P1 and P2 can be assigned. Since this process is time-consuming and may add a lot of unnecessary overheads, test cases could be divided into subsets that are closely related to each other, and each subset is assigned one priority for all the tests within the subset, based on the above formula.

As an example, let's hypothetically give the weights for each factor as shown in Table 8.3. The higher the number, the more weight for the item.

	factors	f_i
1	Business requirements	5
2	Changes and updates	4
3	Frequent defect areas	3
4	Testing time and cost	1

Table 8.3: Weights of factors in determining test case priority

The business requirements have the highest weight in the table, and 'Time and cost' is less important and have a weight value of 1. The ratio of any two weights reflects the relative importance of the two factors.

Table 8.4 lists some sample test cases with their weights in each factor and the final weighted priority for each case. A weight of 5 indicates the maximum a test case can have, and 0 is the minimum which says that the item has no weight at all for that factor. Note, the possible values for 'Time and cost' is from 1 to 5 (a value of 0 for it would mean infinite time and cost). Be careful with 'Time and cost', a value of 5 means less time and cost than that of a value of 4, and so on.

Test case	Requirement (w_1)	Change (w_2)	Defect (w_3)	Time & cost (w_4)	Weighted priority	Priority scaled
1	5	0	2	5	36	P0
2	0	5	2	4	30	P0
4	0	0	5	4	19	P2
5	2	4	0	1	27	P1
6	3	3	0	2	29	P1
7	0	2	0	4	12	P2
8	0	0	5	2	17	P2
9	0	0	1	1	4	P3

Table 8.4: A sample test case priority assignment based on a weighted sum

With 5 as the maximum weight for each factor, and 5 as the maximum for the weight in each factor for a test case, the max possible priority a test case can have is (5+4+3+1)*5 = 65, and the minimum possible priority a test case can have is 1*1 = 1 (account for the minimum with 'Time and cost' item).

For example, for test case 1, from equation (8-1):

$$P \text{ (test case 1)} = \sum_{i=1}^{4} f_i w_i = 5*5 + 4*0 + 3*2 + 1*5 = 36.$$

The scaled priority is based on the following ranges:

(1) $P >= 30$: P0
(2) $30 > P >= 20$: P1
(3) $20 > P >= 10$: P2
(4) $10 > P >= 1$: P3

The range can be modified to serve a different situation.

In the above discussion, we have assumed that the regression test suite has good and balanced test coverage. If the coverages are significantly different in different areas, then coverage may also be added as a factor in test case prioritization. For example, a test case or a set of test cases in a specific feature area may have higher priority if the test coverage in this specific area is low.

8.4 REGRESSION TESTING WITH CONTINUOUS INTEGRATION

Continuous integration is a software development process where developers regularly check in their code changes into a source control repository shared by a group of developers, after which automated builds and tests are executed. Multiple source control repositories from different development groups or teams are merged into a central repository periodically, after which automated builds and tests are again triggered to run.

The purpose of continuous integration is to coordinate the development process better, to find and address defects quicker, and to reduce the time it takes for software release and updates.

Automated tests in continuous integration are not limited to type 0 unit tests, type 1 or type 2 tests are also included, such as API tests, UI tests, performance tests, etc. The whole regression test suite can be included in part or whole in the continuous integration process.

Tools like Jenkins are often used to manage continuous integration including build and test automation. The basic functionality of Jenkins is to call software programs, often software scripts, to execute a predefined list of steps, e.g. to compile Java source code and build a JAR from the resulting classes, to start the software program, and to run the tests. The trigger for this execution can be time-based or event based.

The tool also monitors the execution of the steps, and if one of the steps fails there are various options to send out notifications, including emails and messaging platforms.

The results of the regression testing are available on the Jenkins server. The regression testing process can also be integrated with other services, to make the artifact available on a centralized test development or testing management server. The result (or a summary) is normally also sent via email to a list of team members. Any test failures are to be looked at regularly (daily for example), and actions are to be taken to fix the issues, which could either be due to product defects or due to testing code problems, or any other issues.

It's important to keep the regression test suites up to date, this includes:
(1) Modify relevant tests after any functionality changes.
(2) Remove obsolete tests.
(3) Remove redundant tests.
(4) Rewrite/redesign any tests that are unstable or often fail at runtime with no real product issue.

(5) Rewrite/redesign any tests that take too much resource and/or take too much time to execute.

A regression testing strategy is very important in the software production release cycles, and it's an essential part of software testing.

EXERCISE PROBLEMS:

P8.1: Answer the following questions based on the discussions in this chapter.

    (1) Give a couple of examples of regression testing.
    (2) Why regression testing is needed?
    (3) What are the major changes that require regression testing?
    (4) What are the major techniques for regression test case selection? Explain each of them.
    (5) What are the major factors to consider in identifying test case priorities?
    (6) What you can do to keep regression test cases up to date?

9 UNIT TESTING (TYPE 0 TESTS)

Unit tests (type 0 tests) are discussed in this chapter. Several examples are presented to demonstrate how to use the techniques and principles we have covered in previous chapters to generate type 0 test cases. Automated unit test case writing is then introduced. Mocking and stubbing concepts are also covered with a couple of examples.

9.1 CHARACTERISTICS AND BENEFITS OF UNIT TESTS

We have learned from Chapter 2 that unit tests (type 0 tests) are tests that verify the behaviors of software implementation units. Examples of the units include methods in a class in object-oriented implementation, isolated software components, etc. A unit test is the smallest part of testing for a piece of software implementation.

Unit tests verify the design and implementation of the software and are hidden from the higher-level functional requirements.

So, what should be included in unit tests?

The purpose of unit tests is to verify the implementation of the units of the software, and a unit of a piece of code is a method or function of a class. Thus methods/functions in a class are the primary targets for unit tests. In certain cases, a class or even a set of related classes can be unit tested if the tests won't violate the basic rules or characteristics of unit tests which will be discussed next.

Unit testing intends to verify the logic in the method (or a unit of code component). Even though unit testing is about software implementation, it's still black box testing in this sense. In other words, the implementation may change often, but the tests should change less.

Within a class, certain things normally do not need to be unit tested, such as constructors, properties, configurations, wrappers, a method that calls another public method, and complex multi-threading code (leave it to integration testing).

Generally, only public methods/functions are tested with unit tests. If a private method does important processing and is not exercised through tests from other public methods, then some strategies can be used to test it (sometimes refactoring may be needed if a private method contains complex logic).

For example, in Java you can declare the testing class in the same package with the production class where the private method is residing; and in C++ you can declare the testing class as a 'friend' of the class under test.

There are also certain xUnit extensions to handle testing of private methods, but there are drawbacks in this approach, the testing class is mixed with production code in the same package, for one. There is also a reflection API in Java that can be used to separate testing code and production code, but it makes the testing code complex.

Unit tests have certain unique characteristics:

(1) Unit tests are low-level tests.
(2) Unit tests have fast execution speed.
(3) Unit tests are isolated from external resources.
(4) Unit tests are integrated with the software build process.

Unit tests are closed coupled with the software implementation, so they should be designed at low level (but you should avoid mix testing code with product code). Since they are at low level, the execution of the tests should be extremely fast, on the order of millisecond usually. Also, there can be thousands or more unit tests for a small software application and it's essential to execute fast.

Unit tests are isolated, a set of tests are only associated with a unit of product code such as a method or a function or a class, and can be run in isolation, and should have no dependencies on outside factors such as a file system or a database (stubbing and mocking techniques will be discussed in section 9.4 and 9.5 to deal with relevant situations).

Changes in any code outside the method/component under test cannot affect the unit test results, so the tests can be executed at build time. In consequence, unit tests should be integrated with the product build process and should be run before the application even gets built and leave the testing of the functionalities to integration tests.

The basic testing principles should be followed in writing unit tests, atomicity and independency in particular, and the testing techniques we have covered in this book can be applied in generating test cases, including equivalence partitioning with boundary conditions, decision table testing, combinatorial testing, and various structural testing techniques.

There are many benefits with unit tests, the following are the major ones:

(1) Find defects early in the development cycle.
(2) Enforce good software design and facilitate changes better.
(3) Reduce costs of fixing defects.
(4) Fast regression.

Unit tests are done by developers in the software implementation stage and they provide a more granular examination on the implementation, and defects with the implementation can be found earlier before sending the software for integration testing. The earlier a defect is found, the fewer compound errors occur, and developers can quickly fix the defects and make changes in the codebase. Also, debugging process is made simpler based on failed tests.

Unit tests also push developers to design better early in the cycle, write modularized and reusable code and make code refactoring easier and facilitate changes better. For example, by eliminating dependencies in the code with input parameters (see the example in section 9.3).

Unit tests reduce costs for fixing defects. According to many studies, the earlier a defect is identified, the less the cost.

Since unit tests execute fast and are integrated with the build process, they provide a fast regression of the codebase.

In certain cases, unit tests also furnish live documentation of the implementation since they cover the various behaviors of the coding unit.

9.2 WRITING UNIT TESTS

Let's use a few examples to demonstrate how to approach writing unit tests.

We are going to discuss coding in the context of JUnit, but the ideas behind are not attached to any particular testing framework, you should be able to understand the examples without particular knowledge of the JUnit framework. Also, we are not discussing how to use any of the testing frameworks, resources on how to use a particular testing framework can be easily found elsewhere.

Sometimes the code segments presented here are partial, just enough to demonstrate the concepts to be presented.

Example 9.1: Prime Numbers

A method, *isPrime(n)*, returns '1' (represents true) if '*n*' is a prime number, and '0' (represents false) if '*n*' is not a prime number.

To test this method, a set of input vectors need to be identified. From the nature of the problem, it's easy to come up with test vectors with the equivalence partitioning technique. We will leave the whole treatment as an exercise problem. For now, let's just write a test case for one input value, say, to verify number '5' is a prime number.

After the input vector is identified, the next step is to call the function under test, which is *isPrime(n)*, and apply the input value to the function to get the return value, then compare the returned value with the expected value. The expected value is '1' (true) since 5 is a prime number.

A simple comparison can be done, for example, with an '*if*' clause. The following Java code segment shows one way to handle it.

```java
public void test_isPrime_inputValueFive () {
    if (isPrime(5) == 1)
        System.out.println ("test passed: 5 is a prime number.");
    else
        System.out.println ("test failed: 5 should be a prime number.");
}
```

Code Segment 9.1: A Java implementation of a test for Example 9.1: prime number

For better error handling, you can throw an `AssertionError` when the test fails and catch the error with "`try {} catch {}`" statements, as shown in Code Segment 9.2.

```java
public static void test_isPrime_inputValueFive () {
  int input = 5;
  try {
    if (isPrime (input) == 1) {
        System.out.println ("test passed:" + input + " is a prime number");
    }
    else {
        throw new AssertionError("test failed:" + input + " should be a
                                 prime number");
    }
  }
  catch (AssertionError e) {
      System.out.println (e.getMessage() );
  }
}
```

Code Segment 9.2: Java implementation of a test for Example 9.1 with try catch blocks

It's extra work to implement the logic and to take care of error/exception handling this way. Fortunately, in any common testing framework, this kind of procedure has been implemented. For instance, in Junit, an 'Assert' class is available with various methods, such as assertEquals (expected, actual), which asserts that two objects are equal. If the two objects are not equal, an AssertionError is thrown.

The following code segment is an implementation of the same test case with the JUnit framework.

```java
@Test
public void test_isPrime_inputValueFive () {
  // arrange
  int inputvalue = 5;
  int expected = 1;
  // act
  int actual = isPrime (inputvalue);
  // assert
  assertEquals (expected, actual);
}
```

Code Segment 9.3: A sample test case written in JUnit for example 9.1: prime number

The input value, the expected result, and the actual result are all specified with variables to clearly demonstrate how the test is written. The **'arrange'**, **'act'**, and **'assert'** pattern (or AAA pattern) is a common way to write unit tests. The arrange section sets the values of the testing data and initializes objects needed for the test; the act section invokes the function/method or module under test with the arranged data; the assert section verifies that if the behavior of the action is expected or not.

In practice, when it's appropriate you may write all these in one line, such as:

```
assertEquals (1, isPrime(5));
```

An identifying message can be given for AssertionError, for example, to replace:

```
assertEquals (expected, actual);
```

with:

```
assertEquals ("isPrime() returned false for value: " + inputvalue + ".",
              expected, actual);
```

The code segment below shows this alternative way to write the test.

```
@Test
public void test_isPrime_inputValueFive ()
{
    assertEquals ("5 is a prime number.", 1, isPrime(5));
}
```

Code Segment 9.4: An alternative implementation for the test in Example 9.1

The most commonly used assertions in JUnit are listed in the following table.

Return type	Statement
static void	assertEquals (<T> expected, <T> actual, String message);
static void	assertNotEquals (<T> expected, <T> actual, String message);
static void	assertTrue (boolean condition, String message);
static void	assertFalse (boolean condition, String message);
static void	assertNull (Object actual, String message);
static void	assertNotNull (Object actual, String message);
static void	assertArrayEquals(boolean[] expected, boolean[] actual);
static <T extends Throwable> T	assertThrows (Class<T> expectedType, Executable ex);
static void	assertSame (Object expected, Object actual);
static void	assertTimeout (Duration timeout, Executable ex);
Static void	fail (String message);

Table 9.1: Commonly used assertion statements in Junit

There are many other assertion statements, and for each of the above statements, there are numerous variations as well. Refer to online resources for more information.

When selecting which assertion statement to use for any particular case, use best practices and follow common sense. For example, assertEquals() should be preferred over assertTrue() if possible for better messaging if a test fails.

So, we have written the 1st unit test. Let's take another example and try to write type 0 tests based on test cases generated from the equivalence partition technique, and also make sure that the general testing principles are followed.

Example 9.2: Average of Two Numbers

Example 3.5, a special case of the average of two numbers program, was used to demonstrate how to generate test cases with standard equivalence partitioning technique. In this example, we expand it to the general form of the program.

The program takes two integers and returns the average of the two numbers.

The following code segment shows a Java implementation:

```java
public static double AverageOfTwoNumbers (int x, int y) {
  double result = -1.00;
  result = (x/2 + y/2) + ((x%2 + y%2) / 2);
  return result;
}
```

Code Segment 9.5: Java implementation for Example 9.2

Let's generate the test cases first, then write automated tests for them.

This is a typical case to use the equivalence partitioning technique. For the standard case with edges, there are one valid zone, a square on the 2-dimensional vector space for x and y, and 4 invalid zones on each of the 4 edges. The only difference with Example 3.5 is that the range of valid values for both x and y are [Integer.MIN_VALUE, Integer.MAX_VALUE] instead of [10,10].

Let's define:

INTMAX = Integer.MAX_VALUE (= 2147483647),
INTMIN = Integer.MIN_VALUE (= -2147483648).

The partitions are as following (valid values for x and y are integers):

(i)   { x, y | INTMIN ≤ x ≤ INTMAX, INTMIN ≤ y ≤ INTMAX }
(ii) { x, y | x < INTMIN, INTMIN < y < INTMAX }
(iii) { x, y | x > INTMAX, INTMIN < y < INTMAX }
(iv) { x, y | y < INTMIN, INTMIN < x < INTMAX }
(v)   { x, y | y > INTMAX, INTMIN < x < INTMAX }
(vi) { x, y | INTMIN ≤ x ≤ INTMAX, y ∈ { $\Re$ } }
(vii) { x, y | x ∈ { string }, INTMIN ≤ y ≤ INTMAX }

where $\Re$ is the set of real numbers.

Partition (i) is the valid partition, the rest are all invalid partitions. The last two partitions account for non-integer numbers and strings respectively. By adopting the one-error principle, only one of the variables is a real number or a string, and the other variable has a valid integer value.

For the standard case of equivalence partitioning, 9 input vectors are to be selected (per $4n + 1$ formula, where $n = 2$ for two variables) for the valid partition, and 2 input vectors are to select for each of the invalid partitions.

Here is a selection of the input vectors for the test cases for each of the corresponding partitions, with total 21 test cases:

(i)   { [INTMAX, 0], [INTMAX-1, 1], [0, INTMAX-1], [-1, INTMAX], [INTMIN, 2], [INTMIN+1,-2],[0, INTMIN], [3, INTMIN+1] ,[0,0] }
(ii) { [INTMIN-1, 0], [2*INTMIN, -2] }
(iii) { [INTMAX+1, 1], [2*INTMAX, 4] }
(iv) { [1, INTMIN-1], [-1, 2*INTMIN] }
(v)   { [0, INTMAX+1], [5, 2*INTMAX+1] }
(vi) { [-10, 2.5], [100, -20.00] }
(vii) { ["abc", 25], ["", 1] }

With these input values, it's straightforward to write the tests since the method under test is pretty simple. Code Segment 9.5 shows a sample Java class for the tests in the valid partition (i).

In these tests, a `DELTA` parameter is used in `assertEquals()` to handle precision problem in calculations involving float and double values. For example, in the 1st test, if `AverageOfTwoNumbers(INTMAX, 0)` equals `1073741823.5` with precision 0.001 (in the range of [`1073741823.5 - 0.001`, `1073741823.5 + 0.001`]), then the test passes.

Code Segment 9.6 and Code Segment 9.7 cover the tests in the invalid partitions.

```java
// Unit tests for the valid partition.
// input values: [INTMAX, 0], [INTMAX-1, 1], [0, INTMAX-1], [-1, INTMAX],
// [INTMIN, 2], [INTMIN+1, -2], [ 0, INTMIN], [3, INTMIN+1], [0,0].
public class Type0TestsForAverageOfTwoNumbersValidPartition ()
{
   public static final int INTMAX = Integer.MAX_VALUE;
   public static final int INTMIN = Integer.MIN_VALUE;
   private static final double DELTA = 0.001;

   @Test
   public void testAverageOfTwoNumbersValidPartitionValuesINTMAXandZero() {
      assertEquals (1073741823.5, AverageOfTwoNumbers(INTMAX, 0), DELTA);
   }

   @Test
   public void testAverageOfTwoNumbersValidPartitionValuesINTMAXminusOneAndOne() {
      assertEquals (1073741823.5, AverageOfTwoNumbers(INTMAX-1, 1), DELTA);
   }

   @Test
   public void testAverageOfTwoNumbersValidPartitionValuesZeorAndINTMAXminusOne() {
      assertEquals (1073741823.0, AverageOfTwoNumbers(0, INTMAX-1), DELTA);
   }

   @Test
   public void testAverageOfTwoNumbersValidPartitionValuesMinusOneAndINTMAX() {
      assertEquals (1073741823.0, AverageOfTwoNumbers(-1, INTMAX), DELTA);
   }

   @Test
   public void testAverageOfTwoNumbersValidPartitionValuesINTMINandTwo() {
      assertEquals (-1073741823.0, AverageOfTwoNumbers(INTMIN, 2), DELTA );
   }

   @Test
   public void testAverageOfTwoNumbersValidPartitionINTMINplusOneAndMinusTwo() {
      assertEquals (-1073741824.5, AverageOfTwoNumbers(INTMIN+1, -2), DELTA );
   }

   @Test
   public void testAverageOfTwoNumbersValidPartitionValuesZeroAndINTMIN() {
      assertEquals (-1073741824.0, AverageOfTwoNumbers(0, INTMIN), DELTA );
   }

   @Test
   public void testAverageOfTwoNumbersValidPartitionValuesThreeAndINTMINplusOne() {
      assertEquals (-1073741821.5, AverageOfTwoNumbers(3, INTMAX+1), DELTA );
   }

   @Test
   public void testAverageOfTwoNumbersValidPartitionValuesZeroAndZero() {
      assertEquals (0, AverageOfTwoNumbers(0, 0), DELTA );
   }
}
```

Code Segment 9.6: Sample Java implementation of unit tests for Example 9.2 valid zone

```java
// Unit tests for invalid partitions (ii), (iii), (iv), (v).
// input values: [INTMIN-1, 0], [2*INTMIN, -2]; [INTMAX+1, 1], [2*INTMAX, 4];
// [1, INTMIN-1], [-1, 2*INTMIN]; [0, INTMAX+1], [5, 2*INTMAX+1].
public class Type0TestsForAverageOfTwoNumbersInvalidPartitionsOutOfBound () {
    public static final int INTMAX = Integer.MAX_VALUE;
    public static final int INTMIN = Integer.MIN_VALUE;
    @Test
    public void testAverageOfTwoNumbersInvalidValuesINTMINminusOneAndZero() {
        assertThrows(ArithmaticException.class, () -> {
            AverageOfTwoNumbers(INTMIN-1, 0);
        });
    }
    @Test
    public void testAverageOfTwoNumbersInvalidValuesINTMINtimesTwoAndMinusTwo() {
        assertThrows(ArithmaticException.class, () -> {
            AverageOfTwoNumbers(INTMIN*2, -2);
        });
    }
    @Test
    public void testAverageOfTwoNumbersInvalidValuesINTMAXplusOneAndOne() {
        assertThrows(ArithmaticException.class, () -> {
            AverageOfTwoNumbers(INTMAX+1, 1);
        });
    }
    @Test
    public void testAverageOfTwoNumbersInvalidValuesINTMAXtimesTwoAndFour() {
        assertThrows(ArithmaticException.class, () -> {
            AverageOfTwoNumbers(INTMAX*2, 4);
        });
    }
    @Test
    public void testAverageOfTwoNumbersInvalidValuesOneAndINTMINminusOne() {
        assertThrows(ArithmaticException.class, () -> {
            AverageOfTwoNumbers(1, INTMIN-1);
        });
    }
    @Test
    public void testAverageOfTwoNumbersInvalidValuesMinusOneAndINTMINtimesTwo() {
        assertThrows(ArithmaticException.class, () -> {
            AverageOfTwoNumbers(-1, INTMIN*2);
        });
    }
    @Test
    public void testAverageOfTwoNumbersInvalidValuesZeroAndINTMAXplusOne() {
        assertThrows(ArithmaticException.class, () -> {
            AverageOfTwoNumbers(0, INTMAX+1);
        });
    }
    @Test
    public void testAverageOfTwoNumbersInvalidValueFiveAndTwoTimesINTMAXplusOne() {
        assertThrows(ArithmaticException.class, () -> {
            AverageOfTwoNumbers(5, INTMAX*2+1);
        });
    }
}
```

Code Segment 9.7: Implementation of unit tests for Example 9.2 invalid zones (1)

```java
// Unit tests for invalid partitions (vi), (vii).
// input values: [-10, 2.5], [100, -20.00]; ["abc", 25], ["", 1].

public class Type0TestsForAverageOfTwoNumbersInvalidPartitionsRealValuesAndStrings ()
{
    public static final int INTMAX = Integer.MAX_VALUE;
    public static final int INTMIN = Integer.MIN_VALUE;

    @Test
    public void testAverageOfTwoNumbersInvalidValuesMinusTenAndTwoPointFive() {
        assertThrows(NumberFormatException.class, () -> {
            AverageOfTwoNumbers(-10, 2.5);
        });
    }

    @Test
    public void testAverageOfTwoNumbersInvalidValuesOneHundredAndMinusTwentyPoint() {
        assertThrows(NumberFormatException.class, () -> {
            AverageOfTwoNumbers(100, -20.00);
        });
    }

    @Test
    public void testAverageOfTwoNumbersInvalidValuesStringABCandTwentyFive() {
        assertThrows(NumberFormatException.class, () -> {
            AverageOfTwoNumbers("abc", 25);
        });
    }

    @Test
    public void testAverageOfTwoNumbersInvalidValuesEmptyStringAndOne () {
        assertThrows(NumberFormatException.class, () -> {
            AverageOfTwoNumbers("", 1);
        });
    }
}
```

Code Segment 9.8: Implementation of unit tests for Example 9.2 invalid zones (2)

In the tests, `assertThrows()` asserts that execution of the supplied executable throws an exception of the expected type and returns the exception. If no exception is thrown, or if an exception of a different type is thrown, this method will fail.

For example, `testAverageOfTwoNumbersInvalidValuesStringABCandTwentyFive()`, the test for input vector ["abc', 25], will pass if a `NumberFormatException` is returned by executing `AverageOfTwoNumbers("abc", 25)`.

Each method with annotation `@Test` is one test. There is only one assertion in each test, which satisfies that each test is atomic. These tests can be executed in any order, they are independent of each other.

Let's take another example to illustrate how to assert on exception messages.

Example 9.3: A Set Address Method

Code segment 9.9 is a method to set address in class "Order", the address is a string with a length between 8 and 50 characters inclusive.

Input values to select for testing can be easily generated using the equivalence partitioning technique, we leave it as an exercise, and for now, we are trying to write tests to handle the three exception conditions that appeared in the code segment with three input vectors: { *[empty string]*, *[a string with length less than 8]*, *[a string with length larger than 50]* }.

```java
public class Order {
  private String address;
  public void setAddress (String address) {
    if (address == null) {
      throw new IllegalArgumentException("Address cannot be empty.");
    } else {
      if (address.length() < 8) {
        throw new IllegalArgumentException("Address is too short.");
      } else if (address.length() > 50) {
        throw new IllegalArgumentException("Address is too long.");
      }
    }
    this.address = address;
  }
}
```

Code Segment 9.9: Java implementation for Example 9.3: a set address method

The following code segment shows the implementations of the three tests.

```java
public class Type0TestsForOrderSetAddressMethod () {
  @Test
  public void testOrderSetAddressAddressIsNull() {
    Throwable exception = assertThrows(IllegalArgumentException.class, () -> {
      Order order = new Order();
      Order.setAddress(null);
    });
    assertEquals("Address cannot be empty.", exception.getMessage());
  }
  @Test
  public void testOrderSetAddressAddressIsTooShort() {
    Throwable exception = assertThrows(IllegalArgumentException.class, () -> {
      Order order = new Order();
      Order.setAddress("One St");
    });
    assertEquals("Address is too short.", exception.getMessage());
  }
  @Test
  public void testOrderSetAddressAddressIsTooLong() {
    Throwable exception = assertThrows(IllegalArgumentException.class, () -> {
      Order order = new Order();
      Order.setAddress("1234567890 Abcdefghijklmnopqrsunvxyz St, San Jose, CA");
    });
    assertEquals("Address is too long.", exception.getMessage());
  }
}
```

Code Segment 9.10: Java implementation of unit tests for Example 9.3

The error message is retrieved from the returned exception and can be asserted (optional) using `assertEquals()` as seen in the above examples.

Note, in the above examples JUnit 5 is used to demonstrate how to write the tests. For implementation using other versions of JUnit or other testing frameworks please refer to other resources, the examples here are only to help readers to learn how to apply the testing techniques and principles presented in the book and to learn more on the nature of type 0 tests.

9.3 DEPENDENCIES AND CODING PRACTICES

Commonly, a method in a class needs to interact with members or instances of other classes. In certain cases, the other dependencies are external resources such as file systems, databases, and web services. Given the requirement that unit tests should be executed fast, and be isolated from external resources, several techniques are developed to simulate dependencies.

Before introducing these techniques, let's discuss how the process of unit test design can help on product code design, particularly to reduce dependencies (and leave the testing of the dependencies to integration testing).

Example 9.4: A Customer Can Review Method

The following code segment shows a method in a class to determine if a customer can write reviews depending on a customer ranking value that needs to be retrieved from a database via a method in `TableRecord` class.

```java
public boolean customerCanWriteReview (int customer_id) {
    TableRecord tr = new TableRecord("customer");
    int customerRanking = tr.getCustomerRanking (customer_id);
    if (customerRanking >= 2) {
        return true;
    }
    return false;
}
```

Code Segment 9.11: Java method `customerCanWriteReview()`

This method requires a database connection through a `TableRecord` instance (`tr`) to perform its operations. To test this method, a database connection is required.

Now let's ask, what aspects of the method need to be tested? The only logic in the method is in the *'if'* clause (`if (customerRanking >= 2)`) and `customerRanking` is the only parameter or input vector relevant to the logic.

So, to test this method we will need to generate test cases with various input values for `customerRanking`, but these values have nothing to do with the values of `customer_id`, which is just an identifier for a record in the `customer` table.

In other words, the logic in the method only depends on an integer value for `customerRanking`, and it does not depend on a database connection. Therefore, this dependence should be removed from this method.

The method shown in the following code segment is a refactoring by removing the database dependence, with input parameter `customerRanking` rather than `customer_id`.

```java
public boolean customerCanWriteReview (int customerRanking) {
    if (customerRanking >= 2) {
        return true;
    }
    return false;
}
```

Code Segment 9.12: Refactoring Java method `customerCanWriteReview()`

To get `customerRanking` data sure a database connection is required, but that's the task of the object whoever calls this `customerCanWriteReview()` method, and that part of the code is in the caller method or class.

Now the `customerCanWriteReview` method can be tested easily without any dependencies.

For a method that does have dependencies on external resources, to satisfy that unit tests should be isolated, be fast, and should be run even before the external resources are available, simulations of real resources are needed.

For example, in an e-commerce application, a method in a class in the implementation needs to communicate with a payment provider such as a credit card service, unit tests for the method would be impossible. Also, a test that depends on an external service can become non-deterministic (for example, the service is not available). In this case, mocking of the payment service is required for unit tests.

There are two major techniques to simulate external resources, one is stubbing, and the other is mocking, to deal with different situations by creating objects that simulate the behaviors of real objects in unit tests. Sometimes we can use mocking to refer to both of the techniques and treat stubbing as a special case of mocking. Let's talk about stubbing and mocking in the next two sections.

9.4 STUBBING

Stubbing is to create objects, called stubs, to hold predefined data that need to be obtained from external resources otherwise, and use the data to test the logic in the method or the component.

It's easy to understand with a simple input value needed as in Example 9.4 (Code Segment 9.11). In this example, to test `customerCanWriteReview()`, A `customerRanking` value is needed which resides in the database, but the logic in this method only depends on an integer value of `customerRanking`, it does not matter which customer has the value. Therefore, we can just define a `customerRanking` value to test the logic in the method without getting the value from the database.

Let's look at another example.

Example 9.5: User's Name from a Web Service

In the implementation of an application, a class is defined to handle users' names. A user's name is obtained from a web service based on a user ID. After a name is returned from the web service certain manipulations are done before returning the name.

Code Segment 9.13 is a sample Java implementation of this class.

Method `findUserName()` is the one to be tested, it calls the web service through method `getUserNameFromWebService()` via `getUserName()` from a `DataWebService` object that is a private member of the class.

To simulate the web service call, a stub can be created to overshadow the method. The call to the web service is done through `getUserName(user_id)` method from an object in class `DataWebService`, so we need to create a new class (stub class) to implement the `DataWebService` class, and in the new class, the method `getUserName(user_id)` is defined to just return a fixed value (regardless of the value of `user_id`). A sample implementation is shown in Code Segment 9.14.

In the testing implementation, a `StubDataWebService` object is used in the object under test. A sample test implementation is shown in Code Segment 9.15.

```java
public class UserNameService {
   private final DataWebService dataservice;

   public UserName findUserName (int user_id) {
      UserName user = getUserNameFromWebService (user_id);
      UserName userchecked = checkUserName (user);
      return userchecked;
   }
   public UserName getUserNameFromWebService (int user_id) {
      UserName username = dataservice.getUserName (user_id);
      return username;
   }
   public UserName checkUserName (UserName user) {
      UserName username;
      if ( (isNullUser (user) ) {
         username = UserName.INVALID_NAME;
      }
      // some other manipulation
      else if ( … ) {
      // …
      }
      else {
         username = UserName.setUserName(user);
      }
      return username;
   }
   public void setDataWebService (DataWebService dataservice){
      this.dataservice = dataservice;
   }
   public boolean isNullUser (UserName user) {
      return user == null;
   }
}
```

Code Segment 9.13: Java implementation of class `UserNameService`

```java
public class StubDataWebService implements DataWebService {
   private final UserName username;

   public StubDataWebService (UserName username) {
       this.username = username;
   }
   @Override
   public UserName getUserName (int user_id) {
      return username;
   }
}
```

Code Segment 9.14: Stub class for example 9.5

```java
public class UserNameServiceTestWithStub {

    private UserNameService usernameservice;

    @Before
    public void setUp () throws Exception {
        // create the object to test
        usernameservice = new UserNameService();
    }

    @Test
    public void testFindUserNameWithStub () {
        // setup test data
        UserName user = new UserName (1, "JJ", "", "Shen");
        Usernameservice.setDataWebService (new StubDataWebService (user));
        // call the method under test
        UserName result = usernameservice.findUserName(1);
        // assert the result
        assertEquals(user.getID, result.getID);
        assertEquals(user.getFirstName, result.getFirstName);
        assertEquals(user.getMiddleName, result.getMiddleName);
        assertEquals(user.getLastName, result.getLastName);
    }

    @After
    public void teardown() {
    }
}
```

Code Segment 9.15: A type 0 test with a stub for Example 9.5

In the above code segment, the constructor for UserName takes four parameters, user ID, first name, middle name, and last name.

The method checkUserName() which is called in the method under test (findUserName()) can be unit tested separately (remember modularization principle) without stubbing since it only depends on a user name value which can be generated manually from the category partitioning technique for example.

Examine the method under test findUserName(). It has one call to the web service, and then a call to another method checkUserName() where the business logic resides, there is no logic in the method under test. We followed good coding practice as discussed in Section 9.3 in the implementation by putting the logic into a separate method checkUserName() rather than in findUserName() itself, and eliminated the web service dependency in the method with logic. So we can argue that unit testing for method findUserName() is not needed, therefore, stubbing is not needed. We see that with good coding practice, stubbing is less relevant.

Another benefit of stubbing is to simulate a wide variety of responses that may not be available from an external service to exercise all the code paths or satisfy all the test requirements. But this is more useful in integration testing than in type 0 testing. For example, if a 3rd party service (such as a payment service) is required and there is no control on what data the service may provide during testing, then stubbing is an easy way to get around it.

9.5 MOCKING

Mocking is to create 'fake' objects that simulate the behaviors of real objects that are the dependences of the object under test. Often objects of all other classes that interact with objects of the class under test are mocked.

In a stub, only predefined data are assigned to a stub object, but in a mock object, behaviors of calling a method are to be verified, by imitating the method call without invoking the actual actions of the dependent object.

For example, there is a method to send messages to a user account through another service. To avoid sending actual messages through the service (over and over again), a mock object can be created in which sending the message is configured to do nothing when it's called, and all we need to verify is that the message sending method gets called through the mocked object.

Let's look at an example to illustrate how this works.

Example 9.6: User's Address Updates

The following interface represents a database connection, and the method `setAddress()` sets the address of a user represented by user_id.

```java
public interface DatabaseInterface {
    public void setAddress (int user_id, String address);
}
```

Code Segment 9.16: Java code for `DatabaseInterface` for Example 9.6

The class `UserAddressUpdateService` sets the address into the database using `DatabaseInterface` by calling the `setAddress()` method in the interface, as shown in the next code segment.

The goal is to test method `UpdateUserAddress()` by verifying that `dbaccess.setAddress()` is called (given a new address for a user, the new address is inserted in the database table, but how the data is inserted is not a concern).

CHAPTER 9: UNIT TESTING (TYPE 0 TESTS)

```java
public class UserAddressUpdateService {
   private final DatabaseInterface dbaccess;
   public UserAddressUpdateService (DatabaseInterface dbaccess) {
      this.dbaccess = dbaccess;
   }
   public void UpdateUserAddress (int user_id, String address) {
      if ((address == null) || address.length() == 0 ) )) {
         // error message here
      }
      else {
         dbaccess.setAddress (user_id, address);
      }
   }
}
```

Code Segment 9.17: Java class `UserAddressUpdateService` for Example 9.6

To test `UpdateUserAddress()` without a database, we'll have to mock the database interface, by implementing `DatabaseInterface`, as shown in the following code segment.

```java
public class MockDatabaseInterface implement DatabaseInterface {
   int flag = 0;
   public void setAddress (int user_id, String address) {
      flag = 1;
   }
   public int getFlagValue () {
      return flag;
   }
}
```

Code Segment 9.18: Database interface mocking for Example 9.6

`MockDatabaseInterface` implements the public interface `DatabaseInterface`, so it can be used wherever the interface is used. The method in the mock class does nothing but set a flag, so in the test, if the flag is set as specified in the mocked method, then we know that the method gets called.

Code segment 9.19 shows a test using the mocked database interface to verify `dbaccess.setAddress (user_id, address)` is called in method `UpdateUserAddress()` in class `UserAddressUpdateService`.

In this test, an instance of `MockDatabaseInterface` is created and is used to construct a `UserAddressUpdateService` object, and then the `UserAddressUpdateService` method `UpdateUserAddress()` is called. The success of the test depends on the result of the mock object's method `getFlagValue()`. If the mock is in the expected state, that is, if the flag is set to 1, then the test passes. The mock object verifies that UserAddressUpdateService interacts with it correctly per the implementation of the method UpdateUserAddress() in UserAddressUpdateService.

With the mock, an actual database is not needed to test the method.

```
@Test
public void testUpdateUserAddressWithMock () {
    MockDatabaseInterface mockdbi = new MockDatabaseInterface();
    UserAddressUpdateService uaus = new UserAddressUpdateService (mockdbi);
    // a new address record is created with user_id = 1:
    uaus.UpdateUserAddress (1, "101 Main St, San Jose, CA");
    // assert the flag is set to 1:
    assertEquals(1, mockdbi.getFlagValue() );
}
```

Code Segment 9.19: A type 0 test using a mock for Example 9.6

The mock in the above example only set a flag so the calling of the method can be verified. More complicated mocks can be implemented depends on the situation to verify the state changes of the method under test.

Note, in the above examples, stubs and mocks are created manually. In a mocking framework such as Mockito, various APIs and utilities are developed to assist in creating stubs and mock objects and on the testing. We will not cover any of the frameworks here, there are plenty of good resources online and in other specialized books.

Although mocking is a powerful technique to write unit tests, but there are drawbacks with it such as the overhead with it. So, don't overuse it, if you can't write unit tests for a module without mocking, wait to write integration tests (type 1 tests).

The mocking technique can also be used in type 1 integration testing to a certain extent for the same reason of avoiding interactions with other resources.

EXERCISE PROBLEMS:

P9.1: Seasons of The Year

The following code segment is a Java implementation of a getSeason() method, generate test cases using any technique, and write automated unit tests (in any testing framework or language you prefer).

```java
public static String getSeason (int month) {
    switch(month) {
        case 12:
        case 1:
        case 2:
            return "Winter";
        case 3:
        case 4:
        case 5:
            return "Spring";
        case 6:
        case 7:
        case 8:
            return "Summer";
        case 9:
        case 10:
        case 11:
            return "Autumn";
        default:
            throw new IllegalArgumentException("A month is a number from
                                    1 to 12.");
    }
}
```

P9.2: Right Triangle

The following code segment is a Java implementation of a method to check if a triangle with three integer sides is a right triangle. Generate test cases using any technique discussed in part 2 of the book and write automated unit tests.

```java
public static boolean isRightTriangle (int a, int b, int c) {
    if ( (a<=0) || (b<=0) || (c<=0) ) {
        System.out.println ("All sides are positive numbers.");
        return false;
    }
    return (Math.pow(a, 2) + Math.pow(b, 2) == Math.pow(c, 2)) ||
           (Math.pow(a, 2) + Math.pow(c, 2) == Math.pow(b, 2)) ||
           (Math.pow(c, 2) + Math.pow(b, 2) == Math.pow(a, 2));
}
```

P9.3: Prime Numbers

The following code segment is a Java implementation of a method to check if a number is a prime number, generate test cases with equivalence partitioning technique, and write automated unit tests. Sub-partitioning, 2nd level partitions within a partition, should be considered in certain partitions. Any other concerns?

```
public static boolean isPrimeNumber (int n) {
  if (n <= 1)
    return false;
  for (int i = 2; i < Math.sqrt(n); i++) {
    if (n % i == 0)
      return false;
  }
  return true;
}
```

P9.4: Bank Account Balance Updates

The following code segment shows a bank account update method that takes a customer ID and a deposit amount and updates the total balance in the database. The DatabaseInterface interface is defined with two methods, one to get the current balance, and the other to update the balance.

```
public class BalanceUpdateService {
  private final DatabaseInterface dbaccess;
  public BalanceUpdateService (DatabaseInterface dbaccess) {
    this.dbaccess = dbaccess;
  }
  public void UpdateAccountBalance (int customer_id, float deposit) {
    if ((deposit <= 0.0) || customer_id <= 0)) {
      // error message here
    }
    else {
      float balance = dbaccess.getBalance (customer_id);
      dbaccess.updateBalance (customer_id, balance + deposit);
    }
  }
}
```

```
public interface DatabaseInterface {
  public float getBalance (int customer_id);
  public void updateBalance (int customer_id, float deposit);
}
```

Write unit tests using mocking and stubbing techniques for test cases with valid input vectors (in the valid partition).

10 INTEGRATION TESTING (TYPE 1 TESTS)

We elaborate more on type 1 tests in this chapter. In Chapter 2, we defined type 1 tests as tests that verify the functionalities of the software application and the integration of various pieces of the software working together as a whole. Integration with components or services outside the application itself is also part of type 1 testing since those components or services contribute to the functionalities of the application under test. We will demonstrate how to use the testing techniques and principles we have learned to generate integration test cases, and how to handle integrations with external services.

The goal of this chapter is to introduce the basic concepts and principles. If you wish to dive in further for technical details in certain areas such as how to use a mocking framework for integration testing, refer to other resources.

10.1 INTEGRATION TESTS AND FUNCTIONAL TESTS

Integration testing is to test the behaviors of a group of modules working together. Ideally, the individual modules or units have been tested with type 0 unit tests, and the next step would be to test the module-combined application system. The goal of integration testing is to test the interactions between individual modules.

For a complex software system, the number of individual modules or units can be quite large, and a strategy for module grouping is needed. Layered grouping is one. In these situations, 2nd level grouping (grouping of integration tested module groups) is performed, and higher-level grouping may also be needed until all modules and groups are integrated and tested.

Functional testing is to test the functionalities of the application from the perspective of the functional requirements and the intended usage of the application. Some functionalities can be achieved with a limited number of modules, these functionalities can be tested with only the relevant modules integrated. In practice, most of the time functional testing is performed with all the modules running together. From this point of view, functional testing is a subset of integration testing.

A subset of functional testing is called **end-to-end testing**, in which the workflow behaviors of the application from start to finish are verified when all the components are integrated together.

The relationship between integration testing and functional testing is illustrated in Figure 10.1. The darker triangle to the right on the graph shows the areas of functional testing, whereas the whole rectangle represents the integration testing domain. The graph is only an illustration to demonstrate the concept, and it's not on scale, since the scope (or a number of test cases) of functional testing relative to the whole domain of integration testing is case-specific. On the graph, functional testing is on the far side of the spectrum where the majority of modules are integrated together.

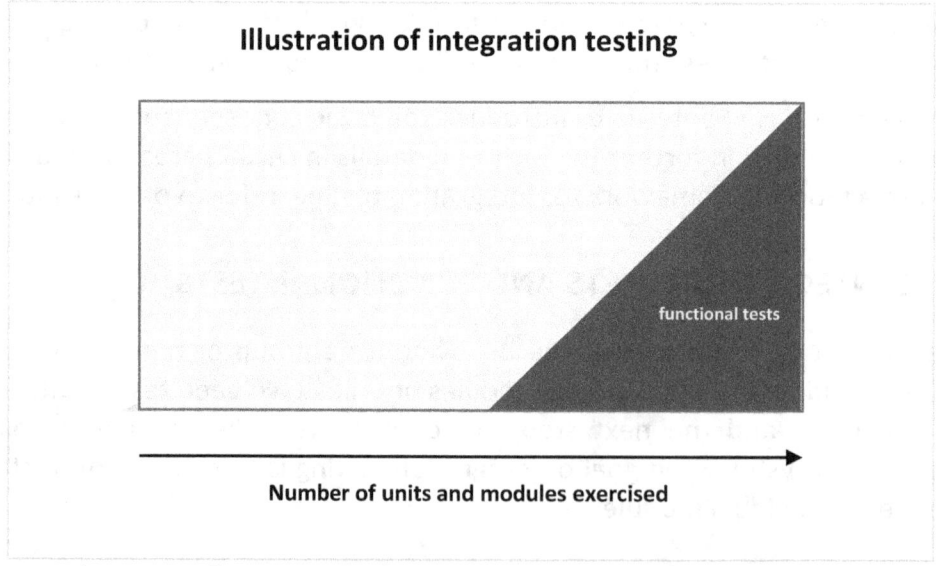

Figure 10.1: Illustration of integration testing and functional testing

While unit testing is done by developers along with the development process, type 1 integration testing and functional testing are the ones that the majority of quality engineers spend their time with. A large portion of automated integration testing is also being written by software developers in practice.

When generating test cases for integration testing, the main focus is on the interfaces between the modules and data transfer between them. When all modules are put together the focus can be shifted to the functionality side and therefore test cases can be generated based on use case categories and business scenarios.

10.2 INTEGRATION TESTING APPROACHES

Several types of integration testing approaches are widely been talked about, namely bottom-up, top-down, mixed (sandwich), and big-bang techniques.

The ***bottom-up approach*** is following the hierarchical modularization principle we have discussed in Chapter 7, where the lowest level modules are tested first, then related modules form a cluster, a higher-level component. The higher-level components are then tested accordingly. The process is then repeated until the clusters of components at the top of the hierarchy are tested.

The ***top-down approach*** is to test the topmost integrated components first, and then the module tree is traversed and the modules at every level are tested one by one until the leaf level of the related modules.

The ideas behind both bottom-up and top-down approaches are illustrated in Figure 10.2.

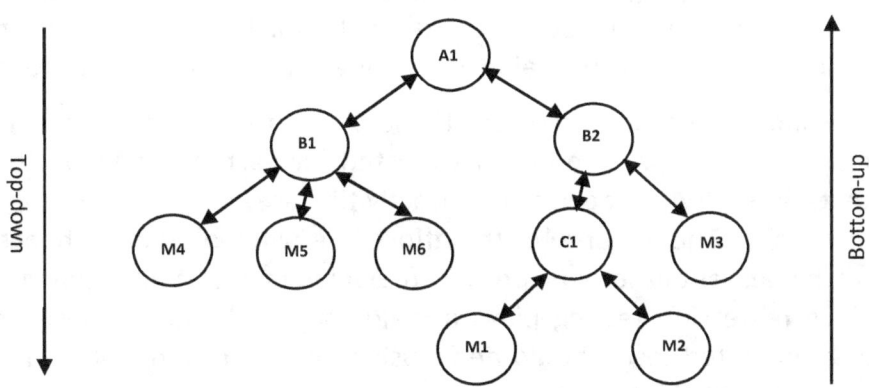

Figure 10.2: Illustration of top-down and bottom-up integration testing approaches

On the above graph, the modules at the bottom of the tree (leaf nodes) M1, M2, M3, M4, M5, and M6 should have been tested with type 0 tests.

For the **bottom-up integration testing approach**, the sequence of integration testing is as following:

1) M1, M2; M4, M5, M6
2) C1, M3
3) B1, B2
4) A1

The branching of the tree also provides a natural way to organize the tests, as we have learned from the modularization principle. In the 1st line in the above list, integration of M1 and M2 is one group, and integration of M4, M5, and M6 is another unrelated group.

For the **top-down integration testing approach**, the sequence of integration testing would be:

1) A1
2) B1, B2
3) C1, M3
4) M1, M2; M4, M5, M6

The **sandwich approach** is to combine bottom-up testing with top-down testing, and the testing starts on both the head of the module tree and the leaves of the tree and ends at some middle nodes.

The **big-bang approach** is to test the application as a whole with all modules working together.

We are not discussing these approaches in greater detail, there are tons of resources online and in other books on them. Besides, not all of these approaches are always applicable in practice, for the reasons that follow.

These approaches are discussed more in the context of software development, and pros and cons are listed for each approach in the same context. But software development activities are not just new application development. The majority of the efforts are with software enhancements and with releases of the same product (newer versions) in an ongoing manner, in which regression testing plays a major part. Therefore, designing and writing integrated tests should be focusing on integration testing as a long-term investment.

With integration testing in mind, a hierarchical modularization approach (bottom-up) should be applied. The big-bang approach is just one part of the testing strategy, where end-to-end functional testing is performed.

An example is given in the next section to demonstrate how integration testing is approached in practice.

10.3 TEST CASE GENERATION STRATEGIES

Let's use an example to demonstrate how to categorize integration tests and generate test cases.

Example 10.1: An Online Shopping Site

Take an example of an online shopping site. Let's assume type 0 unit testing was done on the following individual modules:

   (1) User Login
   (2) Product Catalog
   (3) Product Review
   (4) Shopping Cart
   (5) Billing
   (6) Payment
   (7) Shipping

The next step naturally is to test how each module interacts with other modules, the tasks of integration testing.

What are the integration points? How do we approach the testing? Again, the testing principles and techniques come into play.

In theory, all combinations of the modules should be included in the testing, from pairwise to t-wise, where t is the number of modules. For example, for integrations with Billing, all the rest 7 modules should be included one by one, two by two, and so on. Obviously, the amount of testing effort is impractical to include all the permutations. So, in this example, we choose to test pairwise and three-wise cases.

Furthermore, we have certain knowledge that certain modules are closely coupled together, while other modules have no direct interactions with each other. Therefore, we will eliminate certain combinations based on knowledge of the application architecture.

There are only 7 modules (super-modules) In this example. If the module count is much larger, the hierarchical modularization principle should be applied to separate the modules into clusters for closely associated modules, and then the interactions between cluster modules are handled accordingly at 2nd or higher levels.

Now back to our example, for pairwise testing, the total number of pairs, from equation (2-6), is $C(7,2) = 24$. This is way too large a number and needs to be reduced based on the knowledge of the application. For example, 'Shopping cart' interacts with 'User login', but there is hardly any interaction between 'Product Review' and 'Payment', therefore the latter pair can be removed from integration testing.

The selected 10 pairs are listed in Table 10.1. Pair 1 is [User Authentication, Product Catalog], and so on.

	1	2	3	4	5	6	7	8	9	10
User Authentication	x	x	x	x	x	x				
Product Catalog	x						x			
Product Review		x					x			
Shopping Cart			x					x		
Billing				x				x	x	
Payment					x				x	x
Shipping						x				x

Table 10.1: Module pairs to be included in integration testing for Example 10.1

Similarly, the selected 3-wise items are listed in Table 10.2.

	11	12	13
User Authentication	x	x	x
Product Catalog	x		
Product Review			
Shopping Cart	x	x	
Billing			x
Payment		x	
Shipping			x

Table 10.2: Module triples to be included in integration testing for Example 10.1

Test cases are then generated for each of the 13 categories listed in the above two tables.

Besides pairwise and 3-wise cases, we will also need to include cases with all 7 modules integrated together. The test cases for these can be generated from a functional testing perspective, that is, to exercise use cases and business scenarios.

You may ask why we bother to include module pairs and triples if we have to test with all 7 modules integrated together?

There are several reasons. Firstly, integration between individual modules should be tested thoroughly, and its less likely to cover all required scenarios if only perform testing with all modules integrated together; secondly, it's more expensive to pin down and resolve the issue if a defect is found when all modules are running together; thirdly, since integration testing should be part of the regression testing suite running continuously during product release cycles, a better testing coverage with a smaller number of modules integrated should be preferred.

Now let's try to generate test cases for some of the module combination categories.

Take [User Authentication, Shopping Cart] integration as an example. The following test scenarios demonstrate the interactions between these two modules:

(1) For a valid user, verify that there is a shopping cart associate with the user.
(2) If an item is added to a shopping cart that is not associated with a user, a user is then logged on in the same session, verify that the item is added to this user's shopping cart.

If these two tests are performed on the web UI, then they can be written as:

(1) Sign in with a valid user, verify that a shopping cart icon is seen and clickable.
(2) Go to the website without login, add an item to the shopping cart, then sign in with a user on the same browser window, verify that the item is added to this user's shopping cart (item count increased by 1, and the list view of the shopping cart shows the added item along with others if there is any).

If writing automated tests for these integration cases, non-UI automation is preferred from UI test automation, since UI automated tests are much slower to run and there can be more runtime issues. Also, certain test cases, if performed on the UI, maybe just exercising the relevant UI components. For example, the 1st case in the above list, "Sign in with a valid user, verify that a shopping cart icon is seen and clickable.", the integration of the two modules in the backend framework may be working, but there may be issues with UI rendering of the shopping cart element (which should be part of UI integration testing).

Note, there is no need to repeat all scenarios which are already covered by unit testing. For example, to verify how many items a shopping cart can hold. If the equivalence partitioning technique was used to generate test cases for the unit tests, a list of item numbers should have been selected for testing, such as the numbers in set { -1, 0, 1, 50, 10000, ...}. These test cases are not to be repeated with integration testing.

Stubbing and mocking techniques can be applied in integration testing if necessary. The same testing framework used in unit testing, such as JUnit, can be used for integration testing.

We will skip generating test cases for the rest of the module combinations but discuss the next level of integrations.

The shopping site has a web interface, and the web interface connects to a back end database via the framework we have just discussed above, and there are other outside resources needed for the site to work, namely a payment service to handle various types of payments such as credit card, and a catalog service for product catalog updates.

The following plot shows the high-level architecture.

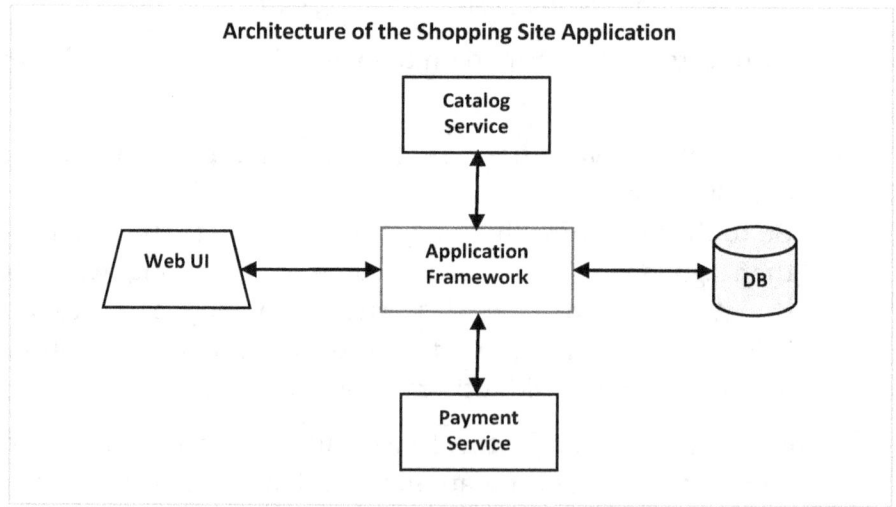

Figure 10.3: Application architecture illustration

The web UI itself also consists of individual units or modules and should be tested with both type 0 unit tests and type 1 integration tests. Again, we are skipping that part of the discussion here.

The next step is to test integration with the higher-level components. The integration points are listed in Table 10.3.

The integration between the application framework and the database is essential since the database is a key component for the application. This integration may already have been covered during integration testing of the modules in the application framework.

For integration testing with databases, it's better to use a real database (e.g. in [User Authentication, Shopping Cart]) rather than use any kind of mocking techniques.

	1	2	3	4
Web UI	x			
Application Framework	x	x	x	x
Catalog Service		x		
Payment Service			x	
Database				x

Table 10.3: Integration points with both database and external services

Integration of the Web UI and the application framework should include testing of proper API calls from the UI, and data flow between the UI and the framework. For example, test cases to verify if the data entered on the UI are properly received and interpreted by the framework, and if the data returned from the framework are presented on the UI properly.

The payment service is a third-party service that we have no control on, and the catalog service is internal but is controlled by other teams, which we have no control over either.

There are several options to test integration with a third-party service. 1st, to have an account on the third-party production service. But the problem is that the actions you can take may be limited, and there may be unwanted side effects. For example, if you use a real credit card account for your testing, you will get charged. 2nd, if the external service provides a testing environment, then you can perform the integration testing without the drawback of production service. But these kinds of external services are rarely available.

The 3rd option is mocking. Since the goal of the testing is to verify if the application under test communicates with the external service properly and if the responses from the external service are processed properly. Whether or not the external service works as specified is not a concern for our purpose, therefore it's fine to use a mock for an external service, to return predefined results.

This kind of mocking can be achieved by running a local mock server. Stubs are created to define the data with the mock server, and responses based on the predefined data and criteria are returned for assertions in the tests.

There are many open-source frameworks for this. For example, WireMock for Java. Relevant resources on how to write tests with mock servers can be found easily online.

Similarly, for integration testing with an internal catalog service, mocking can be used.

The last step of the integration testing is to test the application with all modules integrated together. Most of the time this can be achieved by end-to-end functional testing. For end-to-end testing test case generation, testing technique such as control flow graph (a good example is with Example 6.11) for use cases can be used, as well as other techniques depending on the situation. For example, with the control flow graph technique, test cases around end-user workflow, from logging on to the site, browsing product catalog, adding items to the shopping cart, adding payment and shipping information, to submitting an order, are to be generated.

After all the integration test cases are executed, a real external service may be needed to execute certain tests (in a much smaller scope than the integration tests with the mock) before product release, in a staging environment, or a pre-prod environment. These tests are release-based and are not bound to the development process where integration testing is constantly performed as part of regression testing.

10.4 TEST DATA DESIGN

Testing data are needed for integration testing. Each integration at a certain hierarchical level may require specific data for the particular integration. A common set of data can be used for all levels and end-to-end testing. We presented a few plots in Chapter 7 (Figures 7.1, 7.2, and 7.3) when introducing the hierarchical finite state machine model, and data creations were illustrated on those plots as well.

In Example 10.1 from the last section, common testing data would include:

(1) User accounts for testing.
(2) Product catalog items.
(3) Product reviews from some users.
(4) Shopping carts with different items for some users.
(5) Billing information for some users.
(6) Shipping information for some users.

Data artifacts are also being created on the fly with some of the integration tests, for example, to add/modify billing information. As we have discussed in Chapter 7, independency principle requires that tests won't interfere with each other, therefore, any data artifacts produced from a test or a set of tests in the same test class should be cleaned at the end of the test or the end of the set.

For example, if a new item is added to a user's shopping cart in a test, at the end of the test, the added item should be removed from the shopping cart, as there may be another test depending on the initial state of the shopping cart with the initial items. An alternative approach would be to create its own testing data for a test to avoid dependencies on the general sample data.

For a large application, general sample data set is often provided in the system, also referred to as demo data or seed data. If the system can be easily started from scratch (be built or booted), then the sample data can be loaded after the build, then the freshly started system can be used to run the integration tests. The demo data can be used for certain integration tests, and also for manual sanity checking or exploratory testing during the release cycles.

If the data for the application are all stored in the database, the general testing data can be loaded from a database dump. Test-specific data can be generated via a database API if available.

If an application or a system cannot be booted from scratch, then proper strategies need to be developed for testing data. A bigdata system is an example, in which non-relational databases are used that adding another factor to the complexity of the testing. We are not going to dig further with it in this book, but to note that a proper approach can be designed by applying the basic techniques and principles we have discussed.

Let's take another example.

Example 10.2: Content Visibility on A Social Networking Website

The feature under test is user content visibility on a social network website.

User content visibility refers to what other users' content, profiles, photos, posts, etc., can be viewed by a specific user. A user has connected friends, has 2nd level friends (friends of connected friends), and 3rd level friends, and so on.

The privacy control is achieved by user-specific configuration. For example, one can configure to allow everyone else to see his/her profile. There is a default setting for privacy control. For example, if a new friend is connected to you, the new friend can see all your posts by default.

This feature involves many lower-level modules. Let's assume that the integration of lower-level modules is already tested, and we are now performing end-to-end functional testing of the feature with all the relevant modules integrated together.

We'll need to create users and set relationships between the users for these integration tests.

The testing data are in the following categories:

    (1) Users.
    (2) Connectivity between the users.
    (3) User profile settings.
    (4) Users' contents: posts, photos, messages, etc.

There are other related features like groups, but we are skipping those in this example for simplicity.

The 1st thing to do is to create a set of users, let's give them names Abel, Bob, Carol, David, Ellen, Frank, and so on.

The 2nd part is to set connectivity between the users. Figure 10.2 illustrates a sample connectivity setting for the users, the names are shortened and are represented by the 1st letter in the names, A through M, on the graph.

A solid line between two users indicates that the two users are connected, dashed lines between A and G, A and C, E and C indicate that the two users are 2nd level connected (have a common connection B). The fine dashed line between G and F indicates a 3rd level connection, and the wiggled line between J and K indicates a 4th level connection. There are also 5th level connections, between H and M, for example, which are not marked on the graph.

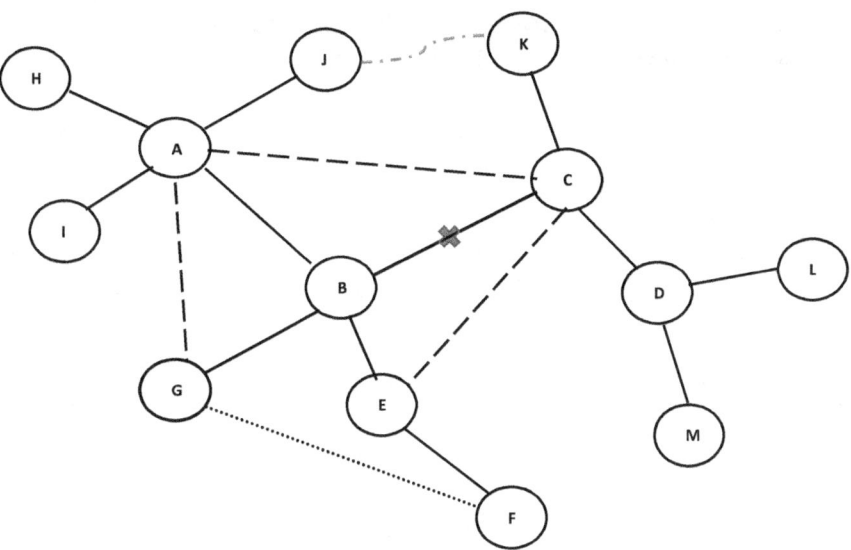

Figure 10.4: User connectivity graph for Example 10.2

User profiles are then created and configured differently for different users to test all the related functionalities. For example, user A can set that only 1st level connections can view his email address, and user C can set to allow 2nd level connections to view her email address.

Posts, photos, and other contents are created for the users with different privacy settings.

The integration testing test cases can be generated with category partitioning techniques, which would include tests in these categories:

(1) verify visibilities for different users according to user settings and connectivity levels.
(2) verify visibilities after configuration changes.
(3) verify visibilities after connectivity changes, such as break the connection between user B and user C, as shown by a cross on the graph in Figure 10.2, and add connections between certain users.
(4) add new users and connections, verify visibility changes.

Test cases can be generated for each of the above categories based on functional requirements. We are skipping the test case generation here.

Note again, after each test, the original state of the data should be restored. For example, if connectivity was broken in the test, the connectivity should be restored after the test, since other tests may depend on this connectivity.

As a final note, there are many open-source testing frameworks for integration testing and for UI testing (such as Selenium), which will not be covered here. Resources can be found elsewhere easily.

11 PERFORMANCE TESTING

Type 2 performance testing is covered in this chapter. Certain mathematical basics used in performance testing are presented first, followed by the discussion of performance requirements, and then common types of performance testing are classified. Processes, principles, and practices with performance testing are also discussed. Finally, one performance testing case study is presented.

11.1 MATHEMATICAL BASICS FOR PERFORMANCE TESTING

Performance testing is about collecting statistical data for performance metrics. Certain statistical concepts are essential to understand and analyze the data. We present here the basic mathematical concepts relevant to performance testing. You may skip the formulas and should still be able to understand the concepts. We start by defining a few terms, then discuss data distribution.

11.1.1 Statistical Terms

Average: Average or mean is just the sum of all the values in a set divided by the total number of items in the set. For example, given a set of integers: {2, 2, 5, 5, 7, 9}, the average is (2+2+5+5+7+9)/6 = 5.

Median: Median is the middle value of the data set when the data set is sorted. In the case of an even number of items in the set, the median is the average of the two center values. For example, in data set {2, 2, 5, 5, 7, 9}, since it consists even number of elements, the average of the two middle values is 5+5/2 = 5, therefore 5 is the median.

In certain cases, the median is a better measure than the average when the distribution of the data samples is irregular. For example, if there are outliers (defined below), as in this data set {2, 2, 5, 5, 7, 9, 30}, since there is an outlier with a value of 30, the average is 10, while the median is 5, the median is a better representation of the variant.

Percentile: Percentile is the value in a dataset below which a percentage of data samples fall. For example, 90% of data have a value below 60 in a data set, then 60 is the 90th percentile. The median divides the items into two equal parts, so the median is the 50th percentile. Percentile is a good indicator especially when the data distribution is irregular (e.g. not following common distributions such as normal distribution, or there are too many outliers).

For example, for a transaction on a web application, taking 100 samples for the response time, if 95 of them have a response time around 1 second, while the rest 5 of them have a response time of 25 secs, then the average response time is 2.2 secs, while the 95th percentile response time is 1 sec. 95th percentile is a better representation of the data sample in this case.

Normal Value: Normal value is the value that occurs most often in a dataset. For example, in set {3, 4, 4, 5, 6, 6, 6, 7, 10}, the value 6 appears most often, the normal value of the set is 6.

Standard Deviation: Standard deviation is a measure of the extent of deviation of samples from the average value, is a measure of the spread of data in a distribution. By definition, the standard deviation is:

$$ $$

(11-1)

where $(x_1, x_2, ..., x_N)$ is the set of sample values, $\bar{x}$ is the average and N is the total number of samples. s is always positive.

When individual values in the set are close to the mean, the standard deviation is smaller, when individual values are spread out far from the mean, the standard deviation is larger. Since the standard deviation is defined using the sample mean, it is a preferred measure of variation for symmetric distributions, such as normal distribution.

Let's take an example to calculate the standard deviation. Suppose a measurement of the time it takes for a person to commute from home to work is done for 5 days, and the numbers of minutes, one for each day, are in the set of {17, 20, 23, 21, 19}. The average time is (17+20+23+21+19)/5 = 20 minutes.

The standard deviation is:

$$s = \sqrt{[(17-20)^2 + (20-20)^2 + (23-20)^2 + (21-20)^2 + (19-20)^2]/(5-1)}$$
$$= \sqrt{[9+0+9+1+1]/4} = 2.24$$

Think time: Think time is the time spent between two actions on an application. Think time is simulated in performance testing, in which it can be a variable with a random number generator, for example, a random number of seconds in the range of [min, max] (e.g.: [1, 30] secs). A think time can also be set to a constant in testing or follow a specific distribution. Use real-time environment application logs as a reference, better still use bigdata analyses of real-time data if available, for accuracy.

Outliers: Outliers are atypical data that are infrequently observed, and do not seem to follow the distribution of the rest of the samples. Typically, any data that are outside, say, 99% percental, are considered outliers and can be dismissed. But if there is a cluster of data that are outliers, caution should be taken to determine if they are true outliers, by rerun the same tests for example.

11.1.2 Normal Distributions

If the events in a measurement of a variable happen randomly and are independent of each other, then the distribution of the values of the variable follows the normal distribution or Gaussian distribution.

Here are some examples of normal distribution.

(a) Measurements of a physical quantity follow the normal distribution.

For example, you are asked to measure the height of a tree multiple times, or a bunch of people is asked to measure the height of a tree. Say there are 15 measurements, the values are (in centimeters): 156, 154, 161, 159, 155, 155, 156, 157, 160, 158, 153, 156, 115, 156, and 148. Each measurement is independent of others, and the measurements are done randomly. All the values are dispersed around a mean value.

(b) Weight of newborn babies.

If you check the weight records of all newborn babies in a hospital (or all hospitals), then the weight follows the normal distribution, with an average value, and all the values are evenly distributed around it. The selection of babies is random, and a baby's weight is independent of any other baby. (same is true for the length of newborn babies).

(c) The time users spent on a website.

For a large sample pool, since each user is independent to other users (an example of a dependent group of users would the ones who are in a gathering and are asked to go to the website and do the same thing in the same period for example), and the time spent for each user is random since users are doing different things and are not correlated to each other.

The probability density of normal distribution is:

$$P(x) = \frac{1}{\sigma\sqrt{2\pi}} e^{-(x-\mu)^2/(2\sigma^2)} \tag{11-2}$$

The probability density function is the probability that the variable has the value x. In the above equation, μ is the mean (average) or expectation value, σ is the standard deviation.

From the density formula, the probability is highest at the average value ($x = \mu$), and is symmetric on both sides of the mean value. The graph in Figure 9.1 illustrates the density function.

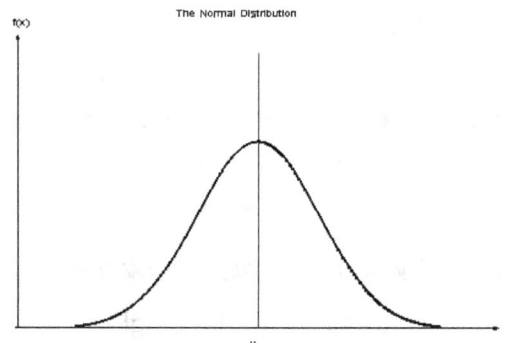

Figure 11.1: Normal distribution density

The probability of the samples that fall in a certain range can be calculated by the integral of the density function for the specified range:

$P([\mu - \sigma, \mu + \sigma])$ = 0.683
$P([\mu - 2\sigma, \mu + 2\sigma])$ = 0.954
$P([\mu - 3\sigma, \mu + 3\sigma])$ = 0.997

That is, the probability of the samples falling in the range of $[\mu - \sigma, \mu + \sigma]$ is 68%, and so on. We can see that 99.7% of the samples lie within the 3σ range, therefore, any value outside 3σ is normally considered an outlier.

The normal distribution is the most used model for performance analysis. Sometimes other distributions may be used, such as Poisson distribution, or logarithm normal distribution.

Given the complexity and non-symmetric nature of other distributions, using percentile as a middle ground is a good approach in those cases.

11.2 PERFORMANCE REQUIREMENT AND INDICATORS

Software performance requirements specify performance capabilities that a system must possess in terms of responsiveness and efficiency. Examples of such capabilities are response time, throughput, capacity, and dependability of the system. We will define the commonly used ones shortly.

Performance requirements are part of the business requirements, such as how many users the system can support, how many transactions the system can handle in a unit time, and to some extents are also part of usability requirements, such as how fast the system responses to user input.

The five major capacities or performance indicators are:
   (1) Response time
   (2) Throughput
   (3) Number of concurrent users
   (4) Resource usages
   (5) Scalability

Response times define how fast requests should be processed and results are returned. Acceptable response times should be defined in each particular case depending on the nature of the request. For example, a time of one second loading a specific web page is good but querying a database to return millions of rows of data could take longer. Response time also depends on the load on the system, so it is necessary to define conditions under which a specific response time should be achieved, for example, response time under average load or peak load.

For the same request or transaction, the response time may be different for different users or at a different time for the same user. Response time measurements often follow a specific distribution. The normal distribution is the most used one to model responses since it's the simplest one to work with, although a lot of times the deviation from a normal distribution is large.

Other distributions such as Poisson distribution, Erlang distribution, or log-normal distribution could also be used, depends on the nature of the variables under measurement.

For the normal distribution, average response time is usually used, with the specification of standard deviation. Another approach is to use average response time or meridian response time with percentiles, such as 50%, 75%, 90% percentiles.

Throughput is the rate at which incoming requests are completed. Throughput defines the load on the system and is measured in operations per unit time. For example, the number of transactions per second.

The number of concurrent users specifies the maximum number of users who are accessing the system at the same time. It is a commonly used indicator for the load on a system. For a complex system, the users are not necessarily making the same kinds of requests, or not at the same time. Also, there is no direct correlation between throughput and the number of users on the system, since the frequency of requests could be quite different for different users. Therefore, what the users are doing and how intensely the transactions are should be part of the performance requirements.

Homogenous throughput with randomly arriving requests is a simplification and is often used in modeling the real-time situation. A lot of software applications use a session or similar approaches to manage users and associated resources, and the number of users (sessions) would be a good indicator and can be used in the performance requirements.

The performance of a system depends on hardware resources and network resources, therefore hardware configuration should be specified, if possible, in line with real-time business requirements of data volume and user capacity. Major resources to consider are CPU, memory, storage, and network bandwidth.

Resource utilization is the most widely used metric in capacity management and production monitoring. Since hardware configuration is not known in the software design phase, a generic policy may be used such as average CPU utilization should be below 50%.

Scalability is the system's ability to meet the performance requirements (e.g. response time) as the load (number of concurrent users, throughput) increases, by adding more resources (hardware) to the system. Response times may increase with load increases, regardless of the hardware resource increases. So, scalability means that relevant performance requirement is specified as a function of load or data. For example, the requirement may be specified to support throughput increase from 10 to 20 transactions per second with response time degradation of no more than 10 percent.

Note, some of the performance capacities may conflict with one another and require the specification to make tradeoffs. For example, high throughput performance can degrade response time.

Performance requirements are not always specified or fully specified. The functionalities of a system are usually quite complex and are in abundance, and end-user behaviors are diverse, so a lot of time it's not possible to specify performance requirements in great detail, in which cases only some general requirements are included.

11.3 PERFORMANCE TESTING TYPES

Here are the main categories of factors that application performance issues are induced:

(1) Software design, architecture, implementation & configuration.
(2) Server hardware resources.
(3) Communication network.
(4) User interfaces (device, browser, etc.).

Network impacts software performance tremendously, especially for mobile and cloud services, but the network is usually considered a condition affecting the performance of an application and is not considered as part of the application itself as far as performance is concerned. Performance requirements may specify the performance matrix under certain specific network conditions (and on what end-user devices or browsers as well). Network latency and bandwidth information could be collected during performance testing.

Also, in a production environment, proper network monitoring is a key to isolate network-related performance issues.

Software performance testing is mainly focusing on the first two items. So, the main goals of performance testing are to examine:

(1) If the software meets the performance requirements.
(2) The impact of hardware resources on software performance.
(3) The behavior of the system with volume/load that exceeds the specified limit.

From the last section, we know that the main categories of performance capabilities are response time and volume, therefore, performance testing should measure these capabilities, and determine the response time under different volumes or loads.

The main condition here is the volume or load, therefore, it's natural to classify performance testing based on volume and workload conditions. From the definition from Chapter 2, we know that performance testing is type 2 testing.

Given that there is another level of complexity with the volume/workload in performance testing, we add another digit to the type number as defined below:

(1) Type 2.0 performance testing: benchmark testing.
(2) Type 2.1 performance testing: load testing.
(3) Type 2.2 performance testing: stress testing.

Type 2.0 performance testing or benchmark testing is to measure performance indicators under normal conditions, with one or a relatively small number of concurrent users (much less than the specified limit) on the system. The goal is to establish a baseline for response time under normal conditions, and the baseline values of response time are called benchmarks. We may call benchmark testing performance 0 testing.

One important aspect of this type of testing is to compare the values after a change is made to the software, as the benchmarks are expected to remain the same after a change. So, benchmark testing should be part of the regression testing, to compare the baseline after a change to the system. Any deviation from the baseline needs to be justified.

Type 2.1 performance testing or load testing is to measure performance parameters under a specified limit of volume or load, that is, with a large number of users or a large number of transactions per unit time up to the limits specified in the performance requirements. The goal of load testing is to verify if the system meets the performance requirements under normal business operational conditions. We may refer to load testing as performance 1 testing.

Type 2.2 performance testing or stress testing is to measure the performance indicators and determine the behavior of the system under high volume or workload that exceeds the limit specified in the performance requirements, in terms of the number of concurrent users or number of transactions per unit time. The idea is to measure the amount of response degrades for load, and to measure the limit of the system if any functionalities wound become unavailable. We may call stress testing performance 2 testing.

Another form of stress testing is to test the system under load for a long period of time, to verify if the system is sustainable.

The goal of stress testing is to determine the capacity of the system, and if it meets the performance requirements, and shed some light on if the limitation is due to resource constraints or due to program internal design limitations. Very often this is not specified, then the goal would be to measure and benchmarking the capacity, limitation, and failure management of the system.

How capacity changes with hardware configuration changes (number of CPUs, amount of memory, amount of storage; allocation change for servers at different software abstraction layers) is a scalability measurement. Extrapolation can be done as well for further volume increase. This would be useful in production deployment architecture design and modification.

There are other terms used in performance testing, for example, capacity testing, scalability testing, and soak testing.

Capacity testing is to identify the maximum capacity of volume or workload the system can support while the response performance requirement is still satisfied. For example, a response time of loading a web page is specified as less than 3 seconds for 90% of the time. When the number of concurrent users accessing the page at the same time exceed, say, 1000, the response time exceeds 3 seconds for 90% of the time, then the capacity is identified as 1000 concurrent users. Keep adding more concurrent users beyond 1000 to further stress the system, further degrading should be observed, and an error condition may be reached.

Scalability testing is to determine if the system scales up with more volumes or workload and still satisfies the response time requirement by adding more hardware resources if needed.

Soak testing is to determine the performance behavior of a system by running load testing for a long period of time, such as longer than 24 hours. With the same amount of volume or load, response time may start to degrade after a long duration, if there are memory leak issues for example. Other factors that may surface for long-duration testing are disk space fill-up, and other periodical processes on the system that may lead to resources (CPU, memory, etc.) to peak, or any process queues filling up.

Table 11.1 summarizes the major performance testing classifications.

	Type 2.0 benchmark testing	Type 2.1 load testing	Type 2.2 stress testing
# of concurrent users	low	Below the limit	at & above the limit
Volume/workload	low	below the limit	at & above the limit
Main goal	baseline responses	performance requirement	capacity, failure handling

Table 11.1: Major performance testing classifications

11.4 PERFORMANCE TESTING PROCESSES

11.4.1 Performance Testing Processes

Performance testing is quite different from type 0 unit testing and type 1 integration testing, and is also quite different from other kinds of type 2 testing such as usability testing or security testing, mainly due to that the volume or load involved is large (vs, for example, number of concurrent users on the system is irrelevant for functional testing, except in some cases that the functionality requires a certain number of users on the system to get verified), and the goal of the testing is quite different.

We have discussed the goals of various types of performance testing in the last section, now let's discuss the differences in the testing process. The main differences from other types of tests are in test case design and scripting, data collection during testing, and testing result analysis.

The main tasks in performance testing include set up the testing environment, design and write testing scripts, execute tests, monitoring resource usage, & analyze testing results.

Here is a list of the major steps in performance testing.
   (1) Gather performance requirements.
   (2) Identify performance testing scope.
   (3) Identify and set up the testing environment.
   (4) Design tests & write test scripts.
   (5) Test execution.
   (6) Resource monitoring.
   (7) Test analysis.

Gather performance requirements include identifying the performance acceptance criteria, including response time requirement, throughput requirement, volume and workload requirement, capacity requirement, etc. Very often, not all performance requirements are specified, and sometimes there maybe none, and in those cases, other business requirements specification may be used to extract certain guidelines for performance, or common industrial standard for similar systems could be used.

Based on the performance requirements, the performance testing scope can be defined. If there is no performance requirement specification, then all kinds of performance testing could be done, including benchmark testing, load testing, and stress testing.

Depends on the nature of the software application, and if there are any performance concern in any area, performance focus may be different. For example, if the main concern is the performance of the system after every major change to the application, then benchmark testing and load testing to verify response time is not degraded under the same load should be performed.

With the performance goal and testing scope in mind, an appropriate testing environment should be identified and configured. These include hardware, software, and network configuration, performance testing tool configuration, resource monitoring set up if needed.

Performance test cases are designed based on the testing scope. Test cases should be selected from typical use cases or key scenarios, with consideration of end-user behavior differences, to better simulate the real-time situations. A performance tool is usually used for writing and executing performance tests.

Some of the essential practices in test scripting include parameterizing variables, adding proper delays (think time) between actions to simulate real users, etc. If no delay is added, some other mechanism or methodologies need to be developed to simulate real-world situations. We will talk more about these in later sections. Testing data including users for testing can be loaded/created as part of the testing scripts.

Test execution is to run the test scripts and collect relevant data (see next section for metrics to collect). Test execution should be planned and run with a specified number of concurrent users, data volume, number of transactions per unit time, etc., and should also include resource monitoring (unless it's not needed, for certain benchmark tests for example). Test re-run is very common given the complexity of the test and the testing environment.

The test execution results then are analyzed and presented and shared with stakeholders, and certain actions may be recommended if certain performance requirements are not satisfied.

11.4.2 Metrics to Collect

There are three major categories for data collection during performance testing, responses of requests or transactions, volumes or load on the system, and resource utilization.

The major metrics to collect in each of the categories include:

1. Response

    (1) Average response time (with standard deviation).
    (2) Percentile responses (e.g. 50%, 75%, 90%, 95%).
    (3) Response latencies; connect time.

2. Volume

    (1) Number of concurrent users.
    (2) Throughput.

3. Resources

    (1) Memory usage.
    (2) CPU usage.
    (3) Disk storage usage.
    (4) Network bandwidth usage.

Response time is the major indicator for performance measurement. The end-user experience of response time is the sum of server response time, plus network latency, and plus UI rendering time. Sometimes it's useful to separate server response time and network latency to understand more on the nature of performance issues if any.

Volume, both the concurrent users on the application and the throughput, in the form of transactions or other specified actions, are the inputs for performance testing.

Resource usages are collected on the servers depending on the types of testing and the requirements. For example, for basic benchmark testing, resource usage is not an issue, and there is no requirement to collect resource usages, then there is no need to collect them. There are also cases where only CPU and memory usages are needed to collect.

11.4.3 Performance Monitoring

Besides performance testing, performance monitoring on production is also necessary. There are two types of performance monitoring on production, one is similar to performance testing where testing user(s) is/are launched on a production system and performance metrics (response time, etc.) are collected for the actions from the testing users on the system. Part of the performance test design and test cases can be used for this type of performance monitoring.

The other is collecting real-time data from real users, and monitor real-time responses, throughput, and resource utilization, and triggering alerts if the values of certain indicators reach or exceed pre-defined thresholds, or if any service is not available (not responding after a certain pre-defined time). This requires more effort on developing a system or use proper tools, and is beyond performance testing, but it's an essential part of the production operation of software production environments.

11.5 PERFORMANCE TESTING PRINCIPLES, & PRACTICES

Two key areas deserve attention in performance testing practices:
- (A) Test case design.
- (B) Valid performance testing simulation.

Let's discuss each of them.

11.5.1 Test Case Design

Performance test cases are normally limited to a handful of typical use cases for a specific performance testing requirement. The following are the major factors to consider in designing test cases:
- (1) Identify key use cases or scenarios.
- (2) Model user behaviors in these use cases.
- (3) Identify the distribution of use cases.
- (4) Randomize user actions.

Unless the use cases are specified in the performance requirement or the performance testing scope, the key scenarios should be identified properly. For example, if the project is to test the overall performance of a web application, then what activities or transactions are performed by the users should be identified.

Let's consider a customer service application that is used by both the customer service representatives and the customers. The purpose of the application is to manage customer issues by creating incidents. Customer service representatives can create, update, and view the incidents, and customers can view their incidents and add comments. So, the main use cases to be selected would include:

(a) Create incidents.
(b) Search/browse incidents.
(c) Update incidents.
(d) Browse/search contents (such as frequently asked questions).

Suppose we selected all the above 4 use cases, then how users are performing those actions need to be modeled. For example, for creating an incident, how often an incident is created, how long does it take to perform each step involved in creating an incident, proper think time is then inserted into the testing script between adjacent steps.

Since multiple virtual users launched from the performance testing tool use the same scripts for each use case, a better practice is to randomize the think time in some way, so to avoid action patterns. Better still, randomize the time or at least control the time each user performs the same action (ramp time in some tools).

For certain testing, what use cases are more frequently performed or what use cases are resource intensive also need to be identified. For example, creating and updating an incident may be resource intensive since database updates are needed.

The performance of each use case should be analyzed after test execution. For the overall performance of the application, the distribution of the use cases should be identified. For example, what percentage of concurrent users are creating incidents, and what percentage of users are browsing the incidents, etc., then a normalized performance indicator can be used (for example, a normalized response time can be calculated based on the weight of each of the use cases).

11.5.2 Valid Performance Testing Simulation

It's extremely important that performance testing is a valid simulation of real user activities in a production environment, so the result is meaningful and valuable. Launching virtual users from a testing tool is different from multiple users log on to an application randomly and perform actions randomly.

The following are the major areas to pay attention to in determining the validity of testing:

(1) Testing environment.
(2) Test execution strategies.
(3) Comparison with production data.

Testing environment should be a typical environment that production is based on, or a scaled-down version of a production environment. Depends on the nature of the application, a testing environment can be very close to a production environment in terms of hardware configuration or far from that of a production environment.

In certain cases, it'd be very costly to have a testing environment that has similar hardware configuration as a production environment, and in this case, a scaled-down version could be used, which means the components are proportionally scaled down (for example, keep a similar ratio of application servers and database servers), then extrapolation can be done in performance result analysis.

In addition, if possible, the testing environment should be set in the same data center where the production environment resides.

For benchmark tests that comparing the performance of different versions of the same application, it's very important to test under the same circumstances, that is, with the same hardware configuration, under the same network condition, and execute the tests from the same server.

When it comes to test execution, multiple runs and experiments should be conducted, to validate the test design and to better mimic the real-time environment. For example, the following are some of the strategies to consider:

(a) Try different think time or randomize the think times between operations in each transaction for each user.
(b) Change the concurrent user (thread) ramp-up speed, that is, to add more users to the system gradually and at different rates. For example, try adding 5 more users every 2 minutes, every 5 minutes, etc.
(c) Execute tests with different amounts of time, for example, run a script or a set of scripts for 30 minutes with 50 concurrent users, and then try a run of the same script(s) for 60 minutes with the same number of users (may also use different ramp-up time).

Another strategy is to use transaction volume and response time data from production as references if the data is available and use those data as a guideline for designing the tests, and for deciding on think time, the number of concurrent users to use, etc. Comparison can be made to assess the validity of the performance testing design as well as that of the resource utilization, to adjust the performance tests accordingly.

11.6 CASE STUDY: PERFORMANCE OF DATABASE OPERATIONS

11.6.1 The Application Under Test & Test Design

The application under test is a cloud service tool for software application developers to design applications under a common platform and to collaborate with other developers who are working on the designing of the same application. A portion of the actions is to create or modify database schemas, done through the web interface of the application.

The purpose of the performance testing is to benchmark the basic database operations, to compare response time for a few major versions of the application, and to determine the capacity of the application. So, this project involves type 2.0 benchmark testing, type 2.1 load testing, and type 2.2 stress testing.

The following database operations are included in the test cases:
    (1) Add new columns to a database table.
    (2) Modify table column values: column length, data type.
    (3) Delete table columns.
    (4) Create new tables.
    (5) Delete tables.

In the above test cases, new tables are created by extending a common base table. New columns are added to the newly created tables, and column types and maximum length are modified in certain columns. Some of the added columns are then deleted. The tables created are also deleted at the last cleanup step.

The test measures the responses for the operation's transactions, such as the time needed to modify a column length, from the action submission [http(s) requests] to getting the response back. There are a lot of other activities behind the scene such as adding entries to other tables to track change versions (similar to a software code source control process). Therefore, these operations will take time. Given the nature of the application, the number of users using the application concurrently is relatively small.

11.6.2 Testing Environment & Testing Approach

JMeter was used for the performance test. The testing data for performance analysis and benchmarking are collected on a single instance of the application at a data center. JMeter scripts are launched from a server in the lab from the command line.

The following strategy is used, and experiments are done to make certain that the tests are valid, and to come up with the range (number of users, wait time, etc.) where the performance data is valid, and to determine the system performance degradation range.

(1) Several different wait time numbers are used between operations (such as between querying table form and modify a table column), ranging from 1/2 second to 5 seconds.
(2) Different numbers of concurrent users, from 1 to 50, are used.
(3) Different script running durations, from 5 minutes to 60 minutes, are used.
(4) Different thread ramp-up periods are used.

The server resource utilization, CPU and memory, on the testing environment is relatively large and is not an issue based on earlier studies, therefore, the resource utilization is not monitored.

11.6.3 Performance Benchmarks & Analysis

Based on the data collected with the different numbers of users and different think time, the data with 5 users and wait time 3 seconds are used for performance benchmark analysis. Firefox 45 was the user agent for the simulation.

Note, the response time for the actions does not include browser rendering time.

A. Response Time

Table 11.2 summarizes the average response time for the operations measured. The data are collected with 10 to 30 minutes run with 5 concurrent users and 3 secs wait time between requests, on a single application instance at the data center.

	Average (msec)	Std. Dev. (msec)
Insert a column	2217	468
Delete a column	1679	342
Modify column length	1576	348
Multiple updates for a column	1620	281
Create table	1562	464
Delete table	4810	998

Table 11.2: Response time for various transactions

From the data above, we noticed the following statistics:

(1) Delete a table takes close to 5 seconds, much longer than creating a table.
(2) Insert a table column takes about 2 secs and delete a table column takes a little bit less.
(3) Update a column takes less than 2 seconds.
(4) Update one value for a column and update multiple values for a column take about the same amount of time in one request.
(5) The standard deviation for all the operations is pretty high. In other words, the response time is highly distributed (see the distribution graphs below for an example).

Taking the 'Insert a column' transaction as an example, the average response time is 2217 milliseconds, with a standard deviation of 468 milliseconds. For normal distribution of response time, this tells us that inserting a column takes between 1949 milliseconds and 2685 milliseconds 67% of the time (average plus/minus delta).

The graph in Figure 11.2 shows the response time distribution for table creation for a situation under load (you can see that the mean response time is larger than the benchmark value as shown in Table 11.2). The x-axis is the response time in milliseconds, and the y-axis is the number of responses with different response times. The distribution of responses is very close to a normal distribution and can be modeled with normal distribution.

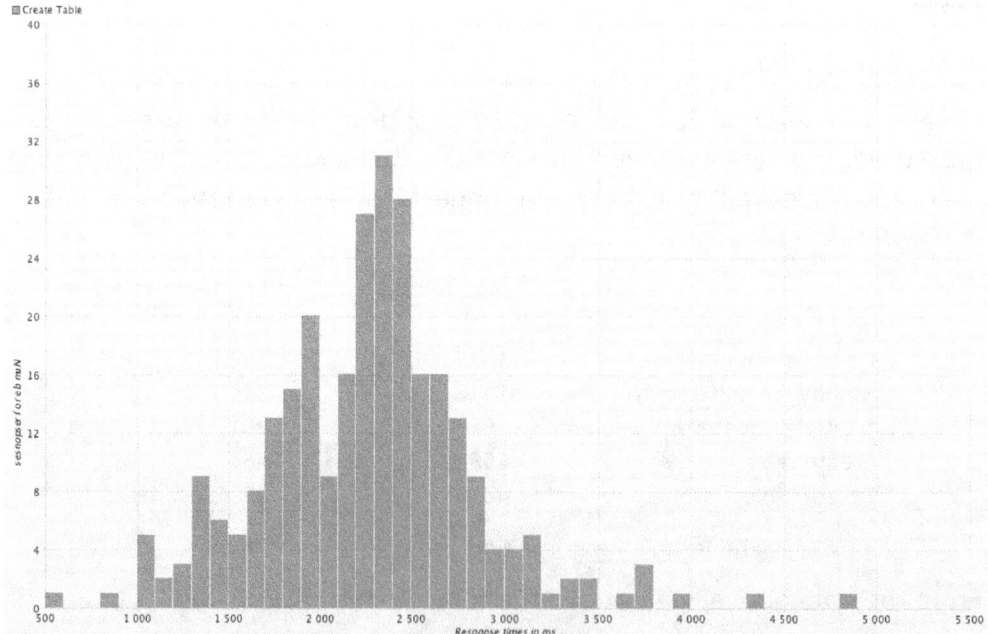

Figure 11.2: Response time distribution for table creation

The graphs in Figure 11.3 show the response times over time and response latencies over time, for a 10 minutes performance test run with 3 through 5 concurrent users, for table creation and deletion.

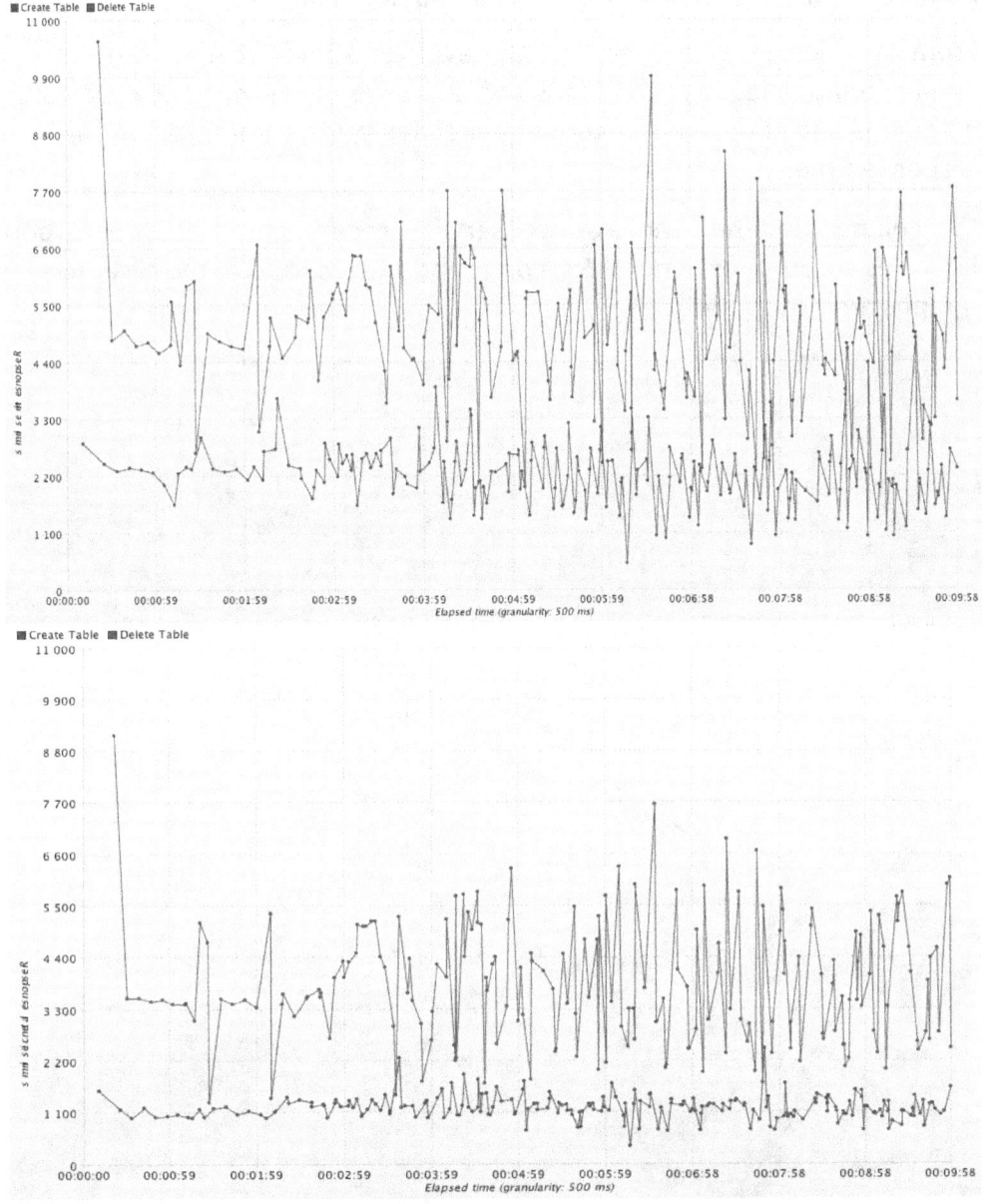

Figure 11.3: Response time over time (1st) and latency (2nd) over time for table creation

From the plots, the average latencies for creating and deleting tables are about 1.1 seconds and 3.2 seconds respectively. Comparing those values with total response time, it's clear that server processing time is about 1 sec and 1.6 secs for creating and deleting a table respectively.

The following graphs in Figure 11.4 show examples of response time over time and the latencies over time for insert and delete columns.

From the plots, we can see that the average server process time and the response latencies account for 1 and 2.1 seconds respectively for column insertion, and 0.6 and 1 seconds respectively for column deletion, in the response time.

For column updates, the average server process time and the response latencies account for about 0.6 seconds and 1.1 seconds, in the response time (graphs are not shown).

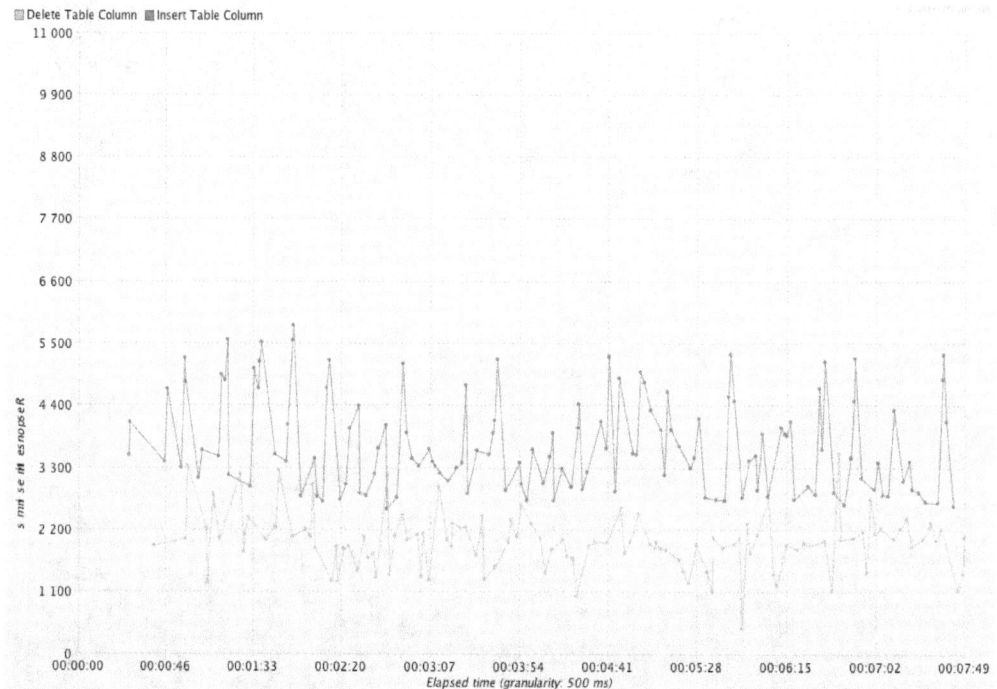

CHAPTER 11: PERFORMANCE TESTING

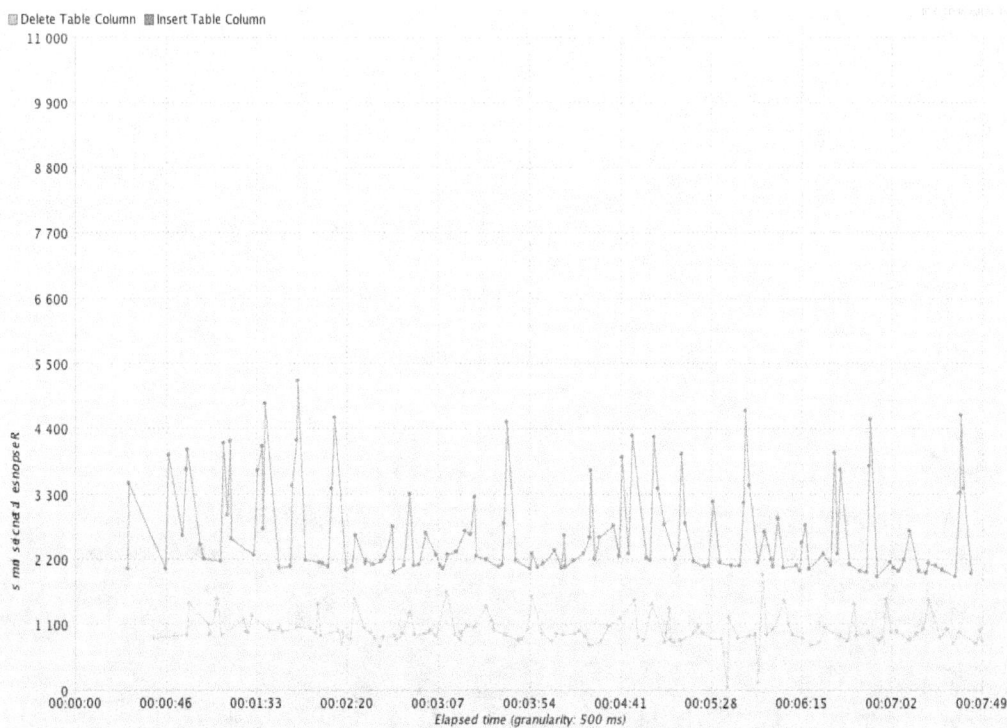

Figure 11.4: Response time (1st) and latency (2nd) over time for column insertion & deletion

B. Performance Under Load

The number of concurrent users is increased gradually in the tests, and to determine performance degradation under load.

Given that the application is for application developers, the number of concurrent users is not big, only a handful most of the time, so there is no heavy load of table operations. There is no performance requirement specified on the capacity of the application, so we will try to find the limit of the performance under load and stress conditions.

For the table operations under the testing environment, where all users are performing table operations, the system responses start to slow down when the number of concurrent user sessions exceeds 10. See Figure 11.5 for the graphs of transaction throughput vs the number of threads, and response time vs the number of threads.

CHAPTER 11: PERFORMANCE TESTING

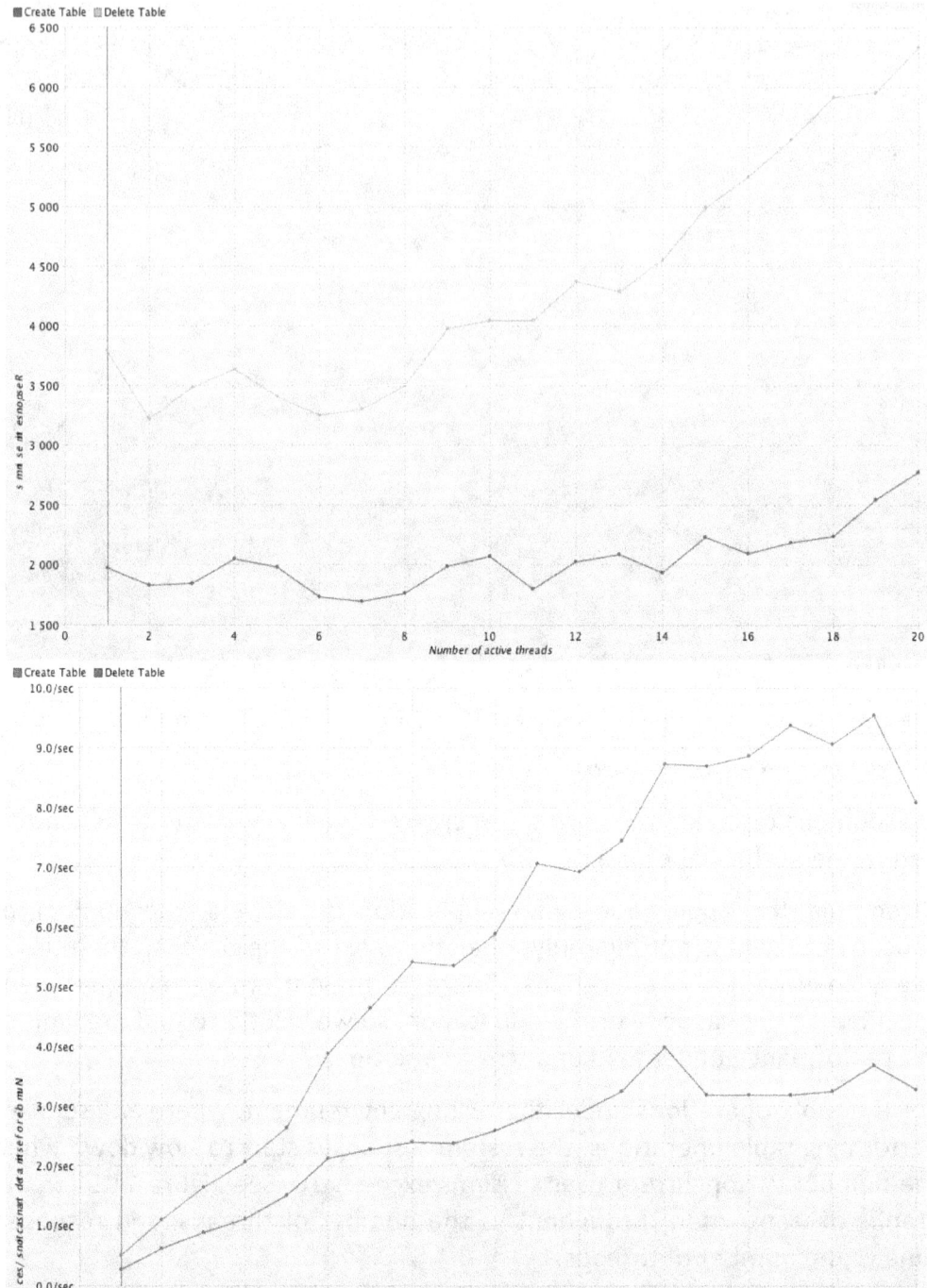

CHAPTER 11: PERFORMANCE TESTING

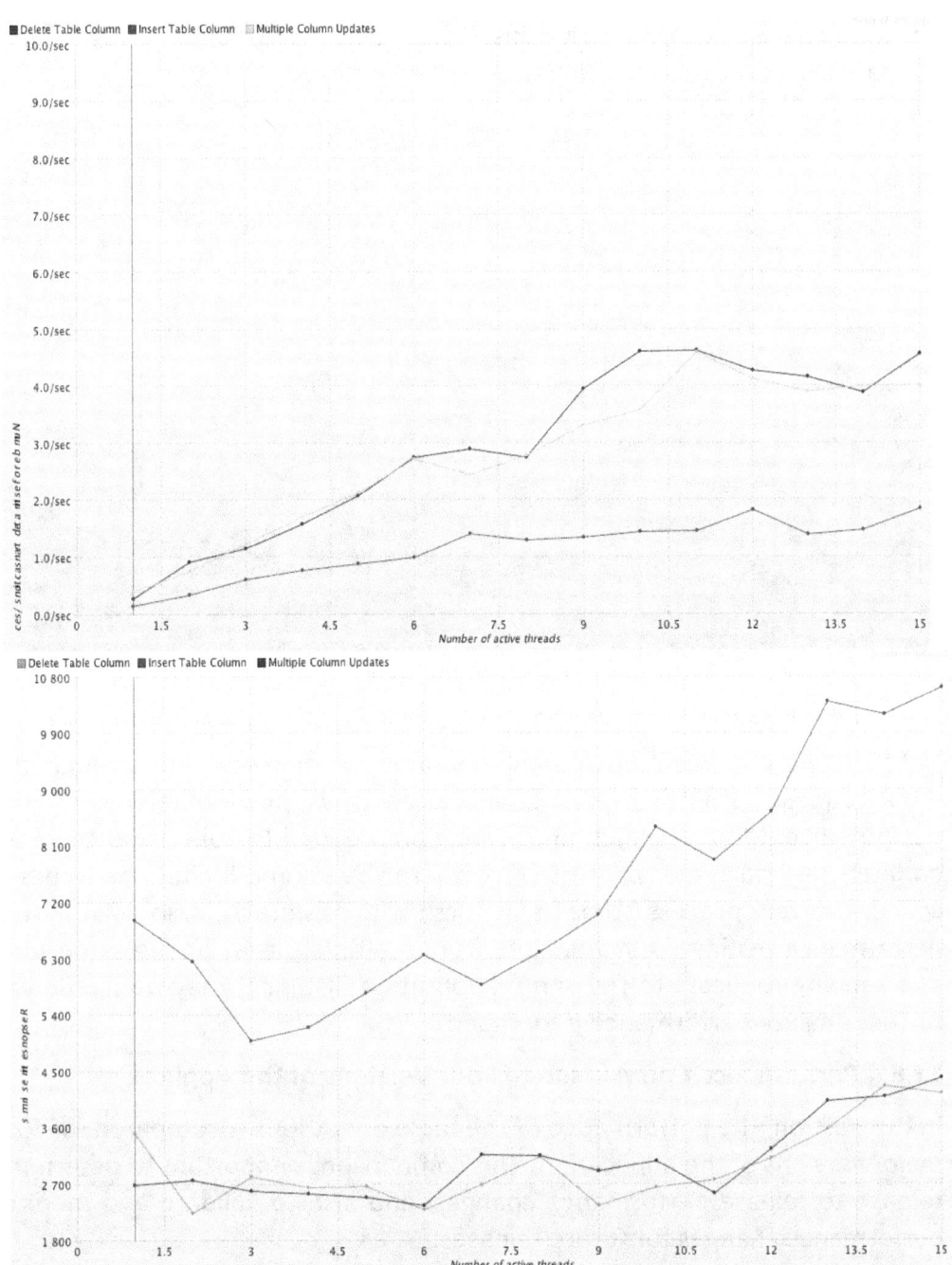

Figure 11.5: Transaction throughput and response time vs number of threads

When the number of concurrent users is larger, the latency becomes larger, and therefore the response time increases dramatically. In this case, the server process time is a small portion of the response time.

The graph in Figure 11.6 shows a case where the number of users is gradually increased from 1 to 25 in 20 minutes or so duration.

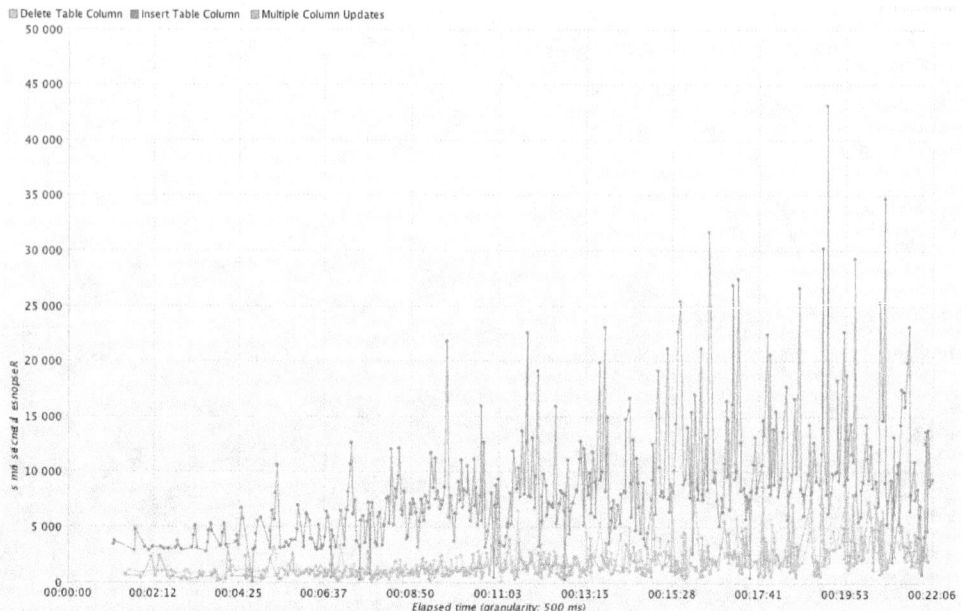

Figure 11.6: Latency over time with the increase of the number of concurrent users

Note, network connections/conditions, amount of data sent through the HTTP requests, JMeter server capacities, etc., all play some roles in the performance. More research and testing are needed to collect more details on latencies and server process time (there were some limitations to easily collect server process time statistics with JMeter). Also distributed performance testing (launch scripts from multiple places at the same time and sending requests to the same application instance) may be needed to further analyze performance under load.

11.6.4 Performance Comparison of Four Versions of the Application

In this section, the performance of the table operations is compared for four major versions of the application. This comparison is important to determine release to release performance changes, and also to validate and monitor performance changes for future releases.

For reliable performance comparison, the testing environment, JMeter settings, and any other conditions should be the same. For example, launch testing scripts from the same server, testing instances are at the same or similar locations and similar state, same network conditions, running with the same number of threads, use the same amount of wait time, same ramp-up time, and same duration.

The average response time values for the four versions of the application are shown in Table 11.3, and also are illustrated in the graphs in Figure 11.7 (unit in milliseconds).

	Version 1	Version 2	Version 3	Version 4
Insert Table Column	2258	2884	2217	2021
Delete Table Column	1768	1831	1679	1941
Table Column Updates	2442	2245	1620	1598
Create Table	1752	2387	1562	1977
Delete Table	2871	3546	4810	3411

Table 11.3: Average response time for testing transactions

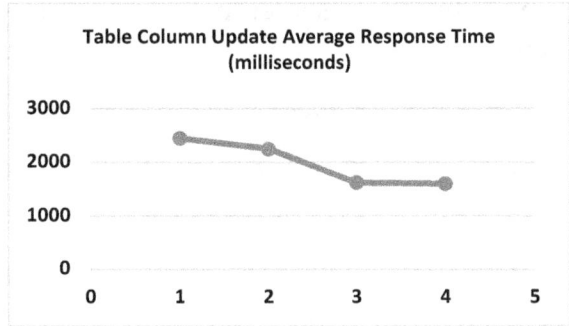

Figure 11.7a: Table column update response time comparison for four versions

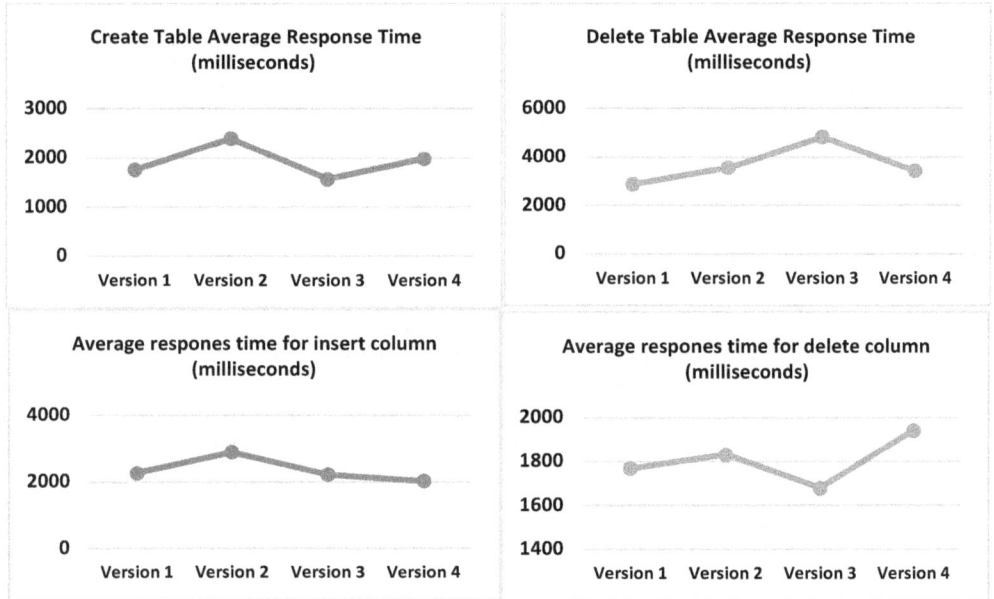

Figure 11.7: Response time comparison for four versions of the application

From the testing data, we can see that there are no significant performance changes for the four versions of the application. Deleting tables take a little bit longer time in version 3 than in others. There is a slight improvement of table column updates performance release by release from version 1 to version 4.

11.6.5 Sever Processing Time Analysis

To show the server processing time clearly, performance testing is run with one concurrent user only, on a datacenter instance. Server processing time is roughly the response time minus latency (the version of JMeter [version 3.2] used for the testing could not measure server time directly), in milliseconds. The following graphs show the server processing time for the different database operations.

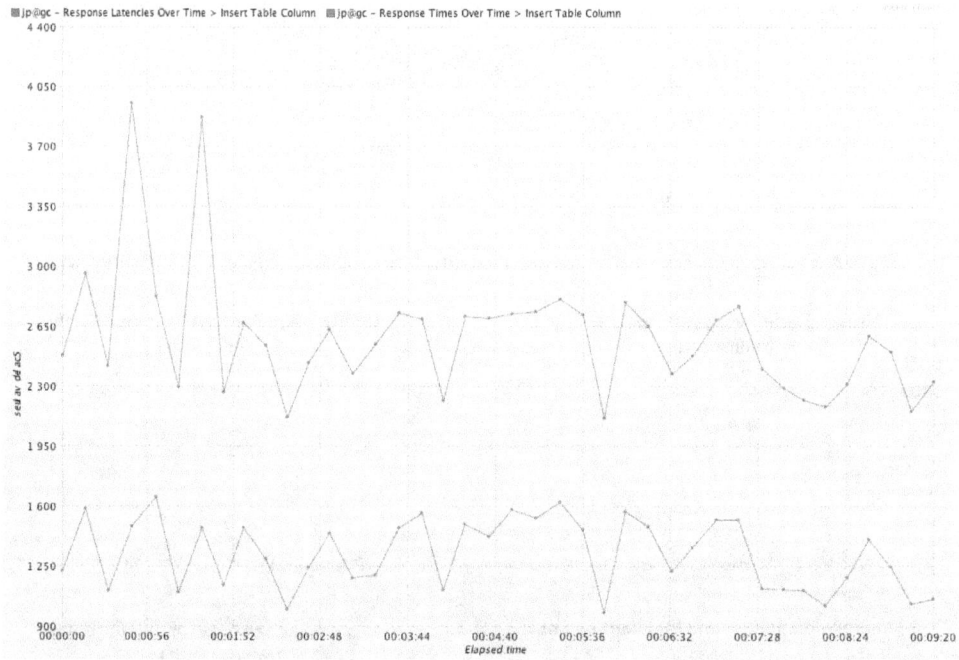

CHAPTER 11: PERFORMANCE TESTING 241

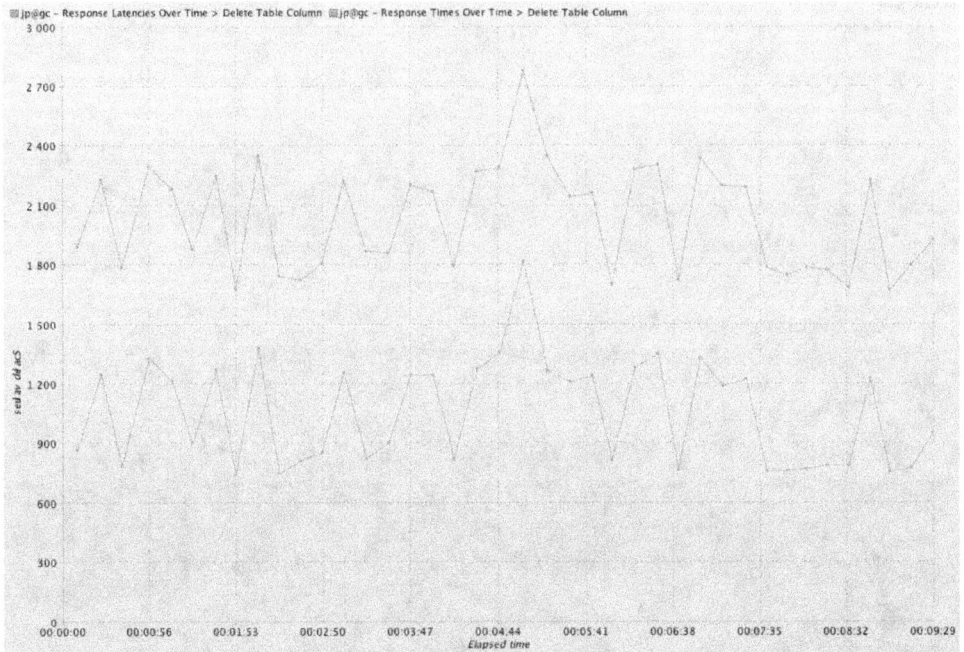

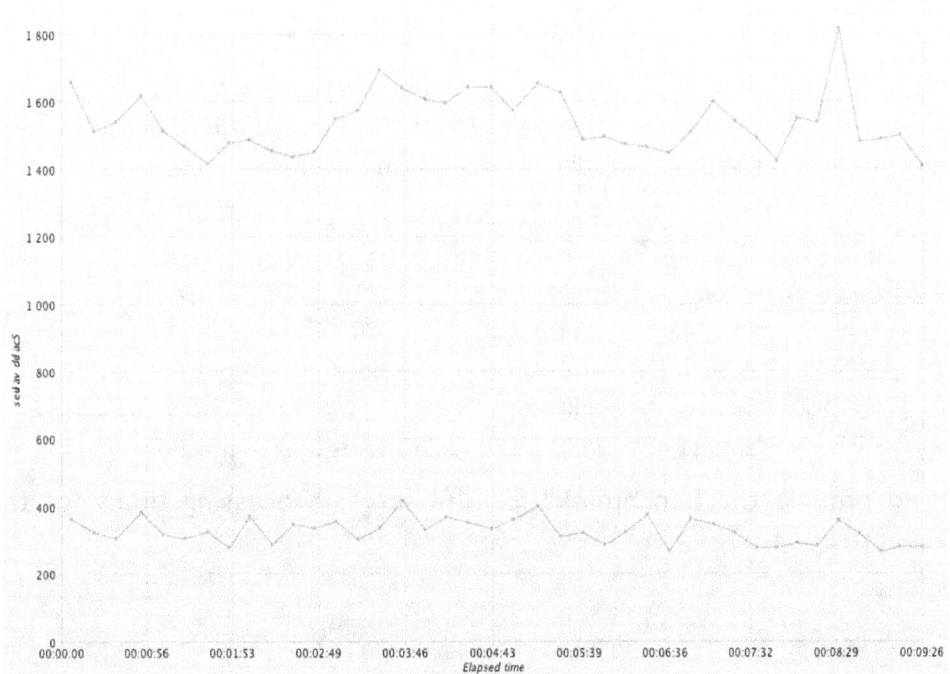

CHAPTER 11: PERFORMANCE TESTING

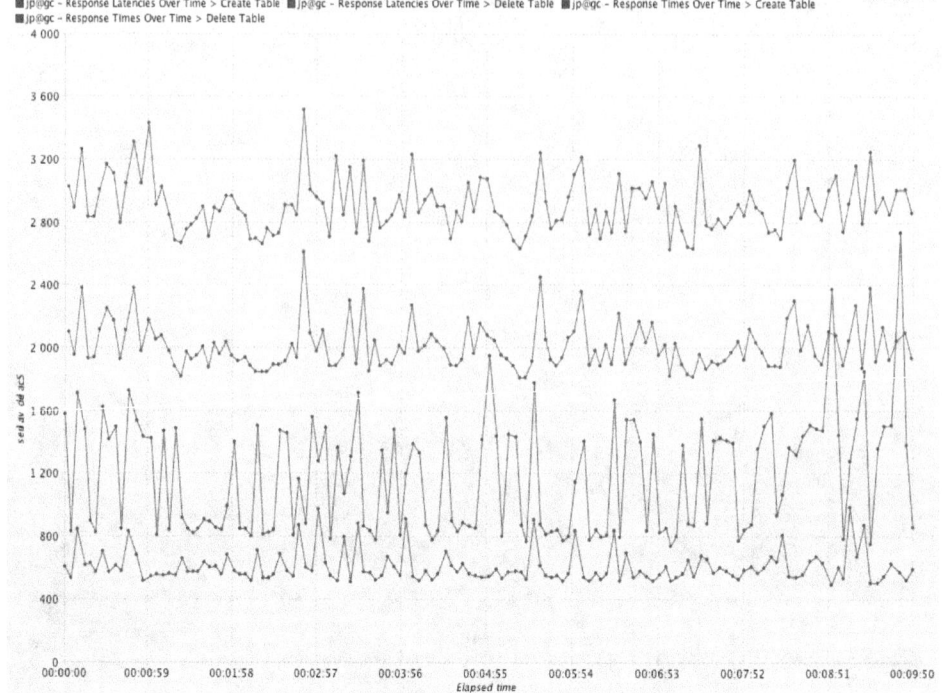

Figure 11.8: Server processing time

The following table summarizes the result for this particular testing (note, response time may be different from that in earlier testing due to environment differences, application version differences, etc.).

	Response Time	*Latency*	*Process Time*
Insert Table Column	2505	1320	1185
Delete Table Column	2007	1020	977
Table Column Updates	1542	480	1062
Create Table	1180	580	600
Delete Table	2909	2000	1909

Table 11.4: Server processing time for testing transactions

These provide the benchmarks for the server processing times for these database operations.

EXERCISE PROBLEMS:

P11.1: Performance Testing Basics
(1) Why percentile is a good performance indicator, and under what conditions it's better than the average indicator?
(2) What kinds of events or processes follow normal distribution? Give an example.
(3) What are the major capacities of performance indicators?
(4) What are the major factors that affect the performance of a software application?
(5) What are the main goals of performance testing?

P11.2: Types of Performance Testing
(1) What are the major types of performance testing?
(2) What does each type of performance testing measure?

P11.3: Performance Testing Processes
(1) What are the major steps in performance testing?
(2) What are the major metrics to collect?

P11.4: Test Case Design and Execution
(1) What are the major factors to consider in designing performance test cases?
(2) How to make sure that a performance test is valid?

12 CASE STUDY ONE: WEB SERVICE API TESTING

In this chapter, we present one case study for testing web service APIs (type 1 tests) to demonstrate how to use some of the techniques and how to apply the basic testing principles we have learned to generate test cases. This case study is an expansion of Example 3.9.

12.1 THE API REQUIREMENTS

In this example, we will concentrate on one web service API. The software application API returns detailed information of product orders consumers placed on an e-commerce site. The parameters of this web service API are listed in Table 12.1.

	Parameters	Data type	Data range	Required	Description
1	start_time	Integer	[800,000,000, 3,000,000,000]	no	Order time in epoch time.
2	end_time	Integer	[800,000,000, 3,000,000,000]	no	Order time in epoch time.
3	order_type	Integer	[1,10]	no	Order type numbers.
4	user_id	String	[a-z0-9]{5,32}	no	User id for the orders.
5	order_id	String	[a-z0-9]{32}	no	Unique id for every order.
6	order_state	Enum	{Open, Finished, Returned, Cancelled}	no	Order states.
7	product_name	String	[a-za-Z0-9]{5,64}	no	Product name.
8	limit	Integer	[0, 1000000]	no	Max # of records to return.

Table 12.1: Parameters for the web service API

Besides those listed in the table, the following is a list of other requirements:

(a) Parameters start_time and end_time are epoch time of the order creation time for starting and ending the search. start_time should be less than or equal to end_time.
(b) Parameter order_type is an integer, there is a one-to-one mapping to a string, such as type 1 is 'books'. The translation of the numerical type to a string is done behind the scene. Multiple values can be specified, separated by commas, any invalid value is ignored.
(c) Parameter user_id is a user's online login id. Multiple values can be specified, separated by commas, any invalid value is ignored.
(d) Parameter order_id is a unique id for each order. Multiple values can be specified, separated by commas, any invalid value is ignored. If order_id is specified all other parameters are ignored.
(e) Parameter order_state is an enum with four choices. Multiple values can be specified, separated by commas, any invalid value is ignored.
(f) Parameter product_name is the name of the product that appears in an order. Multiple values can be specified, separated by commas, any invalid value is ignored.
(g) If no specified parameter is used, return 1000000 orders from the start of time.
(h) If start_time is not specified, 800,000,000 is used by default.
(i) If end_time is not specified, the current time is used by default.
(j) If order_type is not specified, then all types of orders are returned. Same for user_id, order_id, order_state, and vendor_id.
(k) If the limit is not specified, return all records that satisfy other parameters, up to 1000000 records.
(l) Any string that does not match any of the specified parameter names is ignored.
(m) If the value of a parameter is empty or invalid, no record is returned.
(n) If a parameter occurs more than once, then the value of the one which appears 1st in the URL is taken.
(o) The records are returned in a certain format (such as xml), and chronological order.
(p) The sequence of the parameters does not matter.

Let's name the API as api_order, and the API call is in the following form:

https://api_service_url/api_order?start_time=1000000000&end_time=1565733999 &order_type=Open,Finished&user_id=test_user_01&order_state=5&limit=100

In the above example, *api_service_url* is the URL of the server, for example, "https://apiserver.mycompanyname.com". A question mark after the API name starts the parameters, and the parameters are separated by '&'.

12.2 TEST CASE GENERATION

What testing techniques are suitable for this problem? Most of the parameters are distinct and independent, so equivalence partitioning can be applied. Also, the combination of parameters is part of the testing, therefore, combinatorial testing techniques will also be used.

First, let's list all the major categories to consider:

(a) Equivalence partitions of the parameters.
(b) Different parameter orders.
(c) A smaller number of parameters (from 0 to 7) in the API call.
(d) Multiple entries for the same parameter.

Let's work on them one by one.

12.2.1 Equivalence Partitions

We need to determine equivalence partitions for all the parameters. We adopt the standard case of equivalence partitioning for this case study. Remember, for standard case of equivalence partitioning, the number of input values to select is 5 for a valid partition and 2 for an invalid partition. Any special case such as an [empty string] is counted as a single.

Each parameter is independently defined except start_time and end_time. So, start_time and end_time can be handled together as a 2-dimensional vector space (while all other parameters take valid values), and the rest of the parameters can be handled individually.

On the start_time and end_time 2-dimensional vector space, since there is a requirement that end_time must be larger than start_time, the valid partition is a triangle on the 2-dimensional coordinate, and there are 3 edges rather than 4 edges. See the vector space plot in Figure 12.1.

Since the valid partition is a triangle, we identify 3 invalid partitions on each side of the triangle. So, we have total 4 equivalence partitions:

1) { start_time, end_time |
    800,000,000 ≤ start_time ≤ 3,000,000,000;
    800,000,000 ≤ end_time ≤ 3,000,000,000; start_time ≤ end_time }
2) { start_time | start_time < 800,000,000 }

3) { end_time | end_time > 3,000,000,000 }
4) { start_time , end_time | start_time > end_time;
    800,000,000 ≤ start_time ≤ 3,000,000,000;
    800,000,000 ≤ end_time ≤ 3,000,000,000; }

The 1st one is the valid partition, and the rest three are the invalid areas. The number of test input vectors for the two-dimensional space of start_time and end_time can be calculated via (4n + 1) with n = 3 (surfaces), total of 13 cases.

The dots on the graph illustrate the test input vectors for the 13 cases.

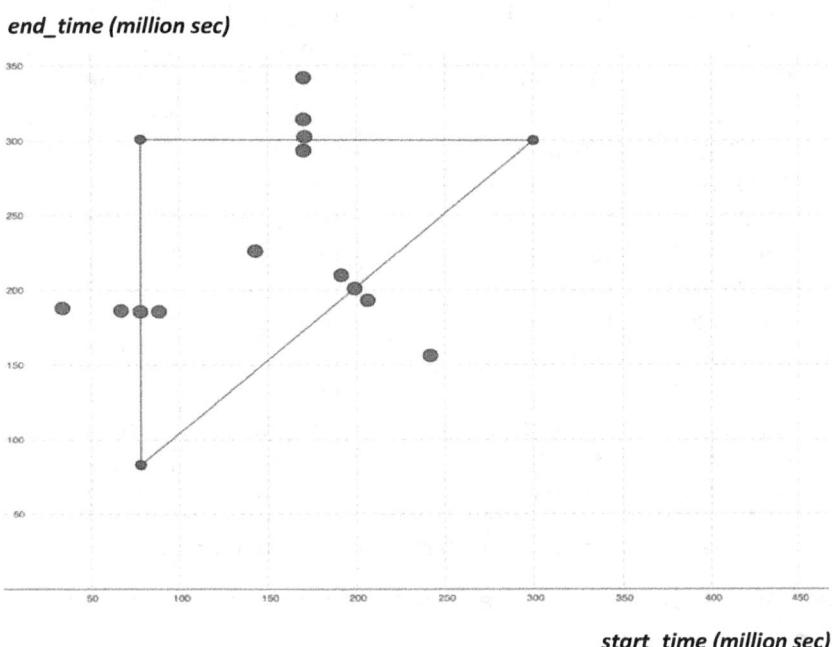

Figure 12.1: Vector space for start_time & end_time

Since both start_time and end_time are integers, there are a few invalid partitions accounting for non-integer cases, and one test case for each partition is sufficient:

5) { start_time | start_time ∈ [strings contain at least one non-integer }
6) { end_time | end_time ∈ [strings contain at least one non-integer] }
7) { start_time | start_time ∈ [empty string] }
8) { end_time | end_time ∈ [empty string] }

Table 12.2 lists sample test cases for the above 8 partitions concerning start_time and end_time.

Note, parameters order_id, product_name, and limit are not listed in the table, those parameters are not specified in the API for the above tests, to simplify the tests (none of the parameters is mandatory per requirements). Parameters order_type, user_id, and order_state are specified to limit the number of records returned (see next section for discussion on test data generation and testing strategies).

Test case	start_time	end_time	order _type	user_id	order _state	Expected result
1	1567550233	1568452435	1	test_user1	Finished	verify data
2	80200000	1568876554	1	test_user1	Finished	verify data
3	80000000	1568876554	1	test_user1	Finished	verify data
4	1567550233	2999000000	1	test_user1	Finished	verify data
5	1567550233	3000000000	1	test_user1	Finished	verify data
6	1800000000	2100000000	1	test_user1	Finished	verify data
7	2000000000	2000000000	1	test_user1	Finished	verify data
8	799999999	1800000000	1	test_user1	Finished	invalid
9	450000000	1800000000	1	test_user1	Finished	invalid
10	160000000	3000000001	1	test_user1	Finished	invalid
11	160000000	3400000000	1	test_user1	Finished	invalid
12	200000000	1900000000	1	test_user1	Finished	invalid
13	240000000	1500000000	1	test_user1	Finished	Invalid
14	567550233	1568452435	1	test_user1	Finished	invalid
15	1567550233	156845243A	1	test_user1	Finished	invalid
16	[empty string]	1568452435	1	test_user1	Finished	invalid
17	1567550233	[empty string]	1	test_user1	Finished	invalid

Table 12.2: Test cases for start_time and end_time partitions

The rest of the parameters are independent of each other, let's find the partitions for them one by one.

For order_type, since the valid values are an integer from 1 to 10, anything else is invalid such as a number outside the range of [1,10] or a string. The value is not for computation as an integer, but rather a choice in an enum set, therefore partitions with a value less than 1 and with a value greater than 10 are in the same partition, the partition with invalid values.

Also, since it's an enum type, there is no order sequence in the values and no boundary conditions, therefore for a valid partition with an enum type, there is no need to have 5 input vectors for each partition. Since the parameter can have one or more values, separated by commas, we will include both single value and multiple values in one valid partition and still generate 5 test cases for each valid partition. The same argument applies to the order_state parameter, another enum type.

Parameters user_id, order_id, and product_name are strings that are either valid (exist in the database) or invalid, the values have no order either. Therefore, the number of test cases can be reduced. For example, only include 3 test cases for a valid partition and one test case for an invalid partition.

With the above arguments, the partitions for these parameters are listed below, including category partitions:

9) { order_type | order_type ∈ [1, 10]+ (1 or more appearances) }
10) { order_type | order_type ∉ [1, 10] }
11) { order_type | order_type ∈ [empty string] }
12) { user_id | user_id ∈ [valid (existing)]+ }
13) { user_id | user_id ∈ [invalid (not existing)] }
14) { user_id | user_id ∈ [empty string] }
15) { order_id | order_id ∈ [valid (existing)]+ }
16) { order_id | order_id ∈ [invalid (not existing)] }
17) { order_id | order_id ∈ [empty string] }
18) { order_state | order_state ∈ [Open, Finished, Returned, Cancelled]+ }
19) { order_state | order_ state ∉ {Open, Finished, Returned, Cancelled}}
20) { order_state | order_ state ∈ [empty string] }
21) { product_name | product_name ∈ [valid (existing)]+ }
22) { product_name | product_name ∈ [invalid] }
23) { product_name | product_name ∈ [empty string] }
24) { limit | 1 ≤ limit ≤ 1,000,000 }
25) { limit | limit < 1 }
26) { limit | limit > 1,000,000 }
27) { limit | limit ∈ [strings contain at least one non-integer] }
28) { limit | limit ∈ [empty string] }
29) { order_state | order_state ∈ [multiples with both valid & invalid values] }
30) { order_state | order_state ∈ [multiples with both valid & invalid values, and non-matching coma] }
31) chronological order returns.
32) no valid parameter exists.

The plus(+) sign after a set denotes one or more appearances of the values in the set. Parameters order_type, order_status, and product_name can have multiple values. For the invalid scenarios with multiple values, only the order_type parameter is included in partitions 29) and 30), and the partitions for the other two parameters are omitted since multiples are handled the same way for different parameters and testing one of them would be sufficient.

The last partition is included to handle the case where no valid parameter exists. Two test cases can be generated in this partition to count for:

a) no parameter is specified;
b) a string is specified with no substring matching any parameter name.

Handling error conditions is a very important part of software testing, not only because it's the area that often has defects but also an error condition that may affect the security and performance of the application. But as we discussed earlier on the nature of the software implementation, when one error condition is met, other error conditions won't be evaluated. Therefore, we adopt two principles to limit the number of partitions and number of input vectors when handling error conditions:

(a) For each parameter, only one invalid sub-parameter is selected, and the rest sub-parameters are valid. For example, order_id is a 32-digit alphanumerical string, and the characters must be lower case ones, and a vector value that is not 32 in length and also contains characters that are not lowercase letters is not selected.

(b) For combinations of parameters, only include partitions where only one of them is invalid. For example, when generating input values to use for parameter start_time, all the other parameters to be selected should have valid values.

Table 12.3 lists the test cases for parameters order_type, user_id, and order_state. An empty cell means that the particular parameter is not in the parameter list in the API call.

Parameter order_id refers to a unique id for each order in the database, the value needs to be known from other means such as from querying a database. The requirement said that when order_id is specified all other parameters are ignored, that is, what's returned from specifying an order_id has no interaction with any other parameters, no further filtering from any other parameters.

CHAPTER 12: CASE STUDY ONE: WEB SERVICE API TESTING 251

case	end_time	order_type	user_id	order_state	Expected
18		2	test_user2		verify data
19		3,4	test_user2		verify data
20		1,5,6,8,9	test_user2	Finished	verify data
21		7,10,1,AA,4,8	test_user2	Finished	verify data
22		1,2,3,4,5,6,7,8,9,10	test_user2	Finished	verify data
23		0	test_user2	Finished	invalid
24		ab	test_user2	Finished	invalid
25		[empty string]	test_user2	Finished	invalid
26	1568452435	1	test_user3		verify data
27		1	test_user1, test_user3	Open	verify data
28	1568452435	1	user_not_exist	Finished	invalid
29	1568452435	1	[empty string]	Finished	invalid
30			test_user3	Returned	verify data
31			test_user3	Returned, Cancelled	verify data
32		3	test_user3	Open,Finished, Returned	verify data
33			test_user3	ReOrdered	invalid
34			test_user3	[empty string]	invalid

Table 12.3: Test cases for parameters order_type, user_id, and order_state

Table 12.4 lists the test cases for parameters order_id and product_name.

Test case	start_time	order _type	order_id	product_name	Expected result
35		1,2,3	a9e428cac61122760075710592216c58		verify data
36			471bfbc7a9fe198101e77a3e10e5d47f, 46f4f4dfa9fe198100063e60278f76ec		verify data
37			46f09e70a9fe198100f4ffd8d366d17b (none existing)		invalid
38			565465grgAA_r5$5kdw		invalid
39			[empty string]		invalid
40	1567550233			prod_a	verify data
41	1567550233	1		prod_b,prod_c	verify data
42	1567550233	2,3		prod_b,prod_c ,prod_d	invalid
43		1		prod_not_exist	invalid
44	1567550233			[empty string]	invalid

Table 12.4: Test cases for parameters order_id, and product_names

To test parameter 'limit', there should be more than 1 million records to be generated in the test data generation step. Table 12.5 lists test cases for parameter 'limit'.

Test case	start_time	end_time	order_type	user_id	Order_state	limit	Expected result
45	1567550233	1568452435		test_user4		1	verify data
46				test_user4	Finished	2	verify data
47			1			500000	verify data
48						999999	verify data
49						1000000	verify data
50					Finished	0	invalid
51			1			-15	invalid
52					Finished	1000001	invalid
53						2000000	invalid
54	1567550233	1568452435				1o1	invalid
55				test_user4		[empty string]	invalid

Table 12.5: Test cases for parameter limit

Table 12.6 lists the test cases for the rest of the partitions. Case 60 is the one to test chronological order return, case 61 is the one to test no parameter exists, and case 62 lists the non-existing parameter names to specify (but the values are valid after '=' sign for these non-existing parameters).

Test case	start_time	end_time	order_type	user_id	order_state	limit	Expected result
56			1		Finished, Oppenn	10	invalid
57				test_user1	Finish, Open, Cancel		invalid
58					Open, Finished,	20	invalid
59					Open,,Return		invalid
60			1	test_user1	Finished		verify data
61							invalid
62	Startime=1567550233	Enttime=1568452435	Otype=1	User__id=test_user1	Orderstates=Open		invalid

Table 12.6: Test cases for partitions from 29) to 32)

12.2.2 Different Parameter Orders

Next, let's work on the test cases for different parameter orders. For testing parameter orders, we only test with valid data for each parameter.

With 8 parameters, the total number of permutations is 8! = 40320. A significant test case reduction technique is needed, and it'll be the combinatorial testing technique discussed in Chapter 4.

We adopt the pairwise testing technique here. If we label the parameters with numbers, as from Table 12.1, start_time is 1, end_time is 2, and so on, and we denote [12345678] as the order that start_time is at 1st position, end_time is at 2nd, and so on, then different orders of the parameters mean that any other order would include at least one pair of numbers which are reversed

CHAPTER 12: CASE STUDY ONE: WEB SERVICE API TESTING 253

numerically. For example, in order [21345678], end_time appears before start_time, [21] is the only reversed one in this order.

With pairwise technique, all the pairs of the 8 parameters should be listed. All the pairs are (total 28 pairs):

[1,2], [1,3], [1,4], [1,5], [1,6], [1,7], [1,8],
[2,3], [2,4], [2,5], [2,6], [2,7], [2,8],
[3,4], [3,5], [3,6], [3,7], [3,8],
[4,5], [4,6], [4,7], [4,8],
[5,6], [5,7], [5,8],
[6,7], [6,8],
[7,8].

Since this is about parameter orders, and the order of any two parameters matters. In other words, each pair can take two values. For example, for pair [1,2], two values should be included, [12] and [21].

Now let's construct the test cases. Starting from pair [1,2], and from [12345678]. We can see that case [12345678] contains these values: [12], [23], [34], [45], [56], [67], [78], then we start next one from [21.....], and if a value is already covered, try a different value. For example, after [12345678], the next set is [21345678], but [34] is already covered, therefore [21345678] is omitted. Next pair after [34] is [35], so the next candidate is [21354678]. Since [67] and [78] are also already covered, the next set should have 7 and 8 reversed, and we end up with set [21354687]. Some pair values may be repeated.

In the construction process, you can keep a list of pairs, and if the two values of a pair are covered, then cross out or remove it from the list, until no item is left in the list. Table 12.7 lists all the test cases constructed this way. In the 'contain pairs' column, the ones in italic are the ones that are already covered by an earlier case.

We end up with a total of 11 test cases, all the 28 pairs and the 28 reverse pairs are covered.

cases	Orders	Contain pairs
1	12345678	[12], [23], [34], [45], [56], [67], [78]
2	21354687	[21], [13], [35], [54], [46], [68], [87]
3	31425768	[31], [14], [42], [25], [57], [76], *[68]*
4	41526378	[41], [15], [52], [26], [63], [37], *[78]*
5	51624387	[51], [16], [62], [24], [43], [38], *[87]*
6	61728345	[61], [17], [72], [28], [83], *[34], [45]*
7	71824365	[71], [18], [82], *[24], [43]*, [36], [65]

CHAPTER 12: CASE STUDY ONE: WEB SERVICE API TESTING

8	81253476	[81], *[12]*, *[25]*, [53], *[34]*, [47], *[76]*
9	32748516	[32], [27], [74], [48], [85], *[51]*, [16]
10	73864512	[73], *[38]*, [86], [64], *[45]*, *[51]*, [12]
11	58471236	[58], [84], *[47]*, *[71]*, [12], [23], [36]

Table 12.7: Test cases for different parameter orders

Now, let's reduce the number of parameters in the API call in the above test cases without reducing any pair coverage, by removing the italic pairs in the above table as much as possible. See Table 12.8.

cases	Orders	Contain pairs
1	12345678	[12], [23], [34], [45], [56], [67], [78]
2	21354687	[21], [13], [35], [54], [46], [68], [87]
3	3142576	[31], [14], [42], [25], [57], [76]
4	4152637	[41], [15], [52], [26], [63], [37]
5	5162438	[51], [16], [62], [24], [43], [38]
6	617283	[61], [17], [72], [28], [83]
7	7182365	[71], [18], [82], *[23]*, [36], [65]
8	815347	[81], *[15]*, [53], *[34]*, [47], *[76]*
9	327485	[32], [27], [74], [48], [85]
10	73864	[73], *[38]*, [86], [64]
11	584	[58], [84]

Table 12.8: Test cases for different parameter orders with a reduced number of parameters

The following table lists these test cases, all the parameters have valid values, and the API returns are the same for all of them (so the verification is the same).

Test case	Orders	Parameter values for all cases	Expected result
63	12345678	start_time=1567550233	verify data
64	21354687	end_time=1568452435	verify data
65	3142576	order_type=1	verify data
66	4152637	user_id=test_user1	verify data
67	5162438	order_id= a9e428cac61122760075710592216c58	verify data
68	617283	order_state=1	verify data
69	7182365	product_name=prod_a	verify data
70	815347	limit=2	verify data
71	327485		verify data
72	73864		verify data
73	584		verify data

Table 12.9: Test cases for different parameter orders

12.2.3 Smaller Number of Parameters

Since every parameter is optional, the number of parameters to provide in the API call is from 0 to 8. The numbers of combinations for the different number of parameters are listed in Table 12.10. The calculations are done using equation (2-6). The number of permutations is very large, we need to find a way to trim it down.

All the cases with only one parameter should be included in the test case set. For the cases with 2 to 7 parameters, there are two questions to ask. 1st, are any of the parameters correlated with or depend on any other parameter(s)? 2nd, from software implementation's point of view, are all the parameters treated the same way or differently?

# of parameters	# of combinations
7	8
6	28
5	56
4	70
3	56
2	28
1	8
0	1

Table 12.10: Permutations for various number of parameters

From the requirements, there is only one that requires start_time to be no larger than end_time, and there is no dependence between any of the 8 parameters.

To answer the 2nd question on how the parameters are treated, we need some knowledge of the design of the API. It's easy to imagine that, since the parameters are given in the form of a URL, then the values of the parameters are obtained by parsing the URL string. In other words, all the parameters are treated the same way. We can also imagine after the parameter values are retrieved from the input API string, the next step is to query the data source, using a specific query language to a relational database or a big data data source. So, we can safely assume that the parameters are not treated differently individually.

Therefore, the chance of a defect with different permutations of the number of parameters is very low. For example, if there is no defect with parameters [12345], then a permutation of [23456] is not likely to lead to a defect related to the number of parameters provided (5 in this case). [similar argument is true to different parameter orders we discussed in the last section].

So, we can trim down the number of test cases for the rest of the cases to only one for each. The new numbers of combinations to test are listed in Table 12.11, with a total of 15 test cases.

# of parameters	# of combinations
7	1
6	1
5	1
4	1
3	1
2	1
1	8
0	1

Table 12.11: Number of permutations to test

Furthermore, we used a various number of parameters in the test cases for testing each of the parameter partitions, as seen in the test cases from the last two sections, therefore the test cases can be further reduced.

From the test cases from the last two sections, all the numbers of parameters are covered except when only one parameter exists.

So, only 8 test cases are left to consider, marked in grey in the above table. Case 36 also covered order_id as the only parameter, so we have only 7 test cases for this section. The 7 test cases are listed in Table 12.12.

Test case	start_time	end_time	order_ type	user_id	product _name	order_ state	limit	Expected
74	1567550233							verify data
75		1567550233						verify data
76			1,10					verify data
77				test_user2				verify data
78					prod_a			verify data
79						2,4		verify data
80							5	verify data

Table 12.12: Test cases for one parameter only

12.2.4 Multiple Entries for the Parameters

From the requirement, if a parameter occurs more than once, then the value of the one that appears 1st in the URL is taken, and the rest is ignored. Here is a list of categories to consider for testing:

  (1) Two occurrences of each parameter:
    (a) 1st occurrence with a valid value;
    (b) 1st occurrence with an invalid value.

CHAPTER 12: CASE STUDY ONE: WEB SERVICE API TESTING

(2) Three or more occurrences of each parameter.
(3) Multiple parameters with more than one occurrence.

As we've mentioned earlier, the parameters are parsed from the URL string, and if a case with two occurrences of a parameter works as expected, there is much less chance that a case with more than two occurrences or a case with multiple parameters occurring more than once would fail. Therefore, we can either eliminate all the cases with the 2nd and 3rd categories above from the testing or only have one test case for each category.

For the 1st category, there are two test cases for each parameter, with total of 16 test cases. Since all the parameters are treated the same way, we could further reduce the number of test cases, by, for example, randomly select only 2 parameters to test, with 4 tests for category (1).

Table 12.13 lists the test cases we would select. A number in both bold and italic indicates an invalid value.

Cases	Orders	Note
1	33*4*	2nd occurrence contains an invalid value
2	**3**436	1st occurrence contains an invalid value
3	**4**46	1st occurrence contains an invalid value
4	34*4*	2nd occurrence contains an invalid value
5	6*6*46	2nd occurrence contains an invalid value
6	88*4*33	1st occurrence of 2nd repeat contains an invalid value

Table 12.13: Test cases for multiple parameter entries

Translate to test cases with the parameter values specified, we have the list in the next table.

To summarize, we have generated total of 86 test cases for order API from several categories and applied both equivalence partitioning technique and the pair-wise combinatorial technique, and the test cases generated satisfy the basic testing principles, atomicity, independence, modularization, and have good coverage.

Test case	orders	order_type	order_type	user_id	user_id
81	334	1	20	test_user1	
82	3436	20	1	test_user1	
83	446			non-exist	test_user2
84	344	1,2,aa		test_user2	non-exist
85	6646				test_user2
86	88433	ii	2,3	test_user2	

Test case	order_state	order_state	order_state	limit	limit	Expected result
81						verify data
82	Open					invalid
83	Open					invalid
84						verify data
85	Open	Done	Finished			verify data
86	2,4	2,4	2,4	10	5	invalid

Table 12.14: Test cases for multiple parameter entries

What's covered in this case study is an analysis of one web service API. There can be many APIs for the same application, and test cases can be generated the same way. But all the APIs are built with the same framework and are in the same codebase calling the same methods/functions/subroutines, and similar parameters are handled the same way, therefore, when testing other APIs, the number of equivalence partitions and the number of test cases can be greatly reduced.

For example, an API api_user returns user information, with parameters user_id, user_state, user_type, user_country, user_zipcode, and limit. Since we have tested api_order thoroughly, and the parameters of this API are similar, and the test cases exercise the same codebase, we can relax the criteria when generating test cases for this API. Table 12.15 lists the suggested strategies for the same categories that were used in generating test cases for api_order.

Categories of testing	Strategies in test case generation
Equivalence partitions of parameters	One test case for each equivalence partition (base case).
Different parameter orders	One test case.
A smaller number of parameters	One test case for no parameters; five each for one parameter; one for three parameters.
Multiple entries for the parameters	Two test cases for one parameter with an invalid value appears 1st and 2nd.

Table 12.15: Testing strategies for the api_user API

12.3 TEST DATA CREATION, VERIFICATION STRATEGIES, & TEST AUTOMATION

Testing data are needed for the test cases to be able to execute. Basic sample or seed data could be loaded as part of the application build process, and specific sets of data can also be loaded to the system for specific sets of tests (remember modularization principle). The data are normally residing in some kind of storage such as a relational database, in which case a database data dump could be used to load the data. Testing data can also be created on the fly from carefully designed scripts through any database access interface.

Based on the test cases generated from section 12.2, we need to create data in these areas:

(1) create testing users: test_user1, test_user2, test_user3, test_user4.
(2) create product order records for each of the users.
(3) create records in each order type, and with each order state.
(4) create products with names [prod_a, prod_b, prod_c, prod_d].
(5) create records across time range [800,000,000, 3,000,000,000].
(6) create orders in the range of [1567550233, 1568452435], with more varieties based on order_type, order_state, and product_name.
(7) the number of order records created should be over 1 million, say 1.1 million in total.

Note, order_id is automatically generated when a record is inserted into the database and is unique.

In these test cases, API returns are to be compared with the testing data, therefore, the testing data creation can be closely correlated with the tests. For example, the product order data for a specific user is generated from an xml file, and the content of this xml file is used as the expected result for the API return for this specific user.

The API returns are parsed in certain ways to be compared with expected results. In general, there are testing automation tools to help web service API testing, you can search on the internet for the proper tools, we won't cover those in this book. You can also write your own parsing functions.

The whole content of what's returned from the API should be compared with the expected result only when the number of records returned is small. For example, when only one order is returned when specifying only an order_id, all tags and their values are to be compared in the xml formatted returns.

For most of the tests, testing data should be designed so that verification should only concentrate on a certain part of the parameters/tags and their values. For example, to test the orders for a specific user, the verification (assertions) should be on the values of the <user> tags for all the orders returned: the value should be the specified user, and no other name appears in the tag.

In any case, the number of order records returned is a basic and powerful verification criterion. The number of orders for each user, in each order type, for each product, at each order state, and between specified times should be carefully designed to be different, then a lot of the tests can be done by just verifying the number of orders returned from the various API calls.

For example, to verify the API returns for one type of order at a certain order state, if the number of orders within these criteria is a number that is different from any other numbers returned by any other test scenarios, then verifying that the number of orders returned from the API call matches the expected number would be a major indicator of the success of the execution of this test case. Then adding one or more assertions of the values of the relevant tags, order_type, and order_state in this case, to make the test complete. If the values of the relevant tags are verified in other test cases in the same equivalence partition, then only the matching record number would be sufficient to fulfill the requirements of the test case.

Code segment 12.1 is a skeleton of a sample test in Java.

In this example, method getAPIReturn() executes the API with the parameters provided and produces the result. Method NumberOfRecordInAPIReturn() parses the result from getAPIReturn(), and gives the number of records in the result. The expected number of records is calculated with the method getNumberOfRecordsFromDBInterface(), which communicates directly with the database where the testing data resizes. If such an interface does not exist, the value of exected_num_case1 could be hardcoded with the corresponding value that was used in testing data creation.

After the record number comparison, the value of each <user> tag is parsed and compared with the expected value (here the xml parsing from the DOM tree is used, you may use other techniques).

```
@Test
void testUserValidCase1 () {
    String user_id = "test_user_01";
    int start_time = 1546304460;
    int end_time = 1567533483;
    String order_status = "Open";
    int expected_num_user_case1 = getNumberOfRecordsFromDBInteface (start_time,
                        end_time, user_id,order_status);
    String APIReturn = getAPIReturn(start_time, end_time, user_id, order_status);
    int record_num = NumberOfRecordInAPIReturn (APIReturn);
    assertEquals ("Number of records does not match for user_case1.",
                expected_num_user_case1, record_num);
    NodeList userTagList = APIReturn.getElementsByTagName("user");
    for (int i = 0; i < userTagList.getLength(); i++) {
        Node node = userTagList.item(i);
        if (node.GetNodeType() == Node.ELEMENT_NODE) {
            assertEquals ("User tag value does not match for user " +
                        user_id + ".", user_id, node.getTextContent() );
        }
    }
}
```

Code Segment 12.1: A testing method for a test case in the valid user partition

One other aspect of designing the tests is to consider performance, by not returning a larger number of records for tests that are not related to the boundary conditions where a large number of records are needed. For example, when testing a case for the valid partition for start_time, end_time pair, other parameters such as user_id and order_type should be used to reduce the size of the API returns, as long as the number of returns is enough to verify the expected results in the concerned tests. For instance, to test the orders are in a specific time range, 5 or so order records should be enough to verify that the orders are in the range, and not outside, rather than say, 50 orders, which does not add any value to the specific test.

A few words on API performance testing. Usually, there are multiple parameters with an API request, and some parameters are value-sensitive, that is, a different value may change the response time of the API request drastically. For example, if a parameter controls how many database records to return, then retuning a large number of records will take more time than retuning a smaller number of records.

How the APIs under test are used, what parameters are used more frequently (if not all parameters are required), and how many data are returned from an API query, all contribute to API load and stress testing design. For example, an API is used by a web interface, then the performance of the web pages utilizing the API is a factor to be considered in the design of load and stress testing test cases.

13 CASE STUDY TWO: RECORD FILTERING TESTING

In this chapter, we present a case study for testing content filtering on a web interface for an enterprise IT management system. These tests are considered type 1 tests.

13.1 THE APPLICATION UNDER TEST

The application is an IT service management tool for both company employees and customers, to report, track, and manage customer issues. The front end is a cloud-based web interface, and the backend has a relational database for data storage. There is a one to one mapping of the columns (fields) in any table in the database onto the web interface, the data in any table in the database can be viewed in either a list of record format or a form format for any record, and the data in each column can be viewed and modified based on a set of rules.

The testing scope is to verify the record filtering in the list view of any table. For a specific filtering operation, the records are listed in a table format with the major columns of the table in the database. Columns can be added or removed for display on UI (column display on UI is not part of the testing).

The filtering of records can be on any column/field of a table, and two logic operators, 'AND' and 'OR', can be used. For example, if 'Access', 'Priority', and 'Worknotes' are a few columns of a table, the following is a filtering option:

((Access is true) AND (Priority is High)) OR (Worknotes contains 'account')

In this example, the type of column 'Access' is Boolean, the type of 'Priority' is Enum, and the type of 'Worknotes' is String. The above filtering returns all records in the specific database table with either the Worknotes column contains word 'account', or satisfies that Access is 'true' and Priority is 'High' (a record with no 'account' in Worknotes field, and Access is 'true,' but Priority is 'Low', will not be returned, for example).

Also, there is a sorting option based on any column with two options, ascending and descending.

There are pre-defined filtering settings on UI navigation to start with, with a default sorting column. Filtering can be performed from any pre-set page, and the result is independent of where it's started, except for sorting, unless a new sorting column is specified.

The filtering operations for each type of column are listed in the following tables.

Column type	Operations	Possible values
Boolean	is	true, false
	is empty	
	is not empty	

Table 13.1: Filter operations and possible values for the Boolean column type

Column type	Operations	Possible values
Date and Time	on	Today, Yesterday, Tomorrow, This week, Last week, Next week, This month, Last month, Next month, This quarter, Last quarter, Next quarter, This year, Last year, Next year, Last 3 months, Last 12 months, Last 30 days, Current hour, Last hour.
	not on	
	before	
	at or before	
	after	
	at or after	
	between	
	is empty	
	is not empty	

Table 13.2: Filter operations and possible values for Date and Time column type

Column type	Operations	Possible values
Integer	is	[0, 100]
	is empty	
	is not empty	
	less than	
	greater than	
	less than or is	
	greater than or is	
	between	

Table 13.3: Filter operations and possible values for Integer column type

Column type	Operations	Possible values
Enum	is	one of a set of values
	is not	one of a set of values
	is one of	one or more selections in a set of values
	is empty	
	is not empty	

Table 13.4: Filter operations and possible values for Enum column type

Column type	Operations	Possible values
String	starts with	a string
	ends with	a string
	contains	a string
	does not contain	a string
	is	a string
	is not	a string
	is empty	
	is not empty	

Table 13.5: Filter operations and possible values for String column type

The possible values for columns with types of Boolean, Date and Time, and Enum, are options that can be selected from a dropdown list except for 'is empty' and 'is not empty' operations.

One database table is to be selected for testing, let's call this table the 'Customer Incident' table, and simply the 'incident' table, and the major columns of the database table are listed in the following table.

CHAPTER 13: CASE STUDY TWO: RECORD FILTERING TESTING

Column name	Data type	Possible values
Record_id	String	[a-z0-9]{32}
Number	String	[A-Z0-9]{5,10}
Active	Boolean	true, false
Priority	Enum	[Critical, High, Moderate, Low]
State	Enum	[New, Awaiting, Resolved, Closed]
Description	String	Any string
Created	Date and Time	[2018 00:00:00 AM, 2050 11:59:59 PM]
Created By	String	Valid user name in the 'user' table.
Change count	Integer	[1,100]
Assigned To	String	Valid user name in the 'user' table.
Release time	Date and Time	[2018 00:00:00 AM, 2050 11:59:59 PM]
Worknotes	String	Any string

Table 13.6: Columns of the database table under test

The values of both 'Record_id' and 'Number' columns are generated automatically by the system based on certain rules.

There are only two levels with logical AND and OR operators. On the top level, there can be as many as AND or OR operators (there is a limit, say, 64, but for practical reason, filtering queries are seldom close to that many logical conditions) on any columns. At the 2nd level, there also can be multiple operators, but the OR operator can only act on the same column. For example, here is a filtering condition:

{(Active is true) AND [(State is New) OR (State is Awaiting)] }
OR (Assigned to user_01)

This logic is simplified to [(a AND (b OR c)) OR d], where conditions b and c are for the same database column.

The test requirements are to verify that the records returned for all operators and operator combinations are as expected.

13.2 TEST CASE GENERATION

From the application testing requirements, the following category partitions are to be included in the testing:

(1) Filtering operations for each column type.
(2) Conditions with AND and OR operators.
(3) Sorting.

There are dozens or more columns in a typical table, testing on each column is not feasible and unnecessary. Since the filtering operations for each data type are different, all the operations should be covered, rather than all the database columns. Therefore, the categories to include are each data type, including Boolean, String, Date and Time, Integer, and Enum.

Based on the modularization principle, when testing filtering operations for each column type, there is no need to involve the condition operators AND and OR, and when testing operator condition operators only use valid values for the filtering operations.

The testing is to verify that the correct records are returned based on the filter setting. For example, if the 'Priority' column is set to 'Critical' in a filter with only this column, then all the records in the table with 'Critical' in 'Priority' field are returned, and no records with other values are returned.

13.2.1 Filtering Operations

According to category partitioning (This categorization is consistent with the modularization principle), testing of filtering operations can be done by covering the following modules:

(a) A Boolean type column, 5 operations.
(b) A Date and Time type column, 9 operations.
(c) An Integer type column, 10 operations.
(d) An Enum type column, 5 operations.
(e) A String type column, 8 operations.

For each of the modules, there are multiple possible values for the operations. For Boolean, Date and Time, and Enum types, since the values are choices in dropdown lists, each of the choices is one test case, and there are no further invalid partitions to include. For any Integer or String type columns, equivalence partitions need to be determined.

Based on the columns of the table under testing in table 13.6, we select the following columns, one for each data type, for testing:

Column name	Data type	Possible values
Active	Boolean	true, false
Release time	Date and Time	[2018 00:00:00 AM, 2050 11:59:59 PM]
Change count	Integer	[1,100]
State	Enum	[New, Awaiting, Resolved, Closed]
Description	String	Any string

Table 13.7: Selected table columns to use in testing

For column 'Change count', there are 3 partitions:

(i) x < 0
(ii) 0 ≤ x ≤ 100
(iii) x > 100

Since the testing is about record filtering, not about testing the data within any column, we can adopt basic equivalence partitioning, with one test case in each partition.

For the String type column 'Description', there is no restriction on the character types in the string, so there is only one partition, one test case is expected for each operation. For the Date and Time type column 'Release time', there are total of 9 operations, and 7 of them have the same 20 possible values for each. The goal is to cover all 20 values, and all 7 operations, so there will be 20 test cases for the 7 operations, and 2 test cases for the other 2 operations. Similar approach to Enum type column 'State'.

The testing data should be created to have records for each of the filters in the test cases.

The following table lists the test cases.

Test case	Column	Operation	Value
1	Active	is	true
2	Active	is	false
3	Active	is empty	
4	Active	is not empty	
5	Release time	on	Last week
6	Release time	not on	Yesterday
7	Release time	before	Tomorrow
8	Release time	at or before	This week
9	Release time	after	Today
10	Release time	at or after	Next week
11	Release time	Between, and	This month, Last month
12	Release time	is empty	
13	Release time	is not empty	
14	Release time	on	Last year
15	Release time	not on	This quarter
16	Release time	before	Last quarter
17	Release time	at or before	Next quarter
18	Release time	after	This year
19	Release time	at or after	Next month
20	Release time	Between, and	Last 3 months, Last 12 months
21	Release time	on	Next year
22	Release time	not on	Last 30 days
23	Release time	before	Current hour

24	Release time	at or before	Last hour
25	Change count	is	2
26	Change count	is	-5
27	Change count	is	110
28	Change count	is empty	
29	Change count	is not empty	
30	Change count	less than	5
31	Change count	less than	-10
32	Change count	greater than	10
33	Change count	greater than	200
34	Change count	less than or is	5
35	Change count	less than or is	200
36	Change count	greater than or is	5
37	Change count	greater than or is	-10
38	Change count	between	0, 20
39	Change count	between	10, 1
40	Change count	between	-10, 50
41	State	is	New
42	State	is not	Awaiting
43	State	is one of	Resolved, Closed
44	State	is empty	
45	State	is not empty	
46	Description	starts with	Can't
47	Description	ends with	server
48	Description	contains	application
49	Description	does not contain	software
50	Description	is	Trouble getting email
51	Description	is not	Can't read email
52	Description	is empty	
53	Description	is not empty	

Table 13.8: Test cases for the five types of columns

13.2.2 Conditions with AND and OR Operators

From the application requirement, we know that there are only two levels of logic with AND and OR operators. The goal here is to decide what compound logic conditions to include and generate test cases for each logic condition.

With 2 levels of Boolean logic and 2 operators, there can be an infinite number of combinations. Given the nature of computer programing languages, and the characteristics of basic logic, combinations with more conditions are just to repeat the basic combinations. Therefore, we will limit the maximum number of operators at the top level to 3.

The following are all the Boolean logic with 2 operators and 3 operators at the top level:

> a AND b
> a OR b
>
> a AND b AND c
> a AND b OR c
> a OR b AND c
> a OR b OR c
>
> a AND b AND c AND d
> a AND b AND c OR d
> a AND b OR c AND d
> a AND b OR c OR d
> a OR b AND c AND d
> a OR b AND c OR d
> a OR b OR c AND d
> a OR b OR c OR d

All the above conditions are to be included in the testing.

At the 2nd level, each of the conditions in the above list can be a logic condition composed with any of the logic items in the list. For example, in (*a* AND *b*), *a* can be replaced by logic in the form of (a AND b), and *b* be replaced by logic in the form of (a OR b) to produce a compound logic:

> (a AND b) AND (c OR d)

As you can see, the number of logic conditions is extremely large if all the above logic conditions are included in each of the 2nd level conditions (with the same list).

Based on the modularization principle, if a logic item has been covered at 1st level, then there is no need to cover all of them again at the 2nd level.

For example, examine the following logic:

> (a OR b AND c) **AND** (e AND f) **AND** c

This expression exercises the logic (a **AND** b **AND** c).

Therefore, we could cover a few 1st level basic logic expressions, and replace the conditions within with certain basic logic conditions, to form the 2nd level logic to cover.

The 2nd level simple cases are:

> a AND (b OR c)
> (a AND b) OR c

We then select a couple of typical ones with more complex conditions at 2nd level containing 2 operators:

> (a AND b AND c) AND (d AND e)
> (a OR b AND c) OR (d OR e OR f)

and one with 2 operators at 1st level, and 3 operators at 2nd level:

> a AND (b OR c) OR (d AND e OR f)

The above 2nd level selections are just some typical ones; other options may also be selected.

The compound conditions in this case study are different from those in Chapter 6 when various condition coverage techniques are covered. The conditions here are filtering of records and are not to be evaluated to true or false. Therefore, it's much easier to generate test cases here by adding one test case for each logic condition.

Table 13.9 lists the test cases for the logic conditions we have just discussed.

Note, a condition noted with the same letter in different logic expressions may not be the same condition. Testing data need to be defined and created according to the test cases, so that, for each logic expression there are records to be returned for assertion.

Case	Logic	Logic expression
54	a AND b	(Active is true) AND (State is New)
55	a OR b	(Description contains access) OR (Worknotes contains access)
56	a AND b AND c	(Active is true) AND (State is Awaiting) AND (Priority is High)
57	a AND b OR c	(Active is true) AND (State is New) OR (Assigned to is user_01)
58	a OR b AND c	(Priority is Critical) OR (State is New) AND (Assigned to is user_01)
59	a OR b OR c	(Priority is Critical) OR (State is New) OR Created on Today)
60	a AND b AND c AND d	(Active is true) AND (State is New) AND (Priority is High) AND (Created by is user_02)
61	a AND b AND c OR d	(Active is false) AND (Assigned to is user_01) AND (Priority is Low) OR (State is Closed)
62	a AND b OR c AND d	(Active is false) AND (Assigned to is user_01) OR (Priority is Low) AND (State is Closed)
63	a AND b OR c OR d	(Active is true) AND (Assigned to is user_01) OR (Priority is Low) OR (State is Closed)
64	a OR b AND c AND d	(Active is true) OR (Priority is Low) AND (State is Closed) AND (Assigned to is user_01)
65	a OR b AND c OR d	(Priority is Low) OR (State is Closed) AND (Active is true) OR (State is Resolved)

CHAPTER 13: CASE STUDY TWO: RECORD FILTERING TESTING   271

66	a OR b OR c AND d	(Priority is High) OR (State is Closed) OR (Created before Last week) AND (Change count is 0)
67	a OR b OR c OR d	(Active is false) OR (Priority is Low) OR (State is Closed) OR (Worknotes contains closed)
68	a AND (b OR c)	(Active is true) AND ((State is New) OR (State is Awaiting))
69	(a AND b) OR c	((State is Resolved) OR (State is Closed)) AND (Created by is user_01)
70	(a AND b AND c) AND (d AND e)	((Active is true) AND (State is Awaiting) AND (Priority is High)) AND ((Assigned to is user_01) AND (Created by is user_02))
71	(a OR b AND c) OR (d OR e OR f)	((Priority is Low) OR (Created before Last year) AND (Assigned to is user_01)) OR ((State is Awaiting) OR (State is Resolved) OR (State is Closed))
72	a AND (b OR c) OR (d AND e OR f)	(Active is true) AND ((Priority is Critical) OR (Priority is High)) OR ((State is New) AND (Assigned to is user_01) OR (Assigned to is user_02))

Table 13.9: Test cases for Boolean logic

13.2.3 Sorting

Test cases for sorting are easy to generate. There are two sorting options, ascending and descending. Therefore, we include one column for each data type, with total of 10 test cases. The filtering setting for testing sorting can be designed to return a relatively small number of records but enough data to demonstrate sorting on each column.

Table 13.10 lists the 10 test cases for sorting.

Test cases	column
73	Active, a to z
74	Active, z to a
75	Release time, a to z
76	Release time, z to a
77	Change count, a to z
78	Change count, z to a
79	State, a to z
80	State, z to a
81	Description, a to z
82	Description, z to a

Table 13.10: Sorting test cases

13.3 TEST DATA CREATION, AND TEST AUTOMATION

Based on the test cases generated from the last section, we need to create records in the database for the table being used for testing, and there should be records with all possible values to be used in the test cases. For example, there should be records for column 'Release time' with values of today, tomorrow, yesterday, last week, and so on.

Also, the number of records with each value, and the values for other columns in the same record, should be spread out so the records returned from various compound conditions are not the same (there can be certain redundancies).

Assume that the record creation in the database can be performed with the testing setup process, then test case execution and testing data creation/deletion can be done in the same automated test class.

Since it's easy to create testing records in the database, any subset of the test cases can use dedicated testing records. For example, test cases 41 through 45 are for Enum type column 'State', re-listed in the following table.

Test case	Column	Operation	Value
41	State	is	New
42	State	is not	Awaiting
43	State	is one of	Resolved, Closed
44	State	is empty	
45	State	is not empty	

Table 13.11: Test cases for an Enum column

These test cases can be put in one class in the automated test suite, and the following is a typical set of processes to design the test execution:

(a) set the 'State' column for all existing records in the table to one value, say, to 'Closed', and save the total count to variable base_record_count. (another option is to delete all records in the table).
(b) create 2 records with 'State' column value 'New'.
(c) create 3 records with 'State' column value 'Awaiting'.
(d) create 4 records with 'State' column value to 'Resolved'.
(e) create 5 records with 'State' column value to 'Closed'.

With these data, verifications are simple. For example, to execute test case 41, you just need to assert that the total number of records returned is 2, and the 'State' tag for these 2 records is 'New'.

The situation with a column type of Date and Time is a bit complex, let's dig more.

Remember, the possible values for Date and Time include Today, Yesterday, Tomorrow, This week, Last week, Next week, This month, Last month, Next month, This quarter, Last quarter, Next quarter, This year, Last year, Next year, Last 3 months, Last 12 months, Last 30 days, Current hour, and Last hour.

Calculation is needed to determine the time the records reside in, depending on the current time - the time a filtering action is performed, that is, the time a test case is executed. For example, suppose the current time is Tuesday, 10 AM, and suppose the filtering is for 'Last 30 days', then a calculation is needed to go back 30 days from the current time. This sounds easy, but the case is further complicated with testing records creation.

Since all the possible values for Date and Time are to be tested, and there are redundancies in the values, which means, for example, when 'This week' is across two months, test data creation for 'This month' and 'Last month' needs to be carefully designed to cover all possible values.

We present one solution to this problem next.

The testing records are created based on a certain date and time values, and the number of records in other dates and times are calculated accordingly.

Code segment 13.1 illustrates a sample implementation of test cases 5 and 14, for Date and Time type column 'Release time' with value 'on' (certain details and omitted).

In this example, the number of testing records to create in each time period for the 'Release time' column is defined first, then the records are created based on the current time (The data are created in setupData () method before running the tests). The numbers are carefully designed to be different for different periods, therefore, certain verifications can be based on the record numbers.

The records falling into a specific time are calculated from the records created with all other relevant periods. For example, there are records created with timestamp 'Yesterday', then to check records for 'Last Week', whether the records from 'Yesterday' need to be included or not depends on the current time, the time the test is executed. If today is the 1st day of the week, then 'Yesterday' belongs to 'Last Week', otherwise it belongs to 'This Week'.

In the tests, the number of records satisfying the filtering is calculated and compared with the number of records returned, and the time value in each of the 'Release time' tags is retrieved on the UI and is asserted with the expected time.

CHAPTER 13: CASE STUDY TWO: RECORD FILTERING TESTING

The automated tests can be run at any time of a day and any date of the year, such as on a leap day, or on a day just after a new year (all these factors should be considered in the test case design and implementation stage).

```java
public class FiltersOperatorsOn extends RecordFilterOperatorsTest {
  SimpleDateFormat dateFormatter = new SimpleDateFormat ("yyyy-MM-dd HH:mm:ss");
  public static int NUMBER_OF_RECORDS_Now = 19;
  public static int NUMBER_OF_RECORDS_OneHourAgo = 17;
  public static int NUMBER_OF_RECORDS_Yesterday = 13;
  public static int NUMBER_OF_RECORDS_LastWeek = 11;
  public static int NUMBER_OF_RECORDS_LastMonth = 7;
  public static int NUMBER_OF_RECORDS_ThreeMonthsAgo = 5;
  public static int NUMBER_OF_RECORDS_LastYear = 3;
  public Calendar now = new GregorianCalendar();
  public Calendar now2 = new GregorianCalendar();
  public static String url_for_last_week = ""; // note: a real value should be added.
  public static String url_for_last_year = ""; // note: a real value should be added.

  @BeforeClass
  public void setupData () {
    timezone = getTimeZone(); // get time zone in the application
    now = Calendar.getInstance(timezone); // now is used to create the data.
    now2 = Calendar.getInstance(timezone); // now2 is used to get the current time.
    now.add(Calendar.HOUR, 7); // local time conversion
    //for existing records, set the 'Release time' to 2 years ago, so they won't interfere with the tests.
    Calendar aYearAgo = ((Calendar) now.clone());
    aYearAgo.add(Calendar.YEAR, -2);
    modifyTableRecords ("Release_time", dateFormatter.format((aYearAgo.getTime()))).toString());
    // create various numbers of RECORDS with different 'Release time' for the tests.
    Calendar calNow = ((Calendar) now.clone());
    String Release_time_Now = dateFormatter.format(calNow.getTime());
    for (int i = 0; i < NUMBER_OF_RECORDS_Now; i++) {
      createRecord("Release_time_Now", "New", 0, Release_time_Now.toString(), true);
    }
    Calendar calOneHourAgo = ((Calendar) now.clone());
    calOneHourAgo.add(Calendar.MINUTE, -30);
    String Release_time_OneHourAgo = dateFormatter.format(calOneHourAgo.getTime());
    for (int i = 0; i < NUMBER_OF_RECORDS_OneHourAgo; i++) {
      createRecord("Release_time_OneHourAgo", "New", 1, Release_time_OneHourAgo.toString(), true);
    }
    Calendar calYesteday = ((Calendar) now.clone());
    calYesteday.add(Calendar.DAY_OF_YEAR, -1);
    String Release_time_Yesterday = dateFormatter.format(calYesteday.getTime());
    for (int i = 0; i < NUMBER_OF_RECORDS_Yesterday; i++) {
      createRecord("Release_time_Yesterday", "Awaiting", 2, Release_time_Yesterday.toString(), false);
    }
    Calendar calLastWeek = ((Calendar) now.clone());
    calLastWeek.add(Calendar.WEEK_OF_YEAR, -1);
    String Release_time_LastWeek = dateFormatter.format(calLastWeek.getTime());
    for (int i = 0; i < NUMBER_OF_RECORDS_LastWeek; i++) {
      createRecord("Release_time_LastWeek", "Resolved", 5, Release_time_LastWeek.toString(), true);
    }
    Calendar calLastMonth = ((Calendar) now.clone());
    calLastMonth.add(Calendar.MONTH, -1);
    String Release_time_LastMonth = dateFormatter.format(calLastMonth.getTime());
```

```java
    for (int i = 0; i < NUMBER_OF_RECORDS_LastMonth; i++) {
        createRecord("Release_time_LastMonth", "Closed", 8, Release_time_LastMonth.toString(), true);
    }
    Calendar calThreeMonthsAgo = ((Calendar) now.clone());
    calThreeMonthsAgo.add(Calendar.MONTH, -3);
    if (calThreeMonthsAgo.get(Calendar.DAY_OF_MONTH) > 1)
        calThreeMonthsAgo.add(Calendar.DAY_OF_YEAR, -1); //to count for any confusion if Feb has 28 days.
    String Release_time_ThreeMonthsAgo = dateFormatter.format(calThreeMonthsAgo.getTime());
    for (int i = 0; i < NUMBER_OF_RECORDS_ThreeMonthsAgo; i++) {
        createRecord("Release_time_ThreeMonthsAgo", "New", 0,
                Release_time_ThreeMonthsAgo.toString(), true);
    }
    Calendar calLastYear = ((Calendar) now.clone());
    calLastYear.add(Calendar.YEAR, -1);
    String Release_time_LastYear = dateFormatter.format(calLastYear.getTime());
    for (int i = 0; i < NUMBER_OF_RECORDS_LastYear; i++) {
        createRecord("Release_time_LastYear", "Awaiting", 3, Release_time_LastYear.toString(), true);
    }
}

@Test
// test case 5: records have "Release time" on 'last week'.
public void testFilterOperatorOnDateTimeLastWeek() throws Exception {
    openNavURI(url_for_last_week);
    int NumOFRecordReturned = getNumOfRecordsOnFilteringResult();
    // if the current date is Monday, then the records created yesterday is from last week:
    //a week is from Mon to Sun.
    if (now2.get(Calendar.DAY_OF_WEEK) == Calendar.MONDAY ) {
        if (now2.get(Calendar.HOUR) == 0 && now.get(Calendar.MINUTE) < 30) {
            assertEquals( NUMBER_OF_RECORDS_LastWeek + NUMBER_OF_RECORDS_Yesterday +
                    NUMBER_OF_RECORDS_OneHourAgo,   NumOFRecordReturned);
        }
        else { assertEquals(NUMBER_OF_RECORDS_LastWeek + NUMBER_OF_RECORDS_Yesterday,
                NumOFRecordReturned); }
    }
    else {  assertEquals(NUMBER_OF_RECORDS_LastWeek, NumOFRecordReturned);
    }
    // validate the date is last week for the records created last week.
    for (int i = 0; i< NumOFRecordReturned; i++) {
        String ReleaseTimeOnUI = getCellValue("release_time", i+1);
        Date ReleaseTimeDate = dateFormatter.parse(ReleaseTimeOnUI);
        Calendar calReleaseTimeDate = Calendar.getInstance();
        calReleaseTimeDate.setTime(ReleaseTimeDate);
        // a week starts from Monday in this application, while in Java Calendar, a week starts from Sunday.
        boolean isMonday = now2.get(Calendar.DAY_OF_WEEK) == Calendar.MONDAY;
        int weekOfYearDiff = now2.get(Calendar.WEEK_OF_YEAR) –
                                    calReleaseTimeDate.get(Calendar.WEEK_OF_YEAR);
        Assert.assertTrue( (isMonday && weekOfYearDiff == 0) // this week and it is Monday
                || weekOfYearDiff == 1 // week before
                || weekOfYearDiff == -51 // week before but this is a new year
        );
    }
}
@Test
// test case 14: records have "Release time" on 'last year'.
public void testFilterOperatorOnDateTimeLastYear() throws Exception {
    openNavURI(url_for_last_year);
```

```
    int NumOFRecordReturned = getNumOfRecordsOnFilteringResult();
    for (int i = 0; i< NumOFRecordReturned; i++) {
      String ReleaseTimeOnUI = getCellValue("release_time", i+1);
      Date ReleaseTimeDate = dateFormatter.parse(ReleaseTimeOnUI);
      Calendar calReleaseTimeDate = Calendar.getInstance();
      calReleaseTimeDate.setTime(ReleaseTimeDate);
      Assert.assertTrue( (now2.get(Calendar.YEAR) - calReleaseTimeDate.get(Calendar.YEAR) == 1) );
    }
  }
}
// create table record (only the signature is shown here)
public void createRecord (String description, String state, int change_count, String release_time,
              Boolean active) {
}
@AfterClass
public void disposeEnvironment() {
}
}
```

Code Segment 13.1: A sample implementation of test cases 5 and 14 for operator 'on'

ABOUT THE AUTHOR

The author has over twenty years of experience with various software companies in Silicon Valley, from startups to well-known established ones. In particular, the author has extensive experience in building test automation frameworks and in leading quality engineering projects for both consumer and enterprise software applications. The author also has several years of software development experience early in his career in the software industry.

The author conducted academic research in radio astronomy particularly in studying molecular clouds in close-by galaxies before entering the software industry and was also involved in designing astronomical spectrometers at an observatory.

The author holds an **MS** degree in Computer Sciences from the University of Illinois at Urbana-Champaign, an **MS** degree in Astronomy (a byproduct of an unfinished PhD program) from the University of Illinois at Urbana-Champaign, an **MS** degree in Astrophysics from the Chinese Academy of Sciences, and a **BS** degree in Physics from Hebei University.

The author lives in San Jose, California, and can be reached by email at jjshen99@gmail.com.

INDEX

A

acceptance testing · 7
alarm system · 145
annotation · 172
atomic principle · 155
average of two integers · 42, 185

B

backend testing · 8
benchmark testing · 222
best effort touring · 124, 125
    tour · 124
    tour with sidetrips · 124
black box testing · 6, 13
branch coverage · 117
browser testing · 9

C

call graph · 136
capacity testing · 222, 223
case study one · 244
    catogory partitioning · 266
    equivalence partitions · 246
    modulization principle · 266, 269
    pairwise testing · 252
category partition · 53
cause-effect graphing · 104
college admission example · 96
combinations from a set · 20
combinatorial testing · 73
compatibility testing · 9
compound condition coverage · 130
condition and edge coverage · 129
condition coverage · 128
    basic condition coverage · 128
    compound boolean expressions · 131
    compound condition coverage · 130
    condition and edge coverage · 129
    MCDC · 132
control flow graph · 110
    basic block · 113
    call graph · 136
    complete path coverage · 118
    control flow · 113
    edge coverage · 117
    edge-pair coverage · 118
    edges · 110
    for loop · 113
    if-else · 114
    nodes · 110
    path · 110
    predecessor · 111
    semantically reachable · 112
    subpath · 110
    successor · 111
    switch · 114
    syntactically reachable · 112
    test graph · 111
    test path · 111
    tour · 124
    use case graph · 138
    while loop · 114
cycle · 111
cycle in a graph · 110
cyclomatic complexity · 128

D

database testing · 8
decision table testing · 91
    cause-effect graphing · 104
    college admission example · 96
    decision table · 91
    decision tree · 95
    do not care · 94
    extended entry table · 99
    impossible conditions · 97
    inconsistency · 103
    limited entry table · 99
    redundancy · 103
    rule count · 93
    table construction · 93
decision tree · 95

E

edge coverage · 117
end-to-end testing · 202
equivalence partitioning · 31
    area of a triangle · 48
    base case · 34
    base case limitations · 36, 37
    base worse case · 43
    category partition · 53
    definition · 31
    input vector space · 44
    multiple dimensions · 42
    principles · 34
    standard case · 41
    standard case with edges · 47, 186, 188
    standard worse case · 43
    test case numbers · 34
equivalence relation · 31
extended entry table · 99

F

faces in the hyper graph · 52
finite state machine · 141
    cat in a black box example · 142
    test case generation · 142
    transaction coverage · 144
functional testing · 202

G

grey box testing · 6

H

hierarchical finite state machine · 162
    superstate · 162

I

independency principle · 156
    environment independency · 159
    order independency · 156
    path independency · 158
    state independency · 158
    time independency · 159

integration testing · 6, 201
    big-bang approach · 204
    bottom-up approach · 203
    sandwich approach · 204
    test case generation · 205
    test data design · 210
    top-down approach · 203
ISO/IEC 25010 · 3

J

Jenkins · 176
JMeter · 231

L

letter to binary code conversion · 41
limited entry table · 99
load testing · 222

M

mocking · 196
modified condition/decision coverage · 132
modularization principle · 160
    manual testing · 164
    test clusters · 163

N

node coverage · 116
normal distribution · 217
    probability density · 217
number of combinations · 20

O

one-error principle · 54
order API example · 61, 244
orthogonal arrays · 84
    definition · 84
    OA(1,2,3,3) · 85
    OA(1,t,k,v) · 86
    runs · 85
    strength · 85

P

pairwise testing · 74
    definition · 74
    limitations · 81
parallel computing · 15
path · 110
performance testing · 9, 215
    benchmark testing · 221
    concurrent users · 220
    indicators · 219
    load testing · 222
    metrics · 226
    monitoring · 227
    normal distribution · 217
    processes · 224
    requirements · 219
    response time · 219
    scalability · 219
    statistical terms · 215
    stress testing · 222
    test case design · 227
    testing validity · 228
    throughput · 220
    types of performance testing · 221
prime path coverage · 119
    best effort touring · 124
    infeasible requirements · 124
    prime path · 119
    simple path · 119

R

regression testing · 8, 168
    continuous integration · 176
    predefined test set · 170
    prioritized test set · 171
    random test set · 172
    regression · 168
    strategic test set · 170
    test selection · 170
    test sets annotation · 172
    weighted prioritization · 173

S

sanity testing · 7
scalability testing · 222
Schrödinger's cat · 150
security testing · 9
server processing time · 240
smoke testing · 7
soak testing · 222, 223
software quality · 3
    defects · 4
software testing · 4
    traditional classification · 5
standard deviation · 216
statement coverage · 117
statistics · 215
    average · 215
    normal distribution · 217
    normal value · 216
    outliers · 216
    percentile · 216
    standard deviation · 216
    think time · 216
stress testing · 222
structural testing · 110
    call graph · 136
    condition coverage · *See* condition coverage
    control flow graph · *See* control flow graph
    prime path coverage · *See* prime path coverage
    use case testing · 138
stubbing · 193
subpath · 111
system testing · 6

T

test case classifications · 21
    type 0 tests · 21
    type 1 tests · 21
    type 2 tests · 21
    type 3 tests · 22
test cases · 5, 10
    atomic · 17
    characteristics · 13
    definitions · 10
    deterministic · 13
    encapsulating · 12
    finite · 12
    genuine · 13
    reproducible · 16
test coverage principle · 165
test path · 111
test vectors · 19
    definition · 19

input vectors · 19
output vectors · 19
transaction coverage · 144
t-wise testing · 83
    deciding · 83
    definition · 83
type 0 tests · 21

U

UI testing · 8
unit testing · 6
unit tests
    benefits · 181
    common assertions · 184
    exception assertion · 190
    isPrime(n) example · 182
    mocking · 196
    reduce dependences · 191
    stubbing · 193
    unique characteristics · 180
    writing of unit tests · 182
usability testing · 9
use case testing · 138

W

white box testing · 6

X

XOR gate · 12

www.ingramcontent.com/pod-product-compliance
Lightning Source LLC
Chambersburg PA
CBHW080539220526
45466CB00010B/2966